The New Americans
Recent Immigration and American Society

Edited by
Steven J. Gold and Rubén G. Rumbaut

A Series from LFB Scholarly

Immigrants and Crime in the New Destinations

Vincent A. Ferraro

LFB Scholarly Publishing LLC
El Paso 2014

Library of Congress Cataloging-in-Publication Data

Ferraro, Vincent A., 1981-
  Immigrants and crime in the new destinations / Vincent A. Ferraro.
    pages cm. -- (The new Americans: Recent immigration and
American
society)
  Includes bibliographical references and index.
  ISBN 978-1-59332-699-9 (hardcover : alk. paper)
  1. Alien criminals--United States. 2. Immigrants--Crimes against--
United States. 3. Immigrants--United States--Social conditions. 4.
Crime--United States--Sociological aspects. 5. United States--
Emigration and immigration--Social aspects. I. Title.
  HV6181.F47 2013
  364.3086'9120973--dc23
                                        2013029597

ISBN 978-1-59332-699-9

Printed on acid-free 250-year-life paper.

Manufactured in the United States of America.

Table of Contents

List of Tables

Acknowledgements

This book would not have been possible without the invaluable help of a number of people with whom I have had the great fortune to work. I owe an enormous debt to Gordana Rabrenovic, Jack Levin, and Samantha Friedman, each of whom provided critical insight from conception through completion. I owe a special thanks to Jacob Stowell, to whom I am forever indebted.

Many thanks are due to Mark Potok, Director of the Intelligence Project at the Southern Poverty Law Center, who provided critical insight during the early stages of the hate crime analyses. Thanks as well to Benjamin Lasalata and Joan Morrone, for their comments on earlier drafts. Thanks to Leo Balk for his guidance in preparing the manuscript for publication. I would like to thank as well Northeastern University's Office of Graduate Studies and its Department of Sociology, both of which provided funding to assist in completing the analyses to follow.

I will be forever grateful to Haley Rosenfeld, a great friend and colleague, for her unwavering support and ever-sound advice, which talked me off more than few ledges. I can only hope to return the favor.

And finally, to Kristina, a woman of whom I will never be worthy. If the only thing harder than writing a dissertation is being emotionally involved with the writer, then her accomplishment has been immense. That she endured the process and put up with my chronic periods of emotional distance, distraction, and detachment is an indication of either profound love or near insanity—either way, I have been blessed to have her in my life. Kris, you are and have always been my rock and I love you more than these few words could ever say.

Though many have contributed in important ways to shaping this final product, all errors remain mine alone.

Preface

In recent years the link between immigration and crime has received renewed interest in academic research and public and political discourse, with the former tending to find little empirical support and the latter continuing to espouse a firm connection. Recent years have also witnessed the expansion of immigration to new destinations far from traditional ports of entry and settlement. While research has begun to address the implications of these new patterns of internal population shifts, the issue of their effect on crime has not been a major focus. Because these new destinations have limited histories of and experience with immigration, they likely lack mechanisms by which to aid in the incorporation process. Whether the lack of a connection between immigration and crime in traditional areas holds within new destinations warrants sociological attention. Moreover, the extant literature on the immigration-crime nexus has tended to address the issue from one direction: whether immigration increases rates of traditional crime via the supply of offenders. Comparatively little research has investigated the inverse: whether the process increases immigrant victimization. As immigrants increasingly settle outside of traditional receiving areas, and again, given the negative cultural context of reception, the potential for victimization is an important issue.

This research seeks to provide a broader account of the nature of immigration and crime by examining the potential effects within new settlement destinations and incorporating the issue of immigrant victimization. Expectations regarding immigration and crime have tended to flow from social disorganization theory, with recent results challenging its applicability. This research offers a test of social disorganization and a developing alternative view: the community resource perspective. Competing hypotheses regarding rates of traditional crime are tested within a large sample of cities and towns (n=1,252) and a sub-sample of new destinations (n=573). With respect to victimization, expectations from the body of work on group threat theory suggest that increasing immigration into new areas may be met with prejudice and acts of retaliation. Additional analyses on the occurrence of anti-immigrant hate crime are conducted for a total sample of 423 places, and a sub-sample of 173 new destinations. For each, longitudinal data are analyzed for the effect of change over time, rather than cross-sectional effects, to determine whether changes in immigration are associated with either changes in traditional crime or changes in immigrant victimization.

Results of the analyses for traditional crime offer stronger support for the community resource perspective, rather than social disorganization theory, and suggest that the lack of a criminogenic effect of immigration in traditional areas is present in nontraditional ones as well. Results of the analyses for victimization lend limited support to group threat theory, with the surprising finding of a buffering effect of immigrant population growth on hate crime victimization. The analyses call attention to the importance of changing patterns of immigrant settlement. Particularly with regard to victimization, results suggest the need for further analysis to elucidate the unexpected finding of a buffering effect, and perhaps a refinement of group threat theory.

Introduction

In the last few years, researchers have highlighted the changing nature of immigrant settlement within the U.S. According to Massey and Capoferro (2008), from 1901 to 1930, thirty-six percent of all immigrants settled in the nation's five largest urban areas, with fifty-four percent settling in the states where those cities were located. These trends intensified after the passage of the 1965 Hart-Cellar immigration reform Act, such that from 1971 to 1993, forty-eight percent of the foreign-born were settling in the top five destination cities, and seventy-eight percent in the top five destinations states. However, the 1990s precipitated a dramatic shift away from these so-called global cities as settlement destinations. By 2005, the number of immigrants settling in the top five destination states had dropped to fifty-two percent (Massey and Capoferro 2008: 35). Instead, many immigrants have begun settling in states that have either not seen significant numbers of immigrants since the early 20th century or have never seen them in significant numbers at all. The annual growth rate to the 45 other states is approaching the growth rate to the top five (Alsalam and Smith 2005). States such as Indiana and Wisconsin saw their share of the total U.S. immigrant population double from 1980 to 2005, while states such as Arizona, Georgia, North Carolina and Nevada saw their shares triple over the same period.

One likely explanation is that these new immigrants followed the jobs. Several authors have noted the link between the opening of large agribusinesses and the arrival of immigrants (Fennelly 2008; Parrado and Kandel 2008; Zarrugh 2008). The labor required for such occupation tends to be intensive and low-skill, consistent with the findings of Donato and colleagues (2008) on changes in the age structure, education, and English language acquisition of recent immigrants. Moreover, the hiring process likely depends largely on word of mouth and thus social networks. As Massey (1985) has noted, the channeling of immigrants into specific locations is in large part a product of migrant networks (see also Massey and Capoferro 2008). It would appear that today, employment opportunities, variable costs of living, and migrant networks are leading newcomers to settle outside major cities and increasingly in suburban and rural areas. A similar process worked in the early and mid-20th century to funnel immigrants into major urban destinations, where they could locate employment and affordable housing and avail themselves of the experiences of their countrymen and women who had come before. The current pattern of settlement, then, may simply be an extension of an old one, just that now employment opportunities are much more diffuse, and developments in transportation make the country's interior much more accessible.[1]

Clearly, something significant is at work. And demographers, sociologists and other immigration researchers have begun to question what the effects on these new destinations might be. Several researchers have noted the rejuvenating effect of immigrant entrepreneurialism on local commerce, a finding consistent with the concept of *immigrant revitalization* in both urban (Nielsen and Martinez 2006) and rural areas (Fennelly 2008; Oberle and Li 2008). Some have focused on the role of racism, and anti-black racism in particular, in structuring the settlement patterns of recent immigrants (Odem 2008; Price and Singer 2008). Others have looked at how newcomers have challenged traditional negative stereotypes and, by extension, weakened some aspects of natives' prejudice while strengthening others (Griffith 2008; Winders 2008). Still others focus on the reactions of the native-born and how these vary along lines of social class (Fennelly 2008; Fennelly and Federico 2008).

---

[1] On the other hand, as Donato, et al. (2008) note, it may only be temporary. The implication is that in a globalizing economy, American businesses and particularly large agribusinesses move to more isolated areas in search of cheaper costs, especially for labor, but also for property. To the degree that immigrants continue to provide low wage work, companies may stick around. But, should costs of production increase, for example by the constriction of the stream of migrants, by demands from those migrants for higher wages, or by the refusal of their children to work the same job for the same pay, those companies may well make their way abroad in search of lower costs.

Yet what is conspicuously missing from the literature on new settlement patterns is whether they exert a significant effect on crime. Despite the recent surge in research on the immigration-crime nexus, few studies have investigated whether rates of criminal offending are consistent across both traditional receiving locations and new host locales, net of other factors. The emerging body of research on new settlement patterns has already begun to offer some intriguing findings for criminologists. It would seem that recent immigrants who settle in new destination locales far from urban centers tend to rate high on what have historically been viewed as the major criminogenic factors: low occupational skill, low educational attainment, and young adulthood. They also tend to be more geographically mobile, which, according to work by Sampson and colleagues (Sampson, Morenoff, and Earls 1999), should weaken collective efficacy, a deterrent to crime. Lastly, they appear more resistant to English language acquisition, an indicator of traditional social disorganization, as well as a constraint on acculturation and impediment to structural assimilation via upward occupational attainment.

Moreover, many of the new areas in which immigrants are settling have limited experience with the process of immigration, certainly when compared to traditional gateways such as New York, Chicago, and Los Angeles, raising questions about the likelihood for immigrants' successful incorporation. From a structural perspective, it is unlikely that such areas have well-developed mechanisms in place that can ease the incorporation of newcomers. Places which have experienced previous waves of immigrants are better able to absorb successive ones into labor and housing markets.[2] From an interactionist perspective, the arrival of these newcomers to these new places, at a time when immigration is a polarizing political issue, may be viewed as a threat by many native-born residents—who may have only minimal prior experience with immigrants—particularly if the immigrants come

---

[2] For example, Card (1990) finds that the influx of Mariel Cubans into Miami had virtually no effect on the wages of Miami's existing workforce precisely because previous waves of immigrants resulted in large numbers of *immigrant* employers who were able to absorb the newcomers.

seeking (and receiving) employment or if they do not speak English or do not speak it well.

And so for criminologists in particular, the questions loom large. What do rates of crime look like in these areas and to what degree are they influenced by immigration? And just as importantly, how are we to understand and make sense of this emerging pattern? Does it conform to existing theoretical expectations or is it something completely new? Uncovering low rates of crime for the foreign-born might necessitate an extension of the so-called Latino Paradox, whereby Mexican immigrants, despite severe socioeconomic disadvantage, are involved in crime—either as victims or offenders—at lower rates than African Americans and at lower rates than would be expected from traditional theories of crime (Sampson and Bean 2006; Martinez 2002). Such a finding might also be consistent with the community resource perspective, which, drawing from the segmented assimilation view, notes the mechanisms by which immigrant communities aid the incorporation of their members and buffer against traditional criminogenic forces. In both cases, it could pose a direct challenge to the idea of social disorganization, which has guided the understanding of immigration and crime for decades.

This research attempts to provide insight into two of these questions. The first of which is whether rates of crime vary systematically across cities by their historical rates of immigration. Which is to say, do cities with recent increases in immigration experience higher rates of crime than those with relatively consistent rates of immigration, controlling for relevant factors? To address this issue, I perform fixed effects regression analyses on a sample of roughly 1,250 places with population of at least twenty thousand, and on a subset of those places wherein the percent of foreign-born has increased more than fifty percent since 1990. In doing so, this research will contribute to the literature on the immigration-crime nexus by determining whether recent findings—that immigration has little effect on increasing crime at either the individual or structural levels—are generalizable first to the place level for cities and towns with populations of 20,000 or higher. Second, it will also contribute to the literature by addressing whether those findings, typically from research on cities with long histories of immigrant incorporation, are generalizable to cities and towns with little or no experience of immigration.

The second question is focused on the native-born population's response to the arrival of immigrants. Specifically, do increases in immigration exert a significant effect on the occurrence of anti-immigrant hate crimes? As with the first question, fixed effects regression analyses are conducted on a sample of all places wherein a hate crime occurred, and a subset of those places wherein the share of foreign-born has increased more than fifty percent in the last twenty years. Few studies have investigated whether changes in immigration systematically impact the occurrence of biased crime, though there are good reasons to suggest this response among the native-born population.

This research is important firstly because of the recent tendency for newcomers to settle in areas with no history of immigration and second, because the bulk of criminological research, especially the subset focusing on immigration, is largely based on the experiences of urban residents. Most of the great works of the canon draw upon research conducted in many of the traditional gateways of our country—New York, Boston, Chicago, Los Angeles, and so on—that have long histories of immigrant incorporation. Few have systematically looked to suburban or rural locations for the effect of immigration on crime, understandably because until now there has been little reason to do so. Third, the research is crucial in light of recent findings that those who settle away from major urban centers might have distinct socioeconomic and demographic characteristics from their metropolitan counterparts (Donato, et al. 2008). Finally, the research is among the first to systematically test whether the arrival of newcomers fosters anti-immigrant activism in the form of hate crime.

As a means of setting the stage for the analyses mentioned above, the chapters that follow review recent changes to what, until recently, have been long standing and remarkably stable patterns of immigrant incorporation, and attempts to uncover—via news reports, scholarly writing, and political policies—dominant American conceptions of immigrants and the recently-arrived in particular.

Chapter 1 seeks to distill prevailing attitudes toward and perceptions of immigration into their component parts. While in sum the American response to immigration can be characterized as generally opposed, that opposition is marked by three distinct foci: perceived threats to native-born employment opportunities; threats of increasing crime and violence; and threats to the "traditional" American way of life. This chapter also attempts to outline the consequences of the prevailing opposition, namely public calls for more restrictive political policies and the nullification of scientific research that time and again have failed to find a positive link between immigration and crime, and more often have found just the opposite: that immigration is associated with reductions in crime, violence in particular. It presents, in sum, a cyclical process, whereby opposition to immigration leads to increased calls for reform, and buffers against research undermining those very fears. Once buffered, fears proliferate, generating further calls for action.

Chapter 2 locates this research within the larger discussion of immigration and crime. It reviews the prevailing theories of immigrant incorporation, both traditional assimilation theory and the segmented assimilation perspective, as an attempt to understand the shifting nature of settlement patterns. Dominant approaches to understanding the potential impact of immigration on crime, namely social disorganization theory and the emergent community resource perspective., are also reviewed along with recent research findings on the immigration-crime link. Finally, this chapter offers a discussion of immigrant victimization, reviewing the major findings of scholarly work in this area. Major theories that can help us understand the causes and correlates of victimization are reviewed, including group threat theory and its variants.

This research draws demographic data from the 2000 decennial census and the American Community Survey's 2005-2007 3-year product. These data are paired with traditional crime data drawn from the Federal Bureau of Investigation's Uniform Crime Reports and biased crime data drawn from the FBI's annual *Hate Crime in the United States* reports. Chapter 3 offers a discussion of the data sources employed, the steps taken to prepare the data for analysis, the variables analyzed, and the analytical techniques employed. It also offers hypotheses to be tested in the analyses presented in subsequent chapters.

Chapter 4 presents the results of the analyses of the effect of changes in immigrant concentration on changes in rates of crime at the place level. Results are offered for the concentration of both the total foreign-born population and those arriving in the last five years. This chapter also presents the results of analyses conducted on a subset of new destinations, to help determine whether the relationship of immigration and crime is in part determined by place and historical patterns of reception.

The second set of analyses, those addressing the impact of changes in immigration on the occurrence of anti-immigrant hate crimes, are presented in Chapter 5. As with the analyses of traditional crime, the analyses of hate crime patterns were conducted for the total and recent foreign-born populations, for the full sample of places and a subset of new settlement destinations.

Chapter 6 offers concluding remarks. The major findings are reviewed and placed into context. This section also offers a discussion of the limitations of the present study, from which are offered suggestions for avenues of future research. Finally, this chapter reviews the implications of this research and its findings, for scholars, politicians, and the public alike.

CHAPTER 1

Making Sense of Immigration

The dramatic changes to what have been fairly stable patterns of immigration over the last several decades hearken back to the early work of Park and Burgess, Shaw and McKay and others of the Chicago School. Their groundbreaking ecological work, which would become part of the foundation of the discipline of sociology, was rooted in a fundamental desire to understand the massive changes occurring in and around the city of Chicago in the early 20th century. At that time, while immigrants accounted for a very sizeable 15 percent of the country's population, they constituted an astounding 33 percent of the population of the city of Chicago.[3] By 1900, some estimates suggest that more than three quarters of Chicago's population was made up of first and second generation immigrants (Bursick 2006). Much as Chicago's social landscape underwent fundamental change at the turn of the 20th century, so too is today's, only on a much larger geographical scale.

The major finding of Shaw and McKay's (1942) research was that, controlling for other factors, immigrant status was not likely to result in increased crime. Immigration *could* result in increased crime but only to the extent that immigrants tended to settle in impoverished inner cities, where most crimes were likely to occur. As immigrants moved out, their *individual* rates of crime were expected to drop, a finding famously displayed in those authors' image of concentric zones, while rates of crime in the impoverished areas they departed were expected to remain fairly stable. However, this finding—that poverty was the key—

---

[3] A high-water mark for the nation's immigrant population that went unmatched for decades.

has largely either been ignored or misunderstood outside of academia. And popular accounts continue to rely on a direct, rather than indirect, correlation: immigrants beget crime. But fears of an immigration-crime link are not the only fears Americans hold toward immigrants. Crime is just one of a number of negative outcomes attributed to an increasing immigrant population. Immigrants have been cast as threats to native employment, implicitly because they are willing to work for lower wages, thereby undercutting native-born workers' incomes. They have also been cast as threats to the American way of life, evidenced most notably perhaps through fears that English will be supplanted by Spanish as the national language. A recent poll of Virginia residents is instructive: seven out of ten respondents believed that recent immigrants don't do enough to learn English or generally fit in (Cohen and Constable 2007). While a common perception, it is largely inaccurate. "Studies of the Hispanic second generation show that while over 98 percent of its members are fluent in English, only about a third (35 percent) retain fluency in Spanish" (Portes 2007: 27).

The sections that follow address both popular and political constructions of immigrants and immigration, relying on academic sources, news reports, and political policies to reconstruct those dominant conceptions. Much as Shaw and McKay's work was an attempt to make sense of the world around them, this research attempts in part to make sense of the constructions by which politicians, pundits, and average citizens interpret and understand the process of immigration, how it may or may not affect them, and what its role is in the broader social world. Throughout, the guiding notion is that the process of sense-making does not occur in a vacuum, and its outcomes can often have tangible and lasting results.

FROM THOUGHT TO ACTION: THE IMPORTANCE OF PERCEPTIONS

While perception is not always reality, the error in and the potential for manipulation of public opinions can have significant consequences (Brader, Valentino, and Suhay 2008). Perceiving or believing that immigrants engage in more crime than natives, or that the process of immigration undermines the American economy will not directly cause either outcome, but it may have other direct effects, and may, as labeling theory has shown, create those outcomes *indirectly*. For example, Feldmeyer (2009) finds that fears of immigrants have created barriers to their upward mobility, increasing, at least theoretically, their likelihood of engaging in crime (see also DeJong and Madamba 2001; Clark 1998). It is also likely that the presence of those barriers has led some immigrants to migrate to other parts of the country in search of better opportunities for advancement. Citizens of California, reacting to fears of threat posed by undocumented immigrants, threw their support behind the 1994 reelection campaign of former Governor Pete Wilson and Proposition 187, which blamed the state's economic problems on immigrants, especially the undocumented, and which, when passed, drastically cut back services to undocumented immigrants and their children (for a discussion, see Massey and Capoferro 2008). In this case, perceptions lead to action, and those actions brought sweeping consequences, not only in California but states around the country to which the foreign-born affected would turn for relief.

Sentiments such as those embodied in California's Proposition 187 tend to create a "perceived reality" of immigration and its relation to outcomes such as crime, employment, culture, and so on. What is meant by "perceived" is that for many, the nature of those relations diverge markedly from objective truth or observable facts. The disjuncture is created often either by the substitution of a biased view of the correlation or by the imposition of causation where none exists. It is, in effect, a construct, and to the degree that it is widespread across demographics, can produce some very real outcomes.

As Massey and Capoferro (2008) note, the restrictive policies of California's Proposition 187 and the Immigration Reform and Control Act of 1986 (IRCA), which were rooted in fears that immigrants posed a threat to American jobs, signaled to newcomers the effective closing of California as a settlement destination, transforming "immigration from a regional to a national phenomenon" (2008: 47). The perception of threat led to direct action to stem immigration, and unintentionally created an "immigrant diaspora." The flows of people across the country in the last fifteen years is unlike anything experienced in the U.S. in over a century, akin in function perhaps only to Chicago and the other urban hubs of the early 1900s. As increasing contact between immigrants and the native-born is likely to parallel the geographic spread, understanding how the arrival of immigrants is likely to be met is crucial, as the degree of acceptance will in large fashion help determine the social, economic, and political fortunes of these new Americans.

The direct effects of the perceived reality that immigration increases crime and undermines the employment opportunity structure for the native-born appear to be three-fold. First, such views reaffirm to the holder and others the image of immigrants as threats. Second, they tend to fuel calls for restrictive policies aimed at curbing future immigration. Third, as those images solidify, they tend to nullify dissonant information, namely research findings suggesting that immigration does not increase crime and may actually reduce it. When these conditions work in concert, the consequences can be profound.

AMERICAN ATTITUDES AND POLICY TOWARD IMMIGRANTS AND IMMIGRATION

In his seminal work, *Ain't No Makin' It,* Jay MacLeod (1987) finds that his group of white working-class boys sees the unfairness of the world that lies ahead for them, but is unable to locate that inequity in the structure of their society. Instead the Hallway Hangers are blinded by racism, blaming their plight on *reverse discrimination.* For MacLeod and others, a fundamental lack of class-conscious language has resulted in an equally fundamental inability to discuss structural factors. In much the same way, public discussions of immigration and its relation to crime rarely push beyond characteristics of the incoming groups to locate explanations within the systems of settlement and incorporation. Many of the same fears and concerns found two decades ago in MacLeod's white teenagers toward their Black peers can be found in the policies advocated by today's native-born adults toward recent immigrants. For native-born Americans, the major threats posed by immigrants include undermining of the traditional American way of life, taking jobs away from natives, and engaging in crime.

Such concerns drifted down from the top of our government, as when on May 15, 2006 then-president George W. Bush claimed in his address on immigration reform that, "[i]llegal immigration puts pressure on public schools and hospitals, it strains state and local budgets, and brings crime to our communities" (quoted from Rumbaut and Ewing 2007). They flowed through California's Proposition 187, which stated that "the people of California...have suffered and are suffering economic hardship [and] personal injury and damage caused by the criminal conduct of illegal aliens in this state" (ibid.). They reached across to the east coast, where in 2006, Hazelton, Pennsylvania proposed the "Illegal Immigration Relief Act Ordinance," which emphatically stated, "illegal immigration leads to higher crime rates," and sought to provide citizens "the right to live in peace free of the threat of crime" and protect them from the "crime committed by illegal aliens" (ibid.). And they filtered down to cities and towns with virtually no immigrants, such that in that same year, Altoona, Pennsylvania, with a population of roughly fifty thousand, enacted a similar ordinance, "which threatens to withdraw business licenses of employers and rental licenses of landlords who hire or rent to illegal immigrants" (Hamill 2006). Though the foreign-born make up only about one half of one percent of Altoona's population, residents reportedly sought to "stay ahead of the curve" (ibid.). Evidently, the curve in question for Altoonans is the perceived tendency for increasing immigration to bring increased numbers of unauthorized immigrants, who, the logic holds, are prone to engage in increased rates of crime (Hegeman 2007). Importantly, these enactments all focus on a particular subset of immigrants, those who enter this country without legal permission. And all purport a link between this subpopulation and crime, despite a fundamental lack of research. Very few studies have been conducted on this population precisely because they are difficult to locate and highly likely to refuse participation when found for fear of being deported. Their numbers are imprecise and demographic data on them are scant.[4] Surprisingly, however, the lack of data on this population has not prevented political leaders at multiple levels of government from drawing firm connections. Even when accurate data on immigration is available, it appears to go unused. Recent research on perceptions of immigration suggest that the American public is largely misinformed about a variety of aspects of immigration, most notably the differing sizes of various ethnic populations (Brader, et al. 2008; Sides and Citrin 2007; Scheve and Slaughter 2001; Espenshade and Hempstead 1996).

Research on *attitudes* toward immigrants reveals a bleak situation. In 2006, ten percent of Americans named immigration as the most pressing problem facing the nation, higher than at any time since the

---

[4] Defining the unauthorized immigrant population is problematic for three reasons: first, they are likely undercounted by the census; second, their rates of emigration and mortality are difficult to ascertain; third, ideological questions persist regarding whether to include in the count those whose visas have lapsed or are awaiting renewal (cf. Passel 2005, 2006; Merrell 2007).

Pew Research Center began asking the question in its surveys (Brader et al. 2008). In a cross-national review of attitudes toward immigrants, Simon and Lynch (1999) note that in a 1993 poll by the American Institute on Public Opinion (AIPO), 59 percent of respondents reported that immigration to this country *in the past* was a good thing, while 31 percent considered it bad for the country (Simon and Lynch 1999). When asked whether it was a good thing for the country *in 1993*, only 29 percent agreed, while 60 percent viewed it as a bad thing, leading the authors to conclude,

> At best the pattern that emerges from the American responses is the tendency to look at immigration with rose-colored glasses turned backwards. The American public expresses positive and approving attitudes toward immigrants who came 'earlier,' but expresses negative sentiments about those who are coming at whatever time a survey is being conducted (Simon and Lynch 1999: 458).

According to some researchers, the current American opposition toward immigrants is the continuation of a trend that began in the 1970s: "Public opinion data show that roughly two-thirds of Americans surveyed in the early 1980s thought that levels of immigration to the United States should be lowered, compared with fewer than 40 percent of respondents who expressed these views prior to 1970" (Espenshade and Hempstead 1996: 536; see also Simon and Alexander 1993). While it may have re-intensified in the last few decades, opposition to immigration is far from a product of the late 20th century.[5] Since at least the mid-1800s, the general tones of public opinion and federal policy toward immigrants can best be described as oppositional. Historians have noted American hostility toward newcomers as far back as the 1840s, when immigration to the northeast and its concomitant influx of cheap labor put pressure on native workers (Burns and Gimpel 2000;

---

[5] And it's far from bounded by American borders. Both immigrant and migrant groups have been viewed as presenting problems to their host countries or locales and have often been constructed as harbingers of disorganization and downfall. See Sniderman, Hagendoorn, and Markus (2004) for native opposition in The Netherlands as well as Tonry's (1997a) edited volume for an excellent discussion of the immigration-related issues faced by a number of countries.

Ernst 1948). That decade also saw the beginnings of the California gold rush, which created a need for cheap labor filled by Chinese immigrants. As mines dried up, these same immigrants helped build the transcontinental railroad. When that work was finished in 1869, they moved into agriculture, only to be accused by recently unionized Irish laborers of taking away American jobs (Espenshade and Hempstead 1996). Despite their notable contributions, the 1882 passage of the Chinese Exclusion Act put an abrupt end to Chinese immigration, though not the demand for cheap labor. For a time, that vacuum was filled by Japanese workers, but their propensity to demand higher wages and strike when those demands went unmet, would ultimately lead to the 1907 Gentlemen's Agreement between the United States and Japan, "which effectively terminated [an immigration] flow that was not revived for fifty years" (Espenshade and Hempstead 1996: 537).

The crude and rather narrow exclusionary powers imposed against the Chinese and Japanese would eventually be replaced with broader reforms. In 1921, the U.S. government instituted the first numerical restrictions on immigration with the passage of the Emergency Quota Act, which limited the annual number of immigrants from any particular country to three percent of their total 1910 population in the U.S., as recorded by the Census Bureau. Three years later, that quota was reduced to two percent when the Johnson-Reed Immigration Act went into effect. The outcome was that for close to forty years the United States existed as a nation of immigrants in reputation only. It was not until 1965 that the doors to immigration were opened again, this time with the passage of the Hart-Cellar Reform Act, championed largely by Congressional members who were themselves the children and grandchildren of immigrants.

Researchers looking for causes of American opposition to immigrants have tended to find them in the economy, with many noting that opposition rises during periods of economic recession (King, Massoglia, and Uggen 2012; Burns and Gimpel 2000; Citrin et al. 1997; Lapinski et al. 1997; Simon and Alexander 1993). Surprisingly, several authors have noted that *personal* economic insecurity is much *less* of a determinant of attitudes than is one's perception of the health of the national economy (Burns and Gimpel 2000; Citrin et al. 1997; Espenshade and Hempstead 1996). When the *country's* economic present and future are viewed dimly, regardless of one's own financial standing, citizens tend to hold more negative views toward immigrants and are more likely to call for restricting immigration inflows.

A more troubling finding is that the effect of economic fears in determining attitudes is diminished once accounting for prejudice. Berry and Tischler (1978), noting the linkage between attitudes and economic conditions, argue that racial prejudice operates as a mediating factor. Worsening economic conditions work to increase racial prejudice, which heightens opposition to minority group members, immigrants in particular. According to Burns and Gimpel (2000: 222), "attitudes on immigration policy are highly contingent upon stereotypical beliefs about the work ethic and intelligence of other groups, especially among whites." These authors note that economic conditions essentially activate latent prejudices, exacerbating preexisting negative views. Similarly, Citrin et al. (1997) find that along with dissatisfaction with the national economy and anxiety over increased taxes, negative views of minority groups and immigrants in particular account for American attitudes toward restricting immigration. These findings have been replicated outside of the U.S. as well. In research on native Dutch opposition to immigrants, Sniderman, Hagendoor, and Markus (2004) find that while concerns over economic well-being contribute to opposition, concerns over perceived threats to national identity—the perception that "Deutsch-ness" would be supplanted by "immigrant-ness"—are the stronger factor. It would appear, then, that "public opinion about immigrants seems to be driven more by stereotype than empirical fact" (Wang 2012: 744; cf. Kposowa, et al. 2009; Ousey and Kubrin 2009; Brader, Valentino, and Suhay 2008; Simon and Sikich 2007; Simon and Lynch 1999).

While most of the research literature has focused on the generalized group *immigrant*, very few studies have disaggregated public opinion by ethnicity or country of origin. Given the relative recency of the immigration boom as well as limitations on available data over the years, this is not surprising. In fact, Burns and Gimpel (2000: 219) find that as recently as 1992, negative stereotypes about Latinos *and African Americans* were associated with a desire to decrease immigration. It would seem that only a little more than 15 years ago, "among many whites, blacks and immigrants may count simply as outsiders," with many majority whites failing to make meaningful distinctions among minority groups. Those authors show, however, that the effect on attitudes toward immigration of holding anti-Black views had worn off by 1996, which they attribute to a changing political context. Because of the 1994 reelection campaign of Pete Wilson for Governor of California, which gave rise to California's Proposition 187 and the presidential campaign of 1996, in which Bob Dole criticized former President Bill Clinton for allowing unauthorized immigrants access to social services (Freedburg 1996), the public quickly received a crash course in immigration. Not surprisingly, these events were followed by "steep increases in anti-immigrant sentiment" among Americans, as Muste's (2013: 398) longitudinal analysis of public opinion toward immigration has shown.

The years since 1996 have seen a dramatic increase in media coverage of immigration.[6] The American public has been inundated with information on the topic, particularly during election seasons, and in consequence they have become increasingly polarized and responsive to stereotypical representations. In an analysis of newspaper coverage of the 2005-2006 immigration debate, Dietrich (2012) finds that race, again, was a central component, though race by then firmly and exclusively referred to Latinos. The "only immigrant group ever specifically referenced with regard to undocumented immigration was Latinos" suggesting that the debate "is not about 'immigrants.' It's about Latinos" (2012: 724).

The issues surrounding immigration were also a major focus, and major turning point, of the 2008 presidential election, with prospective candidates offering agendas that linked immigration and crime control (Mario and Oliver 2012).[7] In the run-up to the Iowa caucus that year, Republicans "picked immigration as the country's most important problem more than any other issue (including war, terrorism, and the economy" (Brader, et al. 2008:959). Candidates Mitt Romney and Rudy Giuliani traded charges that the other was "soft" on immigration,

---

[6] A search of the *New York Times* archive for the terms "immigration" or "immigrant" (and any variations thereof) retrieved 5,669 articles for the 15 year period from January 1, 1996 to December 31, 2010. In contrast, a search for the same terms for the 15 year period January 1, 1981 to December 31, 1995 returned 1,657 results, while a search of the 130 years from 1851 to 1980 returned 4,687 items.

[7] This was despite the fact that opinion polls from the time indicate crime was not a major focus of the voting public. For a discussion of the use of immigration and crime as symbolic politics, see Marion and Oliver (2012).

with the Romney camp claiming Giuliani, the former mayor of New York, ran a "sanctuary city" by allowing unauthorized immigrants, "to send their children to schools, use the public health system and report crimes without fear of arrest because of their status" (Gaouette 2007). Giuliani responded in kind, noting that Romney, former governor of Massachusetts, helmed a state with its own share of "sanctuary cities," notably Cambridge, Somerville, and Brookline (Luo 2007). The attacks on Romney were particularly damning, given reports that he had hired undocumented immigrants to perform landscaping maintenance (Saltzman 2006), had continued to employ them throughout the election campaign (Cramer, Sacchetti, and Paige 2007), and had in a 2005 interview spoken, "approvingly about measures being considered in Congress that would have offered a path to citizenship for the estimated 12 million illegal immigrants in the country" (Luo 2007). The measure in question was the Comprehensive Immigration Reform Act, of which former Arizona senator and eventual Republican presidential candidate, John McCain, was the leading GOP supporter. McCain received heavy criticism for a bill that was labeled by many anti-immigrationists as "amnesty" (Vartabedian and Riccardi 2008). Some have claimed that his support for the bill contributed to the "near collapse of the early front-runner's campaign in 2007" (Brader et al. 2008: 959). That immigration became the centerpiece of the election, especially for Republicans, and that accusations of being "soft" on it could dash political hopes suggests how far the American public has come from lumping African Americans and immigrants into a single marginalized group.

A Growing Awareness

Increasing public attentiveness to the issues surrounding immigration has refined the American public's ability to differentiate between groups of ethnic immigrants. With that increasing sophistication has come a need for researchers to provide more nuanced testing of public perceptions toward newcomers. Brader, et al. (2008) are among the first to compare perceptions across ethnic groups. Like many before them, their findings point to the persistence of prejudice as a mediating factor of opposition toward immigrants. Unlike those before them, however, Brader and colleagues show that prejudice is not applied broadly to *all* immigrants, that some are viewed as more threatening than others, and that those more threatening are met with greater opposition.

Brader at al. (2008) report the results of an experiment designed to test whether public reactions to news items addressing the costs of immigration depend upon who the immigrants are. The experiment involved the distribution of a mock *New York Times* news article of a governors' conference on immigration, paired with the picture of an immigrant. It uses a 2 x 2 design, in which both the tone of the article (positive consequences of immigration paired with positive response of governors, versus negative consequences paired with negative response) were varied along with the ethnicity of the immigrant group discussed, either Latino or European (and specifically Mexican or Russian). Questions distributed along with the article asked whether respondents preferred to reduce immigration and whether they preferred English-only laws. For both groups, opposition to immigration was stronger for the negative story but the effect for the Latino group was two times stronger than the European. On the issue of language, for the European group, news emphasizing costs actually elicited *less* support for English-only laws than news emphasizing costs. In contrast, the negative Latino story elicited significantly more support for such laws than the positive one, suggesting that—all other things equal—the public is more inclined to oppose Latino immigration than European, and particularly when reports key readers to negative consequences.

Using an internet-based survey, the authors also include options testing actual behavior, allowing respondents to request more information, to request more anti-immigrant information, and to send an anti-immigration message to their congressmen and women. The results are striking. For the positive news stories, those with the European version were more likely to request information, to request anti-immigrant information, and to send an anti-immigrant message to Congress. For the negative stories, however, news seeking behavior actually *diminished* for the European group and increased dramatically for the Latino. The results indicate that *positive news stories suppress information seeking behavior* when the group in question is Latino but that negative news stories for that group stimulate respondents to "do something" about it. Over 45 percent of respondents in the negative Latino group sent an anti-immigration measure, close to 20 percentage points higher than when the message was positive. One explanation is that respondents may have been less aware of European immigration and were seeking clarification, while for Latinos they have been aware of the negative consequences such that positive information was discordant and met with opposition.

The authors test for potential causes for these differences, specifically whether they are a product of perceptions of harm or feelings of anxiety. Findings show that perceptions of harm are similar across all four categories, but that a sense of anxiety is significantly higher in the negative Latino group. "In every case, anxiety about immigration influences opinions and action" (Brader, et al. 2008: 969). And while respondents did perceive the threat of harm from immigration, it was not significant enough to alter perceptions or behavior.

In a second experiment, the authors test for the impact of immigrant skill level on perceptions of harm, feelings of anxiety, and behavior by manipulating news stories to suggest the Latino and European immigrant is either low-skilled or high skilled. Results show that the pattern for harm is similar across ethnicity, increasing proportionately from the positive to the negative. For anxiety, while there is virtually no change between the European stories, there is a dramatic increase for news stories focusing on low-skill Latino immigrants over high-skilled ones. This pattern is similar for the behavioral aspect of those with the Latino stories, as negative reports induce many more respondents to send an anti-immigration message. Among respondents in the European group, negative stories lead *fewer* respondents to send messages than when the story is positive.

Collectively the results suggest that Americans perceive immigrants differently depending on their ethnicity or country of origin. Moreover, different ethnic group cues (positive, negative, low-skilled, or high-skilled) elicit varying levels of anxiety, which affects both attitudes and behavior. When group cues are consistent with negative stereotypes—Latino immigrants are low-skilled—opposition is particularly strong. "Citizens *felt* more threatened by Latino immigration, not European immigration, and this feeling triggered opposition to immigration and multilingual laws, prompted requests for information, and led people to send anti-immigration message to congress" (Brader, et al. 2008: 975, emphasis in original). Ultimately, the findings suggest, as the authors note, "the public is susceptible to error and manipulation when group cues trigger anxiety independent of the actual threat posed by the group" (Brader, et al. 2008: 959).

Coupling the above findings with those of two other recent studies is instructive. In their analysis of Dutch citizens' opposition to immigrants, Sniderman and colleagues find that situational triggers, operationalized as threats to national identity, "mobilize support [for exclusionary policies] *beyond the core constituency already predisposed to oppose immigration*" (Sniderman et al. 2004: 46, emphasis added). A perceived threat to national identity posed by newcomers, regardless of whether there is any factual basis for the threat, has the tendency to convert citizens who would normally not be opposed to immigration to advocate for the restriction of migrant inflows. These findings have strong implications for the consequences of constructing immigrants as posing challenges to the American way of life, whether in taking away Americans' jobs or in refusing to assimilate via delayed English language acquisition.

Secondly, work by Sides and Citrin (2007) suggests the rigidity of prejudicial perceptions. Noting that hostility toward out-group members is in part a function of inaccurate beliefs about the group, the authors test whether correcting those beliefs alters perceptions. Since many Americans often overestimate the size of immigrant populations—which may lead them to perceive immigrants as a greater threat—Sides and Citrin test whether beliefs undergo significant change once respondents have been provided with correct estimates of group sizes. Their results show that correcting erroneous numerical perceptions has little effect on how citizens viewed immigrants, as a whole, and unauthorized immigrants in particular. The authors suggest that attitudes toward immigrants may be characterized as *symbolic predispositions*, such that factual information plays a role in attitude formation secondary to ascriptive characteristics. As "immigration is arguably explicitly 'racial'...symbolic predispositions such as national identity or a generalized tolerance for difference, predispositions that are developed early in life and durable over time, may be more potent than an encyclopedia's worth of facts about immigration" (Sides and Citrin 2007: 19).

In sum, American attitudes against immigrants can at best be described as ambivalent, at worst, overtly hostile, with a long history of negative stereotyping, open exclusion, and naked prejudice. The current atmosphere is different not so much in tenor or tone, but volume. In an age when information can be transmitted virtually everywhere, nearly instantly, people who may never have seen an immigrant will almost surely have an attitude ready, when and if the encounter should ever take place. The American public's education on all matters immigration has grown dramatically, and the nature of the underlying message has largely been one of exclusion. It is at least plausible that, given the nature of the discourse, many Americans have been primed to view newcomers in a certain way, perhaps more so for those who have no counterbalance: people for whom the effects of immigration are either new or only distant. The implications for the type of reception immigrants may receive in such places, and the consequences for successful incorporation, are not positive. While the discourse might simply be described as hostile toward "others," there are distinct areas in which that hostility has been rooted in something deeper: fear. A distillation of the discourse reveals that opposition to immigrants and immigration has been sustained, even grown, by the framing of newcomers as threats to the well-being of native-born Americans, in particular as threats to take away jobs and threats of crime and violence.

Threats to "Our" Jobs

One of the most persistent threads in popular discussions of immigration is that immigrants come to take away American jobs. Newspaper testimonials and survey research consistently point to this fear among the native-born population, while research continues to belie the point (O'Neil and Tienda 2010; Oppenheimer 2008; Cohen and Constable 2007; Gorman and Blankstein 2007; Alba, Rumbaut, and Marotz 2005). It is instructive, as Dietrich (2012: 737) notes, that "the rhetoric is not about 'my job' but 'our' jobs—not in a purely self-interested fashion but with a sense of group claim to jobs." True, immigrants do come in search of employment and are very much valued by American industry heads as a cheaper source of labor (Alsalam and Smith 2005; Immigration Policy Center 2005; Borjas 1994), but the immigrants to whom the above criticism is pointed are rarely the ones with whom Americans are likely to compete. Ironically, the very groups who are welcomed as contributing to society—well educated immigrants with high degrees of human and social capital from places like India, Japan, and parts of China—are those most likely to compete for the types of jobs to which Americans aspire. Portes (2007: 1) offers an apt example: "In North Carolina, the annual harvest requires about 150,000 agricultural workers. In a recent year, 6,000 openings were reserved for U.S. workers at $9.02 per hour [well above minimum wage]. A total of 120 applied, 25 showed up to work on the first day, and none finished the harvest." This of course begs the question, *taking jobs away from whom*? Staying with the agricultural example, without immigrants as a cheap source of labor, farms would have to raise wages to such an extent—to attract domestic workers— that the average consumer would be unable or unwilling to buy the product, regardless of how organic it may be. Ironically, Portes (2007) notes, as do Rumbaut and Ewing (2007), that immigration may actually create jobs for native-born workers in what he refers to as the spin-off effect. Rather than competing for skilled positions, immigrants tend to cluster in the secondary market—on farms, in restaurants and landscaping crews, and elsewhere—resulting in "better-paid clerical, administrative, and government service jobs that are attractive to native-born workers" (Portes 2007: 26).

Work by Alsalam and Smith (2005) highlight the need to disaggregate the block group "immigrant" when discussing issues of employment. Their research indicates that there are at least two broad types of immigrant workers in the U.S. labor force: those who are skilled and those who are not. Current immigration policy allots only 5,000 visas each year to low-skill and low-education workers; in 2004, only 1,525 were granted (Immigration Policy Center 2005). Only two of 16 types of visas—H2A and H2B—can be available to low-skill workers. The H2A visa is reserved for agricultural workers and the H2B for seasonal workers. Moreover, H2B visas are capped at 66,000 per year. "In Fiscal Year (FY) 2004 this cap was reached in March, halfway through the fiscal year. In FY 2005 the cap was reached in January, only three months into the fiscal year" (Immigration Policy Center 2005: 15).

In 2004, one in seven U.S. workers was foreign-born, half of whom had arrived after 1990. Forty percent of foreign-born workers were from Mexico and Central America, with another 25 percent from Asia. There is a clear skill divide that manifests the geographies of countries of origin: immigrants who come from the furthest away, tend to have greater skills as a group than immigrants who come from countries closer to the U.S. For example, "40 percent of the immigrants from India who came to the United States in fiscal year 2003 were admitted on an employment-based preference, whereas only 3 percent of immigrants from Mexico and Central America were admitted on that basis" (Alsalam and Smith 2005: 3, n.5). The labor market outcomes of unskilled immigrants differ from natives and their more skilled counterparts along three axes: the likelihood of being employed, the type of employment, and the wages earned. Despite lower educational attainment, men from Mexico and Central America aged 16 or older are more likely to be employed (83%) than native-born men (67.9%) and immigrant men from other parts of the world (72.6%). In 2004, 59.5 percent of immigrants aged 25 and over without a high school diploma were in the work force, compared to only 36.8 percent of natives. This difference is largely explained by the reduced tendencies for Mexican and Central American men to attend school, be disabled, or retire early (Alsalam and Smith 2005).[8] "Given these different educational backgrounds, most native-born workers are not competing directly with foreign-born workers for the same types of jobs" (Immigration Policy Center 2005: 12). Neither the gap in education nor the consequent lack of competition is likely to change in the foreseeable future, as the likelihood for immigrants from Mexico and Central America to be in school are less than half those for natives and other immigrants (Alsalam and Smith 2005).

The type of employment also varies, in part as a function of the lack of educational attainment. Roughly 48 percent of all workers from Mexico and Central America are employed in just three of 22 occupational groups—production, construction and extraction, and building and grounds cleaning and maintenance—while only 14.8 percent of native-born workers are employed in the same types of jobs (Alsalam and Smith 2005). More generally, 75 percent of Mexican and Central American workers can be characterized as being employed in *low-education* occupations, such as grounds maintenance, painting, and construction, compared to 26 percent of natives and 31.8 percent of all other immigrants (ibid.). More pointedly, 34 percent are in *very low-education* occupations, such as agriculture, dishwashing and cooking, maid service, and hand packing, versus 6.7 percent of natives and 9.8 percent of all other immigrants. In contrast, only 3.9 percent of Mexican and Central American men are employed in high education positions, compared to 26.2 percent for both natives and other immigrants (ibid.).

Lastly are the differences in wages earned. Men from Mexico and Central America earn less than natives and immigrants from all other

---

[8] With regard to disability, the authors argue that disabled individuals might be less likely to migrate in general and less likely to migrate in search employment specifically.

parts of the world; weekly earnings among men from Mexico and Central America are roughly half the earnings of native-born men. Mexican and Central American women fare only slightly better, with earnings equivalent to roughly 60 percent those of native women. In contrast, for foreign-born workers from the rest of the world, pay was roughly equivalent to their native counterparts.

Analyses of the impact of immigration—skilled and unskilled, legal and illegal—on labor market outcomes for the native-born depend largely on whether one uses a static or dynamic model of the economy. A static model assumes that immigrants exist only as a labor supply, which would tend to drive down wages, at least for the least-skilled, high-school dropouts in particular (see Alsalam and Smith 2005) and that "immigrants and U.S.-born workers are perfectly interchangeable" (Immigration Policy Center 2005: 7). Estimates from analyses over the last 20 years range from negligible effects to 10 percent earnings reductions for dropouts. Most critics of immigration tend to take a static view when discussing consequences for jobs. Dynamic models, on the other hand, assume that immigrants operate to increase both labor supply and labor demand, most notably as consumers in a consumer culture. This view is analogous to the *immigrant revitalization* perspective, which argues that an influx of immigrants can breathe new cultural and economic life into stagnant areas (Donato, et al. 2008; Nielsen and Martinez 2006; Lee, Martinez, and Rosenfeld 2001). In 2004, "consumer purchasing power totaled $686 billion among Latinos and $363 billion among Asians. Given that roughly 44 percent of Latinos and 69 percent of Asians were foreign-born in that year, the buying power of immigrants reached into the hundreds of billions" (Immigration Policy Center 2005: 7-8).

Smith and Edmonston (1997) find only a weak relationship between the number of immigrants in a city or state and the wages of native-born workers, for all types of workers, whether male or female, members of minority groups, or skilled or unskilled. In fact, their research suggests the only group that "appears to suffer substantially from new waves of immigration are immigrants from earlier waves, for whom the recent immigrants are close substitutes in the labor market" (Smith and Edmonston 1997: 6). An analysis of the effect of the influx of Mariel Cubans—described as the dregs of Cuban society—in the 1980s found it to have no effect on the wages of Miami's existing workforce (Card 1990). A more recent and far reaching analysis finds that the influx of poorly educated, low-skill immigrants from 1980-2000 had virtually no impact on the wages of low-skill native workers and in fact the wages of native workers without a high school diploma relative to those with a diploma "remained nearly constant" (Card 2005: 323).

Rather than being a drain on the economy, immigrants might actually offer beneficial effects. For example, native-born students who might be at risk for dropping out might consider continuing their education or otherwise increasing their skills to gain advantage in the workforce (Alsalam and Smith 2005), which would raise not only their wages but those of immigrants as well by decreasing the labor supply in low-skill sectors. Second, an increase in labor supply in one employment area could affect demand in another. For example, an influx of child care providers could lower rates of child care, enabling native mothers to seek work. Alternatively, a surge in the number of registered nurses from abroad might enable some hospitals to expand, creating new jobs in construction, maintenance, medical, service, and technology fields. The demand for such workers may only grow in the coming years. "Whether the retirement of the baby boomers and the growing demand for a wide range of services associated with an aging population will increase the relative earnings in lower-skill occupations is unknown" (Alsalam and Smith 2005: 26).

Several researchers have noted the absolute need for low-skill immigrant workers. Brauer (2006) points out that higher rates of immigration are beneficial for the Social Security Administration because immigrants tend to be largely of working age and highly likely to be employed, meaning that as a group, they tend to put much more money in than they take out. This source of funding will be particularly important as baby boomers begin to retire. According to the Immigration Policy Institute (2005), immigration is critical to the growth of the U.S. labor force, and consequently the national economy, since it is unlikely that the native workforce will increase its productivity or grow sufficiently on its own, for at least two reasons. First, U.S.-born workers currently work some of the highest hours of any workforce in the industrialized world, and those hours have actually been declining since the 1950s, suggesting it is unlikely that American employees will work longer hours in the future. Second, the U.S. fertility rate hovers slightly above 2.0 children per woman, with UN projections that by 2015-2020 it will fall to 1.91, meaning an inability to recreate the labor force from within the native population alone (Immigration Policy Center 2005). Immigrants are important to growing the economy also because of the type of work they are most likely to perform. Projections for the fastest growing industries indicate 98 percent of employment growth between 2002 and 2012 will occur in service industries, with 80 percent in five areas which produce sizeable low-skilled jobs: education and health services, professional and business services, state and local governments, leisure and hospitality services, and retail trade, the types of employment to which many immigrants are typically drawn.

Immigrants complement, rather than replace, the native-born labor force, which tends to be older, with the baby boomers approaching retirement, and increasingly better educated, as more young adults graduate from college in search of higher skilled and higher paying jobs. In 2004, three out of five native workers had *at least* a high school diploma or some college, while two out of five foreign-born workers had *at most* either a high school education or a four-year degree (Immigration Policy Center 2005). Immigrants—skilled and unskilled—hold the potential to both replace the retiring population and assume available low-skill jobs to which native-born workers are increasingly unlikely to apply.

While today "the popular image of immigrants in the American mind is based on the stereotype of *low-skilled* Hispanic laborers" (Brader, Valentino, and Suhay 2008: 961; emphasis in original), skill is only one aspect of the prevailing stereotype. For many native-born Americans, the "perceived reality" of immigration is that it brings *crime* with it and does so in large numbers.

Threats of Crime and Violence

One of the enduring anomalies of crime is its consistent tendency to be over-perceived. For example, according to Wagner (2003), 71 percent of the U.S. population believed there was more crime in 1996 than the year before and 46 percent believed there was more crime in their *local* area than the year before. In reality, according to the Federal Bureau of Investigation (FBI), serious index crimes declined by slightly more than five percent from 1995-1996. Four years later, the same pattern held, though in lesser numbers. In 2000, 47 percent of the population believed crime had increased since 1999, while 34 percent felt crime in their local area had increased over the previous year. Again, according to the FBI, across the nation as a whole, crime had declined roughly six and half percent from 1999-2000. In fact, rates of crime fell steadily and consistently from 1994 to 2005, when they hit all-time record lows.

Several researchers have noted this misperception may in large part be due to media effects and in particular the daily coverage of violent crimes on the evening news or in local newspapers (Romer, Jamieson, and Aday 2003; Chiricos, Escholz, and Gertz 1997; Williams and Dickinson 1993). The availability heuristic tells us that individuals will tend to overestimate the occurrence of phenomena to the degree that examples of it are readily available for their recall (Tversky and Kahneman 1973). Consequently, the fact that crime rates have been dropping for more than a decade still may come as a surprise to many. The situation becomes even more complicated when addressing immigration and crime, and not just because both are hot-button issues receiving significant attention in print, television, and online media. According to Martinez, Lee, and Nielsen (2004: 131-2), "many associated the rise in drug violence [in the 1980s] with ethnic minorities and immigrants" (see also Lutton 1996; Blumstein 1995; Lockwood, Pottieger and Inciardi 1995; Inciardi 1992). Not surprisingly, then, Dietrich (2012) finds that nearly every negative claim made about immigrants or immigration during the 2005-2006 immigration debate portrayed newcomers as either criminals or, to a lesser degree, terrorists. In fact, recent findings suggest that the growth in immigrant populations may have actually contributed to the dramatic declines in rates of crime since the 1980s (Ousey and Kubrin 2009; Stowell et al. 2009).

Conservative and popular accounts of the immigration-crime connection tend to present the issue as an individual-level phenomenon, ignoring the process of immigration, the structural forces impinging on immigrants, and the specific histories and capitals (human, social, and cultural) immigrants bring with them. The most basic of the individualist approaches is one that views immigrants as making a rational choice to engage in crime. In some cases, a perceived resistance to assimilation is thrown in as a mediating factor. In this way, it's not simply that immigrants engage in crime because of a predisposition, but rather it is a multistage process rooted in their decision to retain traditional ways of life. Conceptually, step one involves immigrants' resistance to "our" customs, which leads the first generation directly to reduced occupational attainment and leads their children, either the second generation (those born in the United States) or what has been termed the 1.5 generation (foreign-born children who immigrated before age 11) to reduced educational attainment, which then accounts for reduced occupational success. Step two is a classic Mertonian approach, wherein these economically marginalized individuals are more likely to engage in crime as a means to achieve classic American goals.[9] Stark findings come from Alba, Rumbaut, and Marotz's (2005) analysis of responses to the 2000 General Social Survey. According to that research, nearly three quarters (73 percent) of the American public believes that it is at least somewhat likely that immigrants cause higher rates of crime, with fully one quarter believing it very likely. Those numbers are even higher than the sixty percent who believed it at least somewhat likely that immigrants caused Americans to lose jobs, and the fifty-six percent who believed it somewhat or very likely that more immigrants made it harder to keep the country united (see also Simon and Sikich 2007).

A variant of this individual-level conception is one that locates the problem within the *culture* of immigrant groups, seeming to offer a more complex explanation than it really does. This approach views all immigrant groups as prone to violence due to some innate cultural deficiency, an idea in circulation for decades (Lewis 1959). One of the major problems with this approach is that it tends to reify the designation "immigrant," into one unified category, subsuming variations in different groups' histories. Typically it does so at the same time that it exempts certain other groups. For example, stereotypical beliefs hold that *all* Mexican (or *all* Guatemalan, all Nigerian, and so on) immigrants refuse to assimilate themselves, and thus should be denied entry via the building of a wall (Robbins 2010; Associated Press

---

[9] One of the conceptual problems with this approach is that it assumes these different groups quickly adopt "our" goals, but fail to adopt "our" means, specifically, the *desire* to *put in the work*. It's a classic example of cultural relativism in that "traditional" American goals are viewed as so good as to be universally desirable while true Americans are the only ones willing to put in the requisite effort. At the same time that it doubly validates the host culture, it doubly stigmatizes the *other*: immigrants' traditional ways of life pale in comparison to "ours" and are rightly abandoned while immigrants themselves are not as hard-working as "true" Americans, and must, in a sense, cheat to get the rewards.

1992).[10] In contrast, *all* Asian immigrants are often viewed as exceptional and contributing to the overall well-being of the country, the so-called "model minority". This is not to suggest that culture plays no role in the process of immigrant incorporation; research continues to show it does, though exactly how and why are as yet unclear (Portes 2009; Waters 2009).[11] What it should point to is the tendency for lay-discussions of culture to become reductionistic; in effect they make too much out of culture. While most sociologists are highly attuned to cultural variations *within* and *between* groups, popular conceptions are often not. "Culture" becomes a very broad, very vague, typically exogenous category. Rather than acting as a *contributing* factor for differences between groups, it becomes the *explanatory* one. Moreover, culture is viewed as innate and immutable, something individuals carry with them across space and time, irrespective of historical events, geographical features, economic conditions, or political relations, when in fact culture evolves precisely because of those events, features, conditions, and relations.

This linkage to crime is perhaps nowhere clearer than in former Republican Senator Fred Thompson's remarks in the matter in his push for the 2008 Presidential candidate nomination. According to Thompson, "Twelve million illegal immigrants later, we are now living in a nation that is beset by people who are suicidal maniacs and want to

---

[10] The idea of a wall to keep out "invaders" has been around since at least the 5th century BCE. Its first reference in this country may well have been circa 1750 when John Jay, first Chief Justice of the Supreme Court, advocated for a wall of brass to keep out "Catholic alien invaders". Its recent popularity in the U.S. can be traced to Pat Buchanan, who made its construction a focal point of his 1992 presidential campaign. With advances in technology, the concept of a physical wall along the U.S.-Mexico border has been replaced by a virtual one. The idea has received surprising support, as when lawmakers in Mississippi proposed imposing fees on international wire transfers made by state residents that could be donated to the federal government to fund the efforts (Newsom 2011; Hurt 2006).

[11] Portes and Waters highlighted this disagreement in a panel presentation they shared at the 2009 ESS Annual meeting, where the one referenced data indicating structural conditions almost entirely explained second-generation outcomes, while the other referenced data suggesting the enduring role of culture and the difficulty in measuring it. I will discuss the place of culture shortly.

kill countless innocent men, women and children around the world" (Sidoti 2007; see also Sampson 2008). While egregious, the sentiment resonates with research on American attitudes regarding immigration and crime. Analysis of the 2000 General Social Survey revealed that, at the time, nearly three quarters (73 percent) of the American public believed that it was at least somewhat likely that immigrants cause higher rates of crime, with fully one quarter believing it was very likely (Alba, et al. 2005). Similarly, research by Simon and Sikich (2007) finds that in 1995, 34 percent of the public agreed that immigration contributed to crime; that number fell only slightly by 2003 to 27 percent. The numbers are similar to research conducted by the Pew Research Center for the People and the Press on attitudes among Whites and Blacks toward immigrants: 34 percent of Whites believed that immigration significantly increased crime, compared to 26 percent of Blacks (Doherty 2006). A recent analysis on the mediating effect of race/ethnicity finds that Whites are more likely than Latinos or Blacks to believe immigration makes crime worse (Higgins, Gabbidon, and Martin 2010). It is likely that opinions on the matter would be stronger, were the group in question unauthorized immigrants, though attitudinal data regarding that population are lacking (cf. Chandler and Tsai 2001). Nevertheless, research on the effect of attitudes has indicated the importance of criminogenic beliefs. Iguarta and Cheng (2009) find that when respondents were primed with a newspaper article framing immigrants as more likely to increase crime, respondents were more likely to view immigration as problematic, to hold a negative attitude toward immigration, and to more strongly disagree with positive beliefs about immigration. Similarly, research has found that fear of crime strongly predicts favoring restrictionist policies (Simcox 1997), and is associated with holding right-wing authoritarian views (Cohrs and Stelzl 2010).

CONSEQUENCES OF ATTITUDINAL OPPOSITION TO IMMIGRANTS

The preceding discussion sought to tease out dominant views toward immigrants and in doing so to show that there exists a generalized opposition to them based upon fears of threats of crime and economic competition. This is not to say of course that all Americans are opposed to immigration; many welcome the benefits diversity brings. Yet the overall attitude toward the foreign-born is not so welcoming, and nowhere is that clearer than in state and federal policies, which with few exceptions have been designed to limit the inflow of non-nationals. Whether the push for new regulations stems from the work of moral crusaders or the democratic outcome of the public's wishes is unclear. What is clear is that the growth of restrictionist immigration policy over the last 20 years has paralleled, and appears to have intensified with, the growth of the nation's immigrant population. Such policies may be seen as the logical response borne from anti-immigrant sentiment generally. As the previous section addressed public attitudes toward immigration, this section looks to the consequences of those attitudes. The most direct outcome has been the proliferation of immigration-focused policy generally, and anti-immigrant policy in particular. Of equal importance, though perhaps to less recognition, has been the concomitant nullification of research. In the midst of policy enactments designed to curb the arrival of newcomers and fueled by rhetoric painting them as dangerous, social scientists over the last two decades have produced a wealth of research indicating that immigrants pose no significant threat in terms of employment or crime. In addition, this chapter will address what are termed the *unintended consequences* of anti-immigrant sentiment and policy, because while they have largely failed to curb the arrival of the foreign-born, whose annual numbers continued to rise throughout the 1990s and early years of the new century, such policies have been successful at changing long-standing patterns of settlement, in effect transforming immigration from local concerns to national phenomenon.

Restrictive Policies

For over a century, immigration law has been used to keep certain populations, defined as undesirable, out of this country of immigrants. The first federal policy initiative restricting immigration was passed in 1875 and barred from entry criminals and prostitutes. Seven years later came the first federal law enacting restrictions based on country of origin, as Chinese immigrants were prohibited from entry, along with persons convicted of political crimes, "lunatics" or "idiots", and any who might become dependent on public charity. In 1929, illegal entry became a federal crime for the first time. In 1988 the penalty for re-entry after initial deportation was increased to 20 years, and the basis for deportation was set at the commission of an aggravated felony (McDonald 1997).

The move to enact more sweeping and forceful immigration policy began in earnest in the mid-1980s. In a review of contemporary policy initiatives on immigration, Hagan and Phillips argue "enforcement as a means of controlling immigration has less to do with deterring illegal crossings and removing suspect immigrants than with symbolically reasserting national and territorial sovereignty" (2008: 84; cf. Aliverti 2012). In 1986, Congress passed the *Immigration Reform and Control Act* (IRCA), designed to curtail undocumented immigration. It increased funding to southwestern border patrols and established penalties for employers who knowingly hired unauthorized immigrants. In a controversial provision, it also granted amnesty to all undocumented immigrants who could prove consistent residence in the U.S. since January 1, 1982. As a result of that provision, legal immigration from Mexico and Central America increased markedly in the 1990s, as existing immigrants were then able to sponsor family members for entry (Brauer 2006).[12] IRCA's attempts at restriction ultimately failed, as undocumented immigration continued to grow throughout the early 1990s. Particularly ineffective were the employer sanctions. From 1990-2003, employer audits declined from 10,000 to 2,200 and warnings dropped from 1,300 to 500. The number of fines fell from roughly 1,000 in 1991 to 124 in 2003.

In response to public outcry over the failure of IRCA, President Bill Clinton enacted a series of strategies in 1993 that came to be known as his "Prevention through Deterrence" program. The overall focus was the militarization of the Mexican border, through Operation Blockade outside El Paso in 1993, Operation Gatekeeper outside San Diego in 1994, and Operation Rio Grande outside Brownsville, Texas in 1997. During Clinton's presidency, the number of border agents increased from 3,400 in 1993 to 7,200 in 1999. By 2006, the number stood at 11,500. Despite these efforts, the number of undocumented immigrants increased and has continued to do so (Passel 2006). One important consequence, however, was the breaking up of migratory employment patterns. Workers from Mexico and Central America, who had previously followed a system of engaging in seasonal work in the U.S. and returning home for seasonal work there, became locked on

---

[12] Unlike employment laws, the family unification aspect of immigration laws has no numerical cap.

either side. Many in the U.S. chose to stay put rather than make the arduous journey home—made more difficult by the border militarization—and sent for their families when they could, increasing the overall population of undocumented workers in this country (Massey and Capoferro 2008). As Dietrich (2012: 726) suggests, anti-immigrant attitudes manifested in anti-immigrant legislation, with the unintended consequence of increasing, and making more permanent, the population of permanent undocumented immigrants.

In 1996, Clinton signed the *Illegal Immigration Reform and Immigrant Responsibility Act* (IIRIRA), which amended the 1952 *Immigration and Nationality Act (INA)* by increasing resources for enforcement and increasing the federal government's deportation powers over non-citizens. It expanded the categories of non-citizens who were "deportable" and expanded as well the offenses for which they could be deported. It also broadened the definition of "aggravated felony"—which had been the basis of deportation since 1988—to include 28 separate offenses. As a result, previously minor offenses became the grounds for deportation. For example, "a conviction for turnstile jumping in the New York City subway system is a 'theft of services' that carries a penalty sufficient to qualify as an aggravated felony and authorizes mandatory deportation" (Hickman and Suttorp 2008: 60; see also Morawetz 2000). Not only were the definitions of deportable offenses expanded, but they were applied retroactively to any pre-1996 cases, even ones for which those convicted had already served time or otherwise made restitution. In March of 1998, the Board of Immigration Appeals added Driving While Intoxicated (DWI) to the list of aggravated felonies. The following September, the Immigration and Naturalization Service (INS)[13] deported hundreds of *legal immigrant residents* with DWI convictions through the retroactive provision of the IIRIRA (Hagan and Phillips 2008: 87, n.3; Koppel

---

[13] The INS handled immigration enforcement until 2002, when the Homeland Security Act (HSA) established the Department of Homeland Security (DHS), under which many of the agencies which exercise the powers of the Patriot act are grouped, and which restructured many of the governmental agencies dealing with national security. As part of the restructuring, since 2002 immigration enforcement has been carried out by 2 agencies: the Bureau of Customs and Border Protection (CBP), which handles inspections of immigrants at ports of entry, and the Immigration and Customs Enforcement Agency (ICE), which enforces immigration laws within the country's interior.

1998). Also in 1996, Clinton signed the Anti-Terrorism and Effective Death Penalty Act (AEDPA), which significantly curtailed the judicial review process, to which previous deportees were entitled, and through which judges could overrule a deportation order if they perceived such a measure as posing hardship to an American citizen such as a spouse or child. The IIRIRA had upped the bar on judicial review by setting "exceptional or extremely unusual hardship" as the benchmark for overruling orders of deportation.

The new century brought heightened efforts as the 2001 Patriot Act took the issues of restrictive immigration policies to new levels. It granted broad powers to detain and deport any persons who were thought to pose a threat, regardless of evidence in support. Those powers did not go unused. Deportations increased from an average of 40,000 from 1990-1994 to 180,000 from 1996-2005, to 208,000 in 2005 (Hagan and Phillips 2008). These "removals" have continued to expand under the Obama administration, though to much less recognition. Analyses of U.S. deportations, as well as federal records on those deported, raise questions about what, in practice, it means to "pose a threat." Research suggests that as many as one out of four and perhaps more than 50 percent of those deported had no criminal record; of those non-criminal deportees, 69 percent were from Mexico, with another 16 percent from other Central American nations (Donohue 2012; Hagan and Phillips 2008; U.S. Dept. of Homeland Security 2006). In a sweeping analysis of a century of U.S. criminal deportations, King, Massoglia, and Uggen find that there exists "no evidence linking criminal deportations with crime rates" (2012: 1818).

As efforts were intensified to remove those who were already here, new policies were being drafted to prevent their re-entry and the entry of new immigrants. In the fall of 2006, Congress approved an additional 700 miles of fencing to be built along the Mexican border, which "if completed, could make it the most heavily fortified international boundary in the industrialized world" (Hagan and Phillips 2008: 91). Meanwhile, 12,380 miles of coast remain unfenced, as are virtually all of the 5,500 miles along the Canadian border. The extension of the border fence would thus give the U.S. both the longest unmanned border in the world as well as the most guarded one.

Beginning at the turn of the 21st century, the focus of the United States Justice Department shifted away from its traditional caseload to one more in line with border control. The period from 2000-2006 saw large declines in the prosecution of what had for years formed the base of the department's cases; organized crime prosecutions dropped 38 percent, bankruptcy fraud declined by 46 percent, white collar crime by 10 percent, and money laundering for drugs by 25 percent (Eggen and Solomon 2007). In contrast, prosecutions related to terrorism and national security increased 876 percent in the years following 9/11, while prosecutions for weapons charges followed at an 87 percent increase and immigration offenses at a 36 percent increase. With regard to immigration, in 2006 more than 19,000 defendants were charged in federal court with immigration-related offenses, more than every other category of crime except for drug crimes (Gamboa 2009). The numbers underscore the Justice Department's transition under the Bush administration to an *immigration enforcement* agency and the result has been a change to the face of the typical offender in federal court. In 2007, 40 percent of offenders sentenced in federal court were Latino, compared to 27 percent white, and 23 percent black (ibid.). Much of the change is fallout from the attacks of September 11th, carried out by groups of militants who entered this country like any other immigrants. According to David Laufman, a former senior official with the Justice Department, "'Prevention and disruption of terrorism was a paramount priority [after 9/11], and immigration prosecutions became one of the government's most favored tools for neutralizing people believed to be a security threat, especially when the government lacked admissible evidence that the individual had committed a terrorism offense'" (Eggen and Solomon 2007). While the actions of those involved in the 9/11 terrorist attacks may have precipitated the sweeping changes, many others with no criminal histories have been caught in the crosshairs and many state and local agencies have been left in the lurch.

Following 9/11, local police agencies were in effect asked to pick up the slack on non-terrorism related crime, while their budgets for doing so were steadily slashed. In 1997, the federal government provided $2.5 billion to local law enforcement agencies. By the time the Bush administration released its 2008 budget proposal, that number had fallen to $1.1 billion (Eggen and Solomon 2007). According to the Attorney General of Arizona, because of the backlog of immigration cases in federal courts, federal attorneys in Southwest border states routinely decline to prosecute drug cases involving less than 500 pounds of marijuana, amounts that can retail on the street for up to $800,000 (Moore 2009). These cases are eventually passed off to local prosecutors, whose offices can as well quickly become overwhelmed.

The effects of the heightened focus on immigration go beyond the drug war. Increasingly, cases involving organized crime, consumer fraud, and environmental injustices have become the jurisdiction of local district attorneys. And federal agents investigating those types of cases are turning to local prosecutors for help, rather than face delays from backlogged federal attorneys. In 2007, federal prosecutors requested 457 wiretaps, the fewest since 1993. In contrast, state and local attorneys requested more than 1,700, three times the number from fourteen years earlier (Moore 2009).

At the same time, local law enforcement agencies were also being asked to pick up the slack on the immigration front, an area historically under the purview solely of the federal government. The call this time came not from above, but rather from local citizens. In Butler County, Ohio, Sheriff Richard K. Jones, claiming to respond to his constituents' wishes, and unsatisfied with the efforts on immigration reform at the federal level, began a push for the state of Ohio to deal with immigration on its own. Jones billed the Department of Homeland Security for the cost of jailing unauthorized immigrants, at a total of $125,000. He also "called on Mexico to authorize payment of $61,141 for 'fair compensation for reimbursement' of costs and other related expenses" for marijuana arrests in Butler County (Seper 2007). But the concern for Jones, as for others, was not simply for those undocumented immigrants who have committed a criminal offense. Rather, he called for making the very status of undocumented immigrant a criminal offense. Nor was his concern, or perhaps the concern of his constituents, limited only to this category of immigrants. As Jones put it, as "the local sheriff, I keep my ear to the ground, and I hear what people are saying. I have the bully pulpit and my constituents don't, so I am determined to speak for them" (Seper 2007). In speaking for his constituents, Jones suggested that Ohioans "make English the official language of the state. Those who live in Ohio should know our language. Taxpayers should not have to pay for interpreters in schools, and U.S. citizens living here shouldn't have to learn another language" (Seper 2007). So it would appear that immigration became a central focus not only for federal law enforcement agencies, but state and local ones as well.

Partnerships between local police and federal agents on issues of immigration are nothing new, nor are Sheriff Jones' billing statements to DHS without precedent. In 1954, Operation Wetback was led by federal agents with the assistance of local police in identifying and rounding up undocumented immigrants. It resulted in the forced expulsion and return of 50,000 Mexicans to Mexico. Throughout the 1970s, the Immigration and Naturalization Service, precursor to the Immigration and Customs Enforcement Agency (ICE), paid police departments in some border communities a monthly per capita fee for detaining suspected unauthorized immigrants (McDonald 1997). The passage of 1986's IRCA included a provision by which the federal government would reimburse states for costs related to the imprisonment of undocumented immigrants. That policy was continued in 1994 with the State Criminal Alien Assistance Program (SCAAP), through which states can apply for funds to defer costs for incarcerating unauthorized immigrants, and the Violent Crime Control and Law Enforcement Act, which allocated $1.2 billion for, among other ends, border control, criminal deportation, reform of the asylum system, the establishment of a criminal alien tracking center, and funds to reimburse states for imprisonment (Hagan and Phillips 2008; Merrell 2007; McDonald 1997). After 1994, the INS instituted the *Law Enforcement Support Center (LESC)* and the *Institutional Hearing Program (IHP)* to streamline deportations of unauthorized immigrants. The LESC allows local law enforcement to quickly determine the legal status of immigrant suspects while the IHP allows for the deportation hearing to be conducted while the suspect is still in custody, ensuring that the accused shows up for court but making his or her access to legal counsel difficult.

While the establishment of the LESC and IHP have raised some serious human rights concerns (McDonald 1997), there are perhaps more pressing civil rights concerns. According to the Migration Policy Institute, since 2003 thousands of non-criminal offenders have been rounded up in sweeps by federal immigration agents. Only 27 percent of those arrested by agents of the Immigration and Customs Enforcement Agency (ICE) between 2003 and 2008 had criminal records (Sullivan 2009). Given the mandates from ICE's leadership to its National Fugitive Operations Program, this finding is unsurprising. In 2004, fugitive operations teams were required to arrest 125 fugitive aliens, of which 94, or roughly 75 percent, were to be convicted criminals (ibid.). From the start, the arrest of non-criminal offenders was built into the system. It was intensified two years later when in 2006 the quota for fugitive arrests was raised from 125 to 1,000. Important here is the term "*non-criminal* offender." In the view of ICE agents, all those arrested are offenders, given that they are present in this country without documentation. The official language of ICE refers to such individuals as fugitives, and in defending the arrests of non-criminal offenders made by ICE agents, the former head of the agency, Julie Myers, stated that "It's bad public policy to allow fugitive aliens to remain in the community" (ibid.).

The individual arrestees are not the only ones who are affected by their arrests, very often their children are as well (Human Rights Watch 2009). In the Dallas suburb of Irving, Texas, parents have taken their children out of school, either because the family is on the run from local law enforcement, which since 2006 has been cooperating with ICE to turn over for deportation suspected immigrants who are here illegally, or because they fear the children will be taken by agents while at school (Seper 2008). Irving has dealt with issues of immigration for years, though it is only recently that the police have begun working to deport local residents who lack documentation.

Irving is one of a growing number of cities and towns around the country that has signed an agreement with ICE to assist in the enforcement of federal immigration law. As of December 31, 2013, 39 law enforcement agencies in 19 states had signed a Memorandum of Agreement (MOA) under the federal 287(g) program.[14] Many are located in the major destination states of California, Texas, Arizona, and Florida, though many are in less likely states, including Arkansas, New Hampshire, Oklahoma, and Tennessee (AP 2007). Surprisingly, the state with the largest number of MOAs is Virginia, with nine, followed by North Carolina with eight. In contrast, California and Texas have a combined total of seven. Still other agencies have begun enforcing federal standards without officially signing an MOA. In New Jersey, local police departments have been aggressively pursuing immigration violations since 2007, when that state's Attorney General ordered state and local police to determine the immigration status of those arrested for indictable crimes.

---

[14] The full list can be found on ICE's website at
http://www.ice.gov/news/library/factsheets/287g.htm#signed-moa.

In 2008, ICE created the Secure Communities Strategy[15] as an attempt to streamline information sharing between DHS and the Department of Justice (DOJ) to expedite the process of removing undocumented immigrants. The strategy works by linking local and state agencies with DHS and FBI databases such that when a person is arrested and processed, his or her fingerprints are run against federal criminal and immigration records. As Donohue notes, while "initially the Strategy was voluntary, it now appears as if the Strategy is mandatory" (2012: 126). As of August 2012, Secure Communities was active in 3,074 communities in all 50 states and the District of Columbia. Its spread has been accompanied by significant controversy, as critics, and even former supports, raise concerns about those deported under its powers (Donohue 2012). An analysis by the Illinois Coalition for Immigrant and Refugee Rights (2011) found that more than three quarters of all immigrants arrested in Illinois under the Strategy had no criminal record. Moreover, in three Illinois counties, not one of the twenty persons arrested in the first six months the Strategy was deployed had any criminal history.

Part of the explanation for why the U.S. continues to enact restrictionist policy "can be found in the commonly held stereotype of illegal immigrants and deportees as hardened criminals who pose a unique threat to public safety, which is a message that in recent years has been fueled by politicians and newsmakers who oppose immigration" (Hagan and Phillips 2008: 91). This stereotype persists despite a wealth of evidence over the last decade suggesting that immigrants are less likely to engage in crime than the native-born. These findings, however, are not exactly new; federal commissions established to determine the effects of immigration at the start of the 20th century consistently came to the same conclusions: immigrants posed no significant threat of crime. Deep-seated opposition to immigrants prevents the acceptance and incorporation of dissonant information, in this case, evidence that immigrants are largely law-abiding. The nullification of that information allows the cycle to continue: perceived threat leads to restrictive policy, which results in unintended consequences that reaffirm the perception of threat.

---

[15] It is possible that the Secure Communities Strategy will ultimately replace the 287(g) program. Since the inception of the Strategy, there has been a slight decline in the number of agencies participating in the 287(g) program.

Nullification of Research

Brader and colleagues (2008: 976) note, "citizen's responses to new information may be held hostage to the past, in the form of anxiety induced by out-group images that may or may not hold contemporary relevance". As early as the turn of the twentieth century, federal reports challenged dominant public perceptions. The U.S. Industrial Commission of 1901 found that while a large proportion of native-born prisoners had parents born abroad, foreign-born whites actually had lower rates of crime than natives (U.S. Industrial Commission 1901). Moreover, in 1911, the United States Immigration Commission found that immigration did not increase rates of crime and may in fact have served to inhibit them (U.S. Immigration Commission 1911). That commission concluded that,

> [n]o satisfactory evidence has yet been produced to show that immigration has resulted in an increase in crime disproportionate to the increase in the adult population....Such figures as are presented...indicate that immigration has not increased the volume of crime to a distinguishable extent, if at all....In fact the figures seem to show a contrary result (ibid.; quoted from Tonry 1997b: 21).

The authors of that report would go on to state, though with limited evidence, that data suggested the children of the foreign-born might be more crime prone than their parents or natives, echoing the findings of the Industrial Commission and laying the groundwork for the "not-immigrants-but their-children" view. Perhaps the most famous of these reports is that by the National Commission on Law Observance and Enforcement of 1931, better known as the Wickersham Commission, which once more found that the foreign-born were *less* likely than natives to engage in crime. The Wickersham Committee concluded that the available data "seem to disagree radically with the popular belief that a high percentage [of contemporary crime] may be ascribed to the 'alien'" (National Commission on Law Observance and Enforcement 1931; quoted from Tonry 1997b: 20). Government documents are not the only sources of evidence for immigrants' law-abiding nature. Martinez (2006) reminds us of Paul S. Taylor's ([1932] 1970) work on Mexican immigrants in Chicago; Taylor found that while Mexicans were arrested in rates greater than would be expected by their population size, the majority of offenses were for property crimes and alcohol use or misuse. Taylor explains this heightened propensity toward offending through the inordinate number of single males in the population, as well as neighborhood poverty, rather than inherent characteristics of the group (see Martinez [2006: 8-9] for a discussion of Taylor's findings). Overall, early sociological empirical research, though relatively scarce, indicated that immigrants were less involved in crime than their native counterparts (Sutherland 1947). Explanations for this finding tended to focus on self-selection processes among immigrants: namely, that people who would uproot themselves or their families to make a difficult and dangerous oceanic crossing to settle in an unknown land out of the hope that they might make a better life for themselves or their children, would likely be conformists to the law (Tonry 1997b). So despite research findings dating back more than a century that consistently indicate no significant connection between immigration and crime, causal or spurious, public perception persists. Many popular accounts still equate immigration with crime, operating on an outdated view of the process of immigrant incorporation and an equally outdated (and largely bastardized) interpretation of Shaw and McKay's (1942) Social Disorganization theory, which posits that immigrants should exhibit higher rates of crime due to their tendency to reside in impoverished urban areas; that is, the process of immigration, which brings together a diverse population, undermines mechanisms of social control. Rather than a criminogenic culture of newcomers, it is this weakened social control, which is a product of immigration that ultimately leads to crime. The work of Shaw and McKay will be addressed in much more detail in the next chapter. For now it is worth noting their major finding, as the results of a number of recent analyses have failed to support it.

A wealth of social research on immigration and crime has developed in the last fifteen years. Largely, these studies confirm the findings of the government commissions published early in the 20th century. Indeed, the results are so consistent as to lead Martinez and Lee (2000: 496) to conclude in their meta-analysis of a century immigration-crime studies, "immigrants nearly always exhibit lower crime rates than native groups." At both the individual and aggregate levels, experts have continued to find either no effect of immigration on crime or—particularly in the aggregate—a dampening effect.

Investigating differences between white, Black, and Latino rates of homicide at the metropolitan level, Phillips (2002) finds no effect of immigration on overall homicide rates. Similarly, Reid, et al. (2005) find that immigration exerts no significant effect on several types of crime. For rates of homicide, immigration actually has a significant *negative* effect, suggesting that, consistent with Martinez (2002), the increased presence of Latino immigrants results in lower rates of murder. For robbery and burglary, immigration has no significant effect. Poverty, in contrast, was positively correlated with all three crimes, a finding consistent with the early work of Shaw and McKay (1942). Reid and colleagues (2005) also find that theft is unaffected by poverty, the overall percentage of the population that is foreign-born or the percentage that is foreign-born Latino, but is reduced by increases in the number of Asian immigrants.

In a cross-city analysis of immigration and crime in 1980s, Butcher and Piehl (1998) find that while cities with high immigrant populations tend to have higher rates of crime, once demographic factors are controlled, recent immigrants exert no effect on rates of crime. Further, in looking at crime changes over time, the authors find that the flow of immigrants has no effect on overall crime rates, consistent with other researchers who note that while crime rates fell throughout the 1990s, immigration rates continued unabated (cf. Hagan, Levi, and Dinovitzer 2008; Rumbaut and Ewing 1997). Similarly, Lauritsen (2001) finds that in central cities, people who live in areas with greater concentrations of immigrants experience lower risk of overall and neighborhood violence. "What is clear is that the annual percentage of immigrants has more than doubled since 1980 and that it rose steadily at the same time as rates of both homicide (per hundred thousand) and robbery (per thousand) at first fluctuated widely (between 1980 and 1994) and then dropped (between 1994 and 2002)" (Martinez 2006: 11).

A recent place-level analysis points to both the disorganizing and crime inhibiting aspects of immigration, showing the need for researchers to look not only at the direct effects, but the indirect and overall effects as well. Feldmeyer (2009) finds that Latino immigration has a direct positive correlation with measures of classical disorganization: Latino poverty, residential mobility, and language and racial/ethnic heterogeneity. He also finds, however, that Latino immigration has a direct negative effect on Latino robbery rates and no significant direct effects on either homicide or the overall occurrence of violence. But areas with greater Latino immigration, and in particular a greater presence of Latino males, tend to have lower overall rates violence, robbery in particular. His findings suggest that immigration indirectly increases violence by directly increasing disorganization (via population turnover and language heterogeneity) but that immigration indirectly decreases violence by strengthening social institutions such as the family (via fewer female-headed households and fewer unemployed males) and support systems (by providing networks for child care). The presence of both positive and negative effects leads Feldmeyer to investigate the overall impact of immigration on crime, finding that the "total effects show that immigration has small, but slightly negative effects on Latino homicide and Violent Index rates but much more sizeable negative effects on Latino robbery rates" (Feldmeyer 2009: 727-8).

Research at the neighborhood level has come to similar conclusions. Looking specifically at Miami, Martinez, Rosenfeld, and Mares (2008) find that rates of violence are lower in Miami communities with large numbers of Latino residents, higher numbers of immigrants, and greater linguistic isolation. Also in Miami, Latino communities have lower rates of robbery and assault than Haitian communities, which in turn have lower rates than African American ones (Martinez and Nielsen 2006). That rates in Haitian communities were closer to those in African American communities suggests that (1) immigration exerts a buffering effect, but that (2) this buffering effect may be mediated by both structural disadvantage and racial status, with Haitians more closely resembling African Americans. Looking at group-specific rates (e.g. crimes occurring in a Latino community in which the victim was Latino), robbery rates in African American communities were four times higher than in either Latino or Haitian ones, which were almost identical. The pattern is similar for aggravated assault, with rates in Latino and Haitian communities approximately equal, and those in African American communities much higher, though the disparity is not as great as with robbery. In a subsequent analysis, Nielsen and Martinez (2006) find that Haitians were much more likely to be victims of violence in largely African American communities and areas that were particularly disadvantaged than they were to be victimized in Miami's Little Haiti, suggesting that "Little Haiti may offer a buffer to victimization" (Nielsen and Martinez 2006: 228). Overall, Little Haiti's victimization rates are on par with rates in the city's Latino communities, both of which are significantly lower than in African American communities. Rates of Haitian violence were highest in two of the most impoverished areas of Miami, both largely African American, while the lowest rates of Haitian violence were found in the least impoverished community.

In a comparison of neighborhoods across Miami, El Paso, and San Diego—three cities with long histories and high rates of immigration—Lee, Martinez, and Rosenfeld (2001) find that immigration does not generally lead to increases in rates of crime for either Latinos or African Americans. The only factor consistently correlated with crime is poverty. Interestingly, the authors also find that single female-headed households may actually provide a suppressive effect on crime, a finding at odds with traditional expectations. Martinez (2002) finds that Latino homicide victimization rates are higher than those of native-born whites but lower than those of non-Latino blacks, which is surprising given that structural disadvantage for Latinos is much more similar to African Americans than to native whites.

Research at the individual-level has also come to similar conclusions. Among residents of Chicago, African Americans were 85 percent more likely than whites to commit a violent act, while Latinos were 10 percent *less likely* than whites to commit one (Sampson, Morenoff, and Raudenbush 2005). The entire gap between whites and Latinos explained by combination of the latter having married parents, residing in ethnic enclaves, and having individual immigrant status, as first generation immigrants were significantly less likely to engage in violence. The results suggest that rather than being criminogenic, immigration serves to buffer and insulate individuals from crime.

Patterns of incarceration rates also belie the notion that immigrants engage in more crime than natives. Pennel, Curtis, and Tayman (1989) find that in both San Diego and El Paso for the 1985-86, the overwhelming majority of serious criminals are native citizens, not immigrants. In San Diego, 81 percent of serious criminals were native-born, while 14 percent were immigrants. The same pattern was found in El Paso, though differences were slightly less stark: 74 percent of offenders were native-born while 22 percent were foreign-born (in each case, the immigrant status for 4 percent of the offenders was unknown).

At the national level, among 18-40 year old men, immigrants are less likely to be incarcerated than native-born individuals, and much less likely to be incarcerated than native-born men, controlling for demographic characteristics (Butcher and Piehl 1997). One estimate suggests that in the year 2000, the incarceration rate for foreign-born men aged 18-39 was five times *lower* than for their native-born counterparts (0.7 percent to 3.5 percent; Rumbaut and Ewing 2007). Disaggregating by race and ethnicity, the rate for foreign-born men was two and a half times *lower* than for non-Hispanic white men, and 17 times *lower* than for native-born African American men (ibid). Meanwhile, rates for foreign-born Mexicans, Salvadorans, and Guatemalans were the lowest of any Latin American group, despite also having the lowest levels of educational attainment and making up the majority of undocumented immigrants in the country. Rumbaut and Ewing (2007) find that nativity status is a stronger predictor of incarceration than education, long a hallmark of criminological theory.

Research has also found a generational difference, whereby earlier immigrants are more likely to be incarcerated than recent immigrants. Butcher and Piehl (1997: 654) find that although, "all immigrant cohorts appear to assimilate toward the higher institutionalization rates of the native-born as time in the country increases, recent immigrants do not increase their institutionalization rates as quickly as one would predict from the experience of earlier immigrant cohorts." Similarly, Morenoff and Astor (2006) find that second and third generation youth are more likely to report hitting someone, throwing objects at someone, carrying a weapon, being involved in gang fight, and picking pockets or snatching purses than first generation youth. They find also that age at immigration matters, with youth who immigrate at younger ages being more likely to offend during adolescence than youth who are older at the time of immigration. The "odds that a first generation immigrant youth who was less than six years old when he arrived in the United States will hit someone are 4.26 times larger than the odds of a similar immigrant youth who arrived at ten or older. Comparable odds ratios for carrying a weapon and being in a gang fight are 8.01 and 2.54, respectively" (Morenoff and Astor 2006: 47). Interestingly, linguistic acculturation increases the likelihood of engaging in delinquency, suggesting that calls for English-only laws might actually lead to higher rates of youth crime. The results are generally inconsistent with traditional theories, social disorganization in particular, in that they suggest that increasing assimilation and acculturation appear to *increase*, rather than decrease, the likelihood of imprisonment.

The persistent finding of a buffering effect of immigration on crime has led Sampson (see Press 2006; Sampson and Bean 2006) to speculate that the enormous decline in crime rates in major cities and at the national level since the early 1990s might in fact be due to rising rates of immigration. At the time, such a statement might have been met with doubt not only from the public but many researchers as well. But recent research has buttressed that claim. While investigating the drug market decline as an explanation for the overall crime drop, Ousey and Lee (2007) find that homicide rates declined in cities that experienced both total population growth and in particular growth in the relative size of their Latino population. Additionally, two recent studies on the effect of effect of changes in immigration on changes in rates of crime each find that violent crime tended to decrease in areas where immigration increased. Stowell et al. (2009) assess annual data for metro areas from 1994-2004, finding that increases in the percent of the foreign-born population were associated with reductions in robbery, aggravated assault, and overall violent crime, with results particularly strong for robbery. Overall, those authors determined immigration to be responsible for a "modest" 6% of the total crime drop between 1994-2004; however, the benefits varied by the degree to which the foreign-born population increased. Metropolitan statistical areas that saw the greatest increases in immigrant concentration witnessed five times as many fewer violent crimes as those which saw the smallest increases in immigrant concentration. Stowell and colleagues also report the results of a cross-sectional analysis for the year 2000, which indicates no significant effect of immigration on overall violence, robbery, homicide, or assault, with a significant but small depressive effect on rape. At the city-level, Ousey and Kubrin (2009) offer an analysis of the effect of change in 159 U.S. cities from 1980-2000. After controlling for percentage of young males, size of the population, residential instability, economic deprivation, labor market conditions, illegal drug market activity, and the size of the police force, they find that "cities that experienced increases in immigration from 1980-2000 experienced a decrease in violent crime rates" (Ousey and Kubrin 2009: 466). The authors attribute the effect to the tendency for immigration to strengthen families: immigration was negatively correlated with divorce and the presence of single-parent families, each of which was positively correlated with violence.

In sum, the last two decades have witnessed an impressive accumulation of scientific research indicating that immigrants are at least no more likely to engage in crime than their native-born counterparts and may in fact be less likely to commit criminal acts, especially those involving violence. At the aggregate level, research has shown as well that the process of immigration is not the criminogenic force popular perception on previous research may suggest. Yet despite these findings, opposition to immigrants and immigration remains high, as does the tendency to equate newcomers with increased crime and violence, a tendency common among the public at large and within the justice system. For example, Wolfe, Pyrooz, and Spohn (2011) find that Latino immigrants—documented and undocumented—have a higher probability than the native-born of being incarcerated, all else equal. Those researchers' findings indicate that "judges' perceptions of blameworthiness and dangerousness depend to some extent on ethnicity, education, and pretrial status" suggesting that cultural stereotypes are reflected in the sentences non-citizens receive" (2011: 361). Restrictionist views of immigration in effect buffer themselves against dissonant information to the contrary, raising concerns as to successful methods of countering such views. Moreover, the persistence of anti-immigrant sentiment and growth in restrictionist policies, untempered by the available research, have led to unintended consequences that ironically have shifted the issues of immigration from traditional settlement areas in urban border communities around the country to new areas of the interior, making immigration a national issue.

Unintended Consequences

Massey and Capoferro (2008) provide one of the most comprehensive analyses of *causes* of the new geography of immigration. Prior to the 1990s, more than 80 percent of immigrants settled in ten states: the "Big 5" of California, New York, Texas, Florida, and Illinois, with a second tier of New Jersey, Massachusetts, Washington, Virginia, and Maryland. During the 1990s and into the first few years of the 21st century, immigrant settlement diversified markedly. From 1985 to 1990, roughly two thirds of immigrants settled in the Big 5 states; by 2005, that number dropped to 52 percent. Second tier states also saw declines, though more modest, from a total of 14 percent in 1985 to 12 percent by 2005. Meanwhile, several "new" states saw dramatic increases in their shares of immigrants for the first time in decades, and in some cases for the first time ever. Georgia saw its share of the nation's immigrants quadruple from 0.7 percent of all U.S. immigrants 1980 to 3.0 percent in 2005; Arizona and North Carolina saw theirs triple, from 1.1 and 0.8 percent to 3.5 and 2.8 percent, respectively; and Indiana's share doubled, from 0.6 to 1.1 percent. In absolute terms, the numbers are striking. Georgia's total immigrant population increased from 10,000 in 1980 to 141,000 by 2005. Arizona's number of immigrants grew from 15,000 to 162,000 and North Carolina's from 12,000 to 131,000.

Beginning with this baseline of change, the authors test whether and to what degree the spread of immigrants across the nation can be explained by the restrictive policies of the Immigration Reform and Control Act of 1986 (IRCA), Proposition 187, the selective hardening of the Mexican border, or changes to labor demand. To help answer this question, the authors disaggregate the geographic diversification by immigrant group: Mexican, Other Latino, Asian, and the residual non-Asian, non-Latino group. To measure geographic spread, they employ a diversity index, a measure of the degree to which immigrants are clustered in only a few states or are spread across many, on a scale of 0-100. In 1980, the diversity indices for the groups in question were polarized, with Mexicans much more cloistered in a few states and non-Asian, non-Latinos much more spread out. Massey and Capoferro, however, show that by 2005, all groups, though Mexicans in particular, had experienced systematic diversification: the Mexican index increased from 38.2 to 66.5, other Latinos increased from 58.7 to 71.2, Asians from 71 to 75.9, and non-Asian, non-Latinos from 76.7 to 80. The authors show also that while 63 percent of Mexican immigrants settled in California from 1985-1990, that number had fallen to 28 percent by 2000. Clearly something significant happened in the 1990s. Because *all* groups experienced diversification, and not just those coming through California, results strongly support the notion that surging labor demands drew immigrants to new areas of the country in search of employment. Because California in particular saw dramatic reductions in its share of immigrants, there is ample reason to suspect that Proposition 187 and IRCA worked to make that state less attractive to immigrants. But because of the extraordinary changes to the Mexican population, still the nation's largest immigrant group and which, given its size, drives overall measures of immigration diversity, strongest support is found for the restrictive and selective border enforcement. These measures had the effect of closing off California as a settlement destination and funneling new immigrants through places like Arizona and Nevada to new locations across the American Southeast and Midwest.

THE PLACE AND CONTEXT OF UNAUTHORIZED IMMIGRATION

Before concluding this chapter, it is worth addressing a special category of immigrants. Any discussion of native-born perceptions of the threats posed by the foreign-born must pay special attention to the issues of *illegal* immigrants.[16] If immigrants in general are viewed negatively, undocumented immigrants may arguably be viewed as one of the most deviant groups in contemporary American society. They bear a double stigma. First, their status as immigrants marks them as outsiders, and dominant rhetoric reinforces the threats these outsiders pose. Second, their status as "illegal" marks them as breakers of law. Here the official language used to denote this population becomes important. Terms such as "illegal immigrant," "illegal alien," "criminal alien," and "fugitive alien," all serve to marginalize and delegitimize. The connotation of "illegal" signals that such individuals have committed crimes against the native population and as criminals must be brought to justice. The term "alien" marks them as other, but in a special way. Often, *othering* is a process whereby the targeted group is constructed as subhuman, possessing but lacking in the essential qualities of the targeting group. Labeling undocumented immigrants as alien, however, constructs them as non-human, a different entity entirely, possessing none of the qualities of the host group, and heightening the threat posed. The result is that discussions of "illegal immigrants" tend to stir latent emotions of insider/outsider and moral/immoral which predispose the native-born to opposition.

While research on undocumented immigrants is limited, the studies that do exist offer little evidence to suggest those immigrants are significantly more prone to engage in crime or to challenge for American jobs than either legal immigrants or the native-born. Evidence suggests similarities to both groups across a host of

---

[16] The terms unauthorized and undocumented are used interchangeably throughout. The term "illegal" is used only where it cannot be avoided: in direct quotations and the formal names of certain policy measures. All three refer to immigrants residing in this country without official government approval and, as such, these include those who evade border agents as well as those whose visas have lapsed.

characteristics. As might be expected, the spread of unauthorized immigrants parallels the spread of immigration in general. In 2004, ten times as many undocumented immigrants lived outside the six major destination states of California, Florida, Illinois, New Jersey, New York, and Texas, as in 1990 (Merrell 2007; cf. Massey and Capoferro 2008). Current estimates of the unauthorized population place the number between 11.5 and 12 million (Passel 2005; cf. Pew Hispanic Center 2006). Nearly half, estimated at 4 to 5.5 million, are individuals who have overstayed their visas, rather than persons who evaded immigration inspectors and border patrol agents, an estimated 6 to 7 million (McDonald 1997; cf. Pew Hispanic Center 2006).

Studies of crime tend to show that the undocumented are no more prone to engage in crime than their legal counterparts and might be less likely to engage in crime than the native-born. In a study of serious crime by unauthorized immigrants in San Diego and El Paso for 1985-86, Pennel, Curtis, and Tayman (1989) find that the vast majority of those arrested in both cities are native-born, with relatively low percentages of undocumented arrestees. In San Diego, those arrested for serious crime were 81 percent native-born, 12 percent unauthorized immigrant, 2 percent authorized immigrant, and 4 percent whose immigration status was unconfirmed. A similar pattern emerged for El Paso, with 74 percent native-born, 15 percent unauthorized, 7 percent authorized, and 4 percent unconfirmed. At the metropolitan level, Hagan and Palloni (1998) find no effect of the size of the undocumented population on either violent or property arrest rates.

A recent study of recidivism in California offers similar results. Hickman and Suttorp (2008) compare the recidivism of deportable (those who enter illegally or overstay their visas) and nondeportable immigrants (legal immigrants and naturalized citizens), finding no significant differences between the two in the occurrence, frequency, or timing of their re-arrest. Reliable predictors of rearrest included age, the number of previous offense, and whether previous offenses included property or drug offenses. The authors conclude that "deportable aliens are no greater threat to public safety than are legal immigrants released from incarceration at the same place and time" (Hickman and Suttorp 2008: 77). Unfortunately, the authors do not compare the recidivism of immigrants to natives, though they note in this regard that the "rearrest rate for [the] entire foreign-born sample is relatively low (38%) compared with an earlier study of all jail releasees in LA County. Petersilia et al. (2000) found that roughly 50% of 1,000 LA County Jail male releasees were rearrested within one year" (Hickman and Suttorp 2008: 77).

Estimates over the last two decades of the financial impact of immigration—legal and illegal—in terms of the services used show that the overall tax revenues garnered surpass the overall costs of services distributed (Merrell 2007). Many estimates, however, suggest that the costs of services to unauthorized immigrants surpass tax revenues, largely because those immigrants tend to earn less, making less income available for taxation. The average yearly income for undocumented families is $27,400, compared to $47,800 for authorized immigrant families and $47,700 for native families (Passel 2005). This lack of income also implies less disposable income that can be captured via sales and usage taxes. The discrepancy, again, is a product of lower wages and earnings, rather than an avoidance of paying taxes. A recent analysis finds that 75 percent of undocumented immigrants had taxes withheld from pay, filed tax returns, or both in 2006 (Cornelius and Lewis 2007), and the Social Security Administration assumes a minimum of 50 percent of undocumented immigrants pay federal and state taxes (Passel 2006).

For years, state and local jurisdictions have borne the brunt of costs associated with unauthorized immigrants largely because federal rules and laws limit states' ability to avoid distributing services to them. States do receive federal aid to help defer the costs, but in general such aid does not cover in full. This has put states in a difficult and arguably unfair position; they have limited say in matters of national immigration policy and enforcement and yet are asked to shoulder all or most of the cost. Tax payers as well are placed in a quandary and many understandably may resent having to, in a sense, "pay for" non-citizens. Fairness and emotion aside, unauthorized immigrants on the whole account for only a small fraction of total state spending. A review of the estimates suggests that typically spending amounts to less than 5 percent of the total annual budget for most states (Merrell 2007).[17]

Discussions of the costs associated with undocumented persons often concern their use of health services. Because they are less likely

---

[17] California is the exception, with the highest annual spending on undocumented immigrants but that amount is still less than ten percent of the total state budget.

to have insurance, they are more likely to rely upon emergency care or public hospitals. Reviews of those costs, however, indicate they are often overstated. For example, in 2006 the Oklahoma Health Care Authority (OHCA) estimated emergency Medicaid expenses to undocumented immigrants would total $9.7 million. In absolute terms, the number may appear quite high but in relative terms, it amounts to only a fraction of total spending. In 2006 OHCA's total spending was $3.1 billion, meaning the projected expenses for undocumented immigrants were equivalent to 0.3 percent of total spending. Since 2003, undocumented immigrants have accounted for less than 1 percent of all individuals served and total dollars spent by the OHCA (Merrell 2007).

Regarding employment, McDonald (1997) argues that the political and legal crackdown on the undocumented clashes with the need for new labor to replace an aging and increasingly better educated population (see also Pew Hispanic Center 2006; Alsalam and Smith 2005). Unauthorized male immigrants are more likely to be employed than either legal male immigrants or native-born males (Merrell 2007). Of males aged 18-64, 94 percent of unauthorized immigrants are in the labor force, compared to 86 percent of authorized and 83 percent of native-born. The discrepancy is largely a product of their age—because unauthorized immigrants tend to be younger, they are less likely to be retired or disabled—and their lack of formal education—fewer are enrolled in post-secondary education. Consequently, undocumented immigrants tend to work in occupations that require little or no formal education, require no licensing, and wherein training is on-the-job. Contrary to the popular view of taking jobs away from Americans, undocumented workers tend to be employed in sectors where native-born workers are underrepresented. For example, unauthorized workers are three times more likely to be employed in agriculture and construction and extractive jobs than native-born workers and twice as likely to work in service occupations. Conversely, while 62 percent of native-born workers are employed in "management, business, and professional occupations," only 23 percent of unauthorized immigrants are employed therein (Merrell 2007).

In sum, unauthorized immigrants constitute a doubly-stigmatized group, one toward whom general anti-immigrant ire flares most strongly. While research on this population is limited, given the nature of their status, what studies do exist have tended to show that the unauthorized do not pose the level of threat popular rhetoric ascribes to them in terms of crime or employment. Unauthorized migrants do not come exclusively from Mexico, nor are they exclusively dark-skinned and poorly educated, as stereotypes purport. Even when they do fit stereotypical demographics, available research does not suggest those demographics translate directly to negative outcomes. This discussion is warranted because the data to be analyzed by this research do not disaggregate the foreign-born by legal status, but as the preceding sought to show, there is at least a modicum of evidence to suggest that the unauthorized population may well share many similarities with the overall foreign-born population.

CONCLUSIONS

The sociopolitical climate into which contemporary immigrants arrive and through which they must navigate in order to achieve their own particular goals, is largely oppositional. While that opposition has intensified in recent years, it is ultimately the continuation of a historical pattern of anti-immigrant public sentiment and political legislation. Generalized opposition manifests itself in the form of at least two distinct perceptions of threat: threats of crime and threats to employment. The proliferation of these perceptions appears to have had important consequences. The first is the explosion of restrictionist immigration legislation over the last two decades, such that places with virtually no history of immigration have found it necessary to pass laws aimed at excluding the foreign-born. The second is the tendency for research whose findings belie the negative outcomes attributed to immigration to be overlooked or marginalized. Despite a boom in academic research on the topic, traditional stereotypes have proven particularly resilient. When these biases promote action, the results can be profound. As research suggests, the dispersion of immigrants outward from the American southwest can be traced in large measure to anti-immigrant legislation.

As immigration begins to spread to new areas around the country, and given the cultural context discussed above, important questions remain as to whether patterns of reception and incorporation will differ from those observed in traditional receiving areas. Will academic findings of null or depressive effects on crime hold in new areas? Will the local response to newcomers be more hostile? The next chapter reviews in detail the dominant theoretical views on pathways to immigrant incorporation as well as the major theories seeking to explain the relationship between immigration and crime.

CHAPTER 2

Divergent Perspectives: Social Disorganization and Segmented Assimilation

Sociological theories of immigrant criminality have tended to flow from the dominant conception of immigrants' broader integration into the host society, pointing to the role that the larger socioeconomic structure plays in determining outcomes. For the better part of the last century, the guiding lens through which scholars understood the structural connection between immigration and crime was social disorganization theory, which was rooted in a particular view of the process of incorporation: traditional, or straight-line, assimilation theory. In the last few decades, owing to the legal, political, and economic changes discussed in the previous chapter, researchers have noted that contemporary immigration no longer appears to follow this traditional pattern; nor do the tenets of social disorganization seem as applicable as they once did. In the sections that follow, traditional and contemporary theories of immigrant incorporation are reviewed, as are their correlates for interpreting the link between immigration and crime.

IMMIGRANT INCORPORATION

The Traditional Assimilation View

Traditional assimilation theory developed out of the early Chicago school in the first few decades of the last century. Park and Burgess (1924) termed the process through which ethnic minorities become incorporated into mainstream culture, assimilation. Park viewed it as the final stage of a process that begins with "the breakdown of social order...initiated by the impact of an invading population, and completed by the contact and fusion of native with alien peoples" (Park 1928: 885). The process, as Park envisions it, can be viewed as a *necessary blending* of sorts. It is a diffusion from high pressure to low, wherein the dominant and more pervasive host culture, which surrounds the newcomers, leaks into their way of life, transforming them from Italians to Italian-Americans, from Irish to Irish Americans, and so on.

In more direct terms, this process plays out as a product of the newcomers' differentness. For example, to the degree that they lack proficiency in the English language, immigrants are precluded from employment positions that require direct communication between workers, most notably managerial positions, and are more likely to find employment in positions where this is not an essential feature of the job, such as manufacturing. In other words, lack of English language proficiency prevents access to higher paying, higher status positions. Over time, however, the skill is developed either formally, via enrollment in local schools or the taking of formal classes in programs like English for Speakers of Other Languages (ESOL)[18], or informally, through repeated interactions with native-born acquaintances and the institutions of the host country, including the police, banks, markets, all of which the immigrants may at times need to avail themselves. This development enables entry into those higher paying positions. The

---

[18] ESOL is an emergent variation on what has previously been referred to in the U.S. as English as a Second Language (ESL), and what is referred to elsewhere as English as an additional language (EAL), and English as a foreign language (EFL). ESL is eschewed here in favor of ESOL because latter more clearly acknowledges the multilingualism of many who take these classes—that is, many already speak a second (or third, or even fourth) language, just not English.

acquisition of language has been shown particularly easy among children, one of the key reasons for the pattern of increasing generational attainment. As newcomers adopt the host language and assume roles within the host employment structure, they begin more and more to "look like" the native-born, in the sense that their daily routines become similarly patterned around work, they speak the same language, and may come to value the same things. As they and their children gain access to higher paying positions, income and wealth may grow, enabling many to purchase items like new cars, and importantly, "nice" new homes outside of their initial place of settlement. For many immigrants, and many students of immigration and assimilation, this major step of moving to the suburbs has been a key indicator of "making it," whether envisioned as the attainment of socioeconomic parity or simply a parity of status—the transition from outsider to insider.

The above is an oversimplification of a very complex process and language is only one factor of many that affects the flow from contact to assimilation. And the above presents the situation as the inevitable outcome of a largely *structural* process, when in fact the choices, actions, and reactions made by both the native-born and newcomers greatly impact the end result. Two crucial phenomena are left out: native racism and immigrant isolationism. Their omission has received notable attention in recent years, posing a significant challenge to the early assimilation theory. Nonetheless, Park's "race-relations cycle" of contact, competition, accommodation and ultimately assimilation set the foundation for much work to come. Importantly, Park and Miller (1921) note that the assimilation process entails significant within-group variation, meaning that, for example, the amount of time between *contact* and *assimilation* will vary not only across different nationalities but also for different individuals and families of the same nationality.

Warner and Srole (1945) pick up on the theme of intragroup variation, noting that the process of assimilation will vary from group to group based on characteristics of the newcomers, including their skin color, language of origin, and religion. For Warner and Srole, these factors combine with socioeconomic status to determine the speed of assimilation. While these authors recognize variability in the process, they also ultimately accept Park's version of inevitable assimilation. Milton Gordon (1964) further extends assimilation theory by distinguishing between what he calls *structural assimilation* and *acculturation.* The former refers to immigrants' entry into primary group relations with members of the dominant group, while the latter refers to immigrants' adoption of the dominant group's cultural patterns. For Gordon, structural assimilation is the key to attaining full assimilation. Acculturation, while certainly not irrelevant, is inevitable in Gordon's view, given enough time in the host society, and in itself is not necessary for assimilation. Together, these early works share two key hypotheses that form the bulk of traditional assimilation theory: first, that integration into primary group relations with the majority group drives full assimilation and upward mobility, and second, that intergenerational change—the tendency for successive generations to more quickly adopt the lifestyles of the native-born—precipitates the process (Morenoff and Astor 2006). In this way, each generation moves one step closer toward the majority group.

A contemporary variant of traditional assimilation theory is spatial assimilation theory (Alba and Nee 1997; Massey and Denton 1985). Spatial assimilation theory combines the status attainment perspective with an ecological model (Massey and Denton 1985), and views residential proximity to whites "as a key indicator of, and in some cases precursor to, more general processes of assimilation" (South, Crowder, and Chavez 2005: 497; see also Alba and Nee 1997). Increasing residential proximity to native whites is seen as an indicator of both a decline in the insularity of ethnic enclaves and an acceptance of the minority group by the majority; conversely, rejection by the majority would be manifested in what has been termed "white flight." In essence, the more the residences of the foreign-born and their children are embedded among native communities, the more *blended* are they with the host. Close proximity to the majority enables interethnic relationships, friendships and marriages, via shared businesses, workplaces and schools, which are exactly the types of primary group relationships that fuel assimilation (South et al. 2005; South and Messner 1986; Massey and Denton 1985). As with traditional assimilation theory, spatial assimilation theory assumes a generational component, whereby successive generations should experience increasing proximity to the white majority.

Research on spatial assimilation has found that it is positively correlated with socioeconomic status (Massey and Denton 1985), English language proficiency (South, et al. 2005; Alba, Logan, and Stults 2000; Alba and Nee 1997), and generational change (South, et al. 2005). As income and education increase, minority group members are more likely to have greater contact with native-born whites. As immigrants' grasp of the English language increase, they are more likely to move into neighborhoods with greater proportions of white residents. Lastly, as South, et al. (2005) note, for Mexicans and Latinos more generally, the 1.5 generation (i.e., foreign-born children who immigrated before age 11) and later ones are more likely than their parents to move to increasingly Anglo neighborhoods.

Traditional assimilation theory, and those theories which stemmed from it, was the accepted version of events for earlier waves of immigrants primarily from southern and eastern Europe arriving in the 19th and early 20th centuries. Research on immigration and its effects dwindled in the middle of the 20th century due in part to restrictive immigration policies (Martinez 2006), the absence of recorded data on ethnicity in official statistics (Morenoff and Astor 2006), and challenges from cultural theories whose findings defied the "straight-line" path of immigrants (Bursik 2006; cf. Whyte 1943). The passage of the 1965 Hart-Cellar Immigration Reform Act made immigration from non-European countries easier, resulting in an influx of Asian and Latino immigrants. The last few decades have witnessed a return to importance for the study of immigration, and findings from that research have suggested for some that the experiences of the "new immigrants" (those arriving after 1965) differ markedly from their European counterparts in the earlier wave. Consequently, many believe the notion of a straight-line assimilation to "the mainstream" is no longer the appropriate way of understanding the process of immigration.

The Segmented Assimilation View

The most articulated challenge to traditional assimilation theory has come from those embracing the idea of segmented assimilation. In one sense, it is quite similar to traditional assimilation theory, which accepts that incoming groups over time become more like members of the host society. Segmented assimilation theory acknowledges that this is the case *for some immigrants*, though not for all. It holds that *under certain conditions* incoming groups can adapt to the host society by acculturating to dominant norms and becoming economically integrated in such a way as to enable upward mobility, that is, to structurally assimilate. Where it differs from traditional assimilation theory is in rejecting, or rather problematizing, what the latter takes for granted. The question for segmented assimilation theorists becomes, "assimilated *to what*"? Implicit in traditional assimilation theory is the notion of a unified "middle ground," a middle class that is not only economically homogenous but culturally as well.[19] This is the straight-line (or as Gans [1992] has re-envisioned it, "the bumpy-line") approach. Yet scholars of the new immigration point out that in an increasingly pluralistic society, the idea of a singular core culture is unlikely, as is the incorporation of immigrants into it. Depending on a number of factors, newcomers may find their way to this preferred structural location, or they may find themselves someplace else.

In their introductory piece on segmented assimilation, Portes and Zhou (1993) note that the experiences of new immigrants—again, those arriving after the 1965 Immigration Act—differ markedly from the previous wave of mass immigration—occurring from the late 19th to the early 20th centuries—for two reasons: skin color and fundamental changes to the national and global economies. European immigrants predominated in the last wave and, while in some cases slightly darker in complexion than the native population, their skin color created no lasting barriers. This is not the case for recent immigrants, who tend to come from Latin America, Asia, Africa, and the West Indies. The second factor has been the shift of the U.S. economy from industrial-manufacturing to service-oriented. While the former may not have made immigrant workers wealthy, it at least provided steady pay for those without technical skill sets and the promise of employment for their children as well. The loss of manufacturing has led to a restructuring of employment opportunities and the creation of a two-tiered or "hourglass economy," with high skill, high wage jobs, typically requiring college degrees, at the top and low skill, low-wage positions at the bottom (Crutchfield 1989; Bluestone 1970; Piore 1970).

According to segmented assimilation theory, the new immigrants exhibit three distinct patterns of adaptation to American society. First is *upward assimilation*, akin to the traditional view, in that growing acculturation is accompanied by integration into the white middle class. The second pattern, often termed *downward assimilation*, involves immigrants' acculturation to and integration into what Wilson (1987) has termed the underclass. The third pattern entails rapid economic

---

[19] For discussions of some of the broader problems with this view, see Kivisto and Rundblad (2000), Kivisto (2005) and Modood (2007).

advancement and the intentional preservation of ethnic identity, values, and solidarity. To put this in Gordon's terms, it is essentially structural assimilation without—or with a delayed or lagged—acculturation. As mentioned, while Gordon viewed acculturation as unnecessary for assimilation, he nevertheless viewed it as inevitable given time in the host society. As recent research suggests, some immigrant groups, including those who have had established residence in the U.S. for several decades, continue to retain their ethnic identity and culture (for discussions of Miami's insular Cuban population, see Martinez and Nielsen 2006; Nielsen and Martinez 2006; Velez 2006; Lee, et al. 2001; Portes and Zhou 1993). While traditional assimilation theory suggests that the maintenance of ethnic identity should serve as an obstacle to advancement—most notably by marking the newcomer as an outsider and potentially inviting discrimination—researchers have pointed to a number of benefits offered by such maintenance. In particular, a strong established ethnic community offers economic opportunities to newly arrived immigrants and the children of immigrants that don't require college degrees but still offer the potential for upward mobility (Portes and Rumbaut 2006; Zhou 1997; Portes and Zhou 1993). Strong co-ethnic communities can also offer educational support in the form of access to college grants and the presence of a private school system, which works to reinforce ethnic values and parental views and insulate youth from oppositional cultures (Portes and Zhou 1993). Lastly, strong ties to one's home culture can aid in enforcing norms against divorce and family disruption, as well as reinforcing parental authority over children, particularly important in cases of *dissonant acculturation*, Portes and Rumbaut's (2006) term for challenges to parental authority that occur when children's learning of English and American customs is faster than or conflicts with their parents'.

The path of adaptation taken is the result of individual and family characteristics as well as contextual factors like the political relations between the sending and receiving country, the nature of the host country's economy, and the size and structure of preexisting co-ethnic communities[20]. Portes and Rumbaut (2006; see also Portes and Zhou

---

[20] The term "co-ethnic community" refers to a community inhabited largely by members from the same country of origin and so is fairly homogenous. As such, the term is akin to and often used interchangeably with "ethnic enclave".

1993) offer the concept of *modes of incorporation* to describe how the host country accepts newcomers. These modes are the result of the interactions of a complex of variables: the policies of the host government (whether receptive, indifferent, or hostile), the values and prejudices of the host society (whether primarily prejudiced or not), and the characteristics of the co-ethnic community (whether its organization is weak or strong). Three features of the contexts into which newcomers settle can increase the likelihood of downward assimilation. The first is skin color. Generally, the darker the skin color of the incoming group, the more likely it is that members will be ascribed a lower social status. Second is location. Specifically, residential concentration in urban areas puts the immigrant group in contact with native-born minorities, which leads the majority white population to identify one with the other and potentially exposes children of immigrants to an oppositional youth subculture. Third is the lack of mobility ladders in an increasingly bifurcated employment structure (Crutchfield, Matsueda, and Drakulich 2006), which impels adult immigrants to try to bridge the wide gap from entry-level to professional positions in one generation, in order to afford sending their children to competitive colleges and show them that hard work can yield success (Portes and Zhou 1993). Not surprisingly, many are unable to do so. Segmented assimilation theory suggests, then, that immigrants who enter this country possessing darker skin, who settle in our inner cities, and who lack either access to or the skills required for the primary employment sector, are likely to experience downward assimilation or what Gans (1992) has termed "second-generation decline," whereby rather than reaping gains in human and financial capital across generations, groups experience loss. This *segment* of the immigrant population—rather than all or even most immigrants, as traditional assimilation suggests—are more susceptible to criminal involvement precisely because of their economic marginalization.

IMMIGRATION AND CRIME

As mentioned, theories of the link between immigration and crime have tended to flow from our understanding of the process by which the foreign-born are incorporated into the host society. The sections that follow review the classic and emergent contemporary theories of this link and locate the theories within their larger respective theoretical frameworks.

Social Disorganization Theory

With respect to crime, the dominant theoretical view of the link to immigration has remained Shaw and McKay's (1942) social disorganization theory, which drew heavily from the assimilation perspective developed by Park and Burgess (1924). As Bursik (2006) notes, Shaw and McKay likely even borrowed the term, *social disorganization* from Thomas and Znaniecki's (1918) much earlier work on the experiences of polish immigrants in America. Not surprisingly, then, discussions of immigration and crime have tended to accept the view that immigrants are more prone to engage in crime than the native population. Shaw and McKay's theory posits that the criminogenic effects of immigration stem from structural factors rather than qualities of racial and ethnic groups themselves, as is often posited by theories of the cultural deficiencies of minority groups.[21] In their analysis, those authors indicate that no matter from where the immigrant groups travel, their experiences will be similar and crime will be an option for many, again not because of innate dispositions, but rather a lack of viable legitimate alternatives.[22] What is key is that Shaw and McKay accepted that assimilation was a largely uniform process, rather than segmented, and that most immigrants would experience it in the same way and have similar outcomes. Their study was one of the first ecological analyses of crime in America, and in mapping rates of juvenile delinquency in Chicago, offered a number of

---

[21] Here the term *minority* is used in Wirth's original sense, rather than the constrained contemporary sense, which tends to denote only marginalized racial minority groups and in particular African Americans and Latinos. According to Wirth, a minority group is any "group of people who, because of their physical or cultural characteristics, are singled out from others in the society in which they live for differential and unequal treatment, and who therefore regard themselves as objects of collective discrimination" (1945: 347).

[22] Interestingly, Shaw and McKay differentiated immigrants not only by country of origin, but also by specific *regions* of their home countries. Contemporary research has abandoned this approach (perhaps because statistical procedures require the aggregation of small groups to get large enough counts to run analyses) and is only now returning to it.

key findings.[23] First, rates of delinquency varied inversely to the distance from the center of the city and inversely to socioeconomic status. Second, delinquency persisted despite changes to the racial and ethnic composition of a community. Third, in slum conditions, the researchers found gangs to be natural responses to the living conditions, rather than a collection of innate deviants. Finally, and most importantly, Shaw and McKay found no direct correlations between immigration status and crime *or* between poverty and crime. Rather immigration status and poverty each worked indirectly through residential instability and population turnover to produce a socially disorganized community, no longer able to enforce norms against crime and delinquency.[24]

According to this school of thought, large scale processes of rapid industrialization, urbanization, and immigration result in a heterogeneous population that is residentially unstable. Heterogeneity and instability undermine a community's formal and informal sources of *social control*, which Bursik and Grasmick (1993: 15) define as the "effort of the community to regulate itself and the behavior of residents and visitors to the neighborhood." Communication between neighbors becomes difficult as they lack linguistic, cultural, or historic commonalities. Community members' familiarity with each other and attachment to local institutions and organizations are consequently weakened. Essentially, it is no longer possible to know everyone. Residents begin to treat one another with indifference, creating an environment wherein informal controls are ineffective, leading to a greater reliance and eventual strain on formal social control in the form of police or other official agents.

The micro-social process leading to crime, particularly among young people, may go something like the following: in disorganized communities, the family breaks down as an agent of social control, putting added pressure on schools and the police who must then do double duty, carrying out their assigned tasks—education and rule

---

[23] Byrne and Sampson (1986) later extended this work on the ecology of juvenile crime to adult crime.

[24] Social disorganization theory is often categorized as a pure theory of social structure, though one can see that from its earliest conception, the focus on population heterogeneity and turnover point to the importance of social interaction, making it more a theory of social process than strictly social structure.

enforcement, respectively—as well as socializing youth into dominant norms. Schools experience their own unique problems. Large numbers of new and different students—students with different languages, ways of learning, cultural and social capital, perhaps learning disabilities, education levels, and so on—that similarly make communication and familiarity difficult. Further, in areas that experience rapid increases in population size, due for example to immigration, the influx of students puts a strain on the resources of school systems. Many students in such schools are pushed to the margins; their different forms of knowledge and expression having no conversion value within their new schools (Fordham 1996). Consequently, they are viewed as inferior by the grading standards of the school, which are typically slow to adapt (Carter 2005; Hargreaves 1967). Precisely because they are overburdened and their resources to educate and indoctrinate are spread thin, schools can respond to delinquent behavior with only the limited (official) sanctions available to them: detention, suspension, and expulsion. As these approaches fail to address the underlying causes of delinquent behavior—the inability to communicate needs and have needs met and the devaluation of students' social and cultural capital—they do little to curb the undesired behavior and in fact may foster a mistrust of the school among the students and ultimately may alienate those youth further (Carter 2005; Vigil 2002).

As they enter adulthood, these alienated youth stand greater risk of involvement with the last agent of community social control, the police, for two reasons. First, alienated youth may come to reject school, start skipping classes or drop out altogether. Second, youth who are alienated but who do not drop out, will likely have much difficulty in school, experience a reduction in academic success and ultimately in occupational achievement. Due to racism, many will be met with blocked opportunity upon graduation, and be subject to the social strain that motivates so many to engage in illegitimate opportunities (Martinez 2002; Vigil 2002; MacLeod 1987).

Sampson, Morenoff, and Earls (1999) offer as well a model for the ways in which the structural factors of social disorganization play out at the micro level in their concept of *collective efficacy*. In their view, three aspects of neighborhood social (dis)organization affect the criminal involvement of youth. First, *intergenerational closure* is the degree to which different age groups—juveniles, young adults, adults and elderly—are linked and interact. Second, *reciprocal exchange* is the degree of interfamily and adult interaction with respect to child rearing. Third, *mutual support of children* is the degree to which neighborhood residents can and will intervene on behalf of children. These factors are found in neighborhoods that are wealthy and residentially stable. In poorer, less stable areas residents tend to move in and out often, know each other less well, have fewer resources for mutual support (less time, greater personal concerns such as money, safety), and have higher rates of crime that tend to increase fear of and isolation from neighbors. The authors note that collective efficacy is not necessarily geographically bounded. It can spillover, such that neighborhoods with high collective efficacy will tend to increase that of surrounding communities. Conversely, those with low collective efficacy will tend to reduce that of surrounding communities.

In sum, immigrants face disadvantages relative to the native-born, which may lead them to engage in crime for economic gain (Lee et al. 2001; Merton 1938) or violence out of frustration or retaliation (Messner and Rosenfeld 2000; Tonry 1997b; Agnew 1992). This is the conventional explanation for crime and violence within immigrant communities. It is routinely, though not exclusively, applied to immigrants because of the tendency in the past for those groups to locate themselves in transitional urban areas (cf. Gans 1962). The theory works well irrespective of immigrant status and has been applied to native-born whites and blacks in low-income areas (MacLeod 1987). It is important to note, however, that Shaw and McKay implicated the *process of immigration* as criminogenic, rather than immigrants themselves. For nativists, however, that gap has shown fairly easy to bridge and explanations abound pointing to the cultures of migrant populations as deficient and the source of criminality (Mullen 2005; Huntington 2004; MacDonald 2004a, 2004b).

Community Resource Perspective

Drawing largely from the literature on segmented assimilation theory, and in particular its focus on ethnic enclaves, scholars have begun to question whether the traditional notion of immigration as disorganizing applies as readily today as it may have in the past. An emerging line of thought holds that increasing immigration to an area, rather than fostering disruption, may in fact strengthen community cohesion, thereby possibly acting as a suppressant to local rates of crime, at least in certain communities. This view has received growing attention in recent years, though, testifying to its emergent nature, that attention has come under a variety of names. It has been referred to as an *immigrant concentration* view (Desmond and Kubrin 2009), the *ethnic community model* (Logan, Alba, and Zhang 2002), the *enclave hypothesis* (Portes and Jensen 1992), and a *residential instability* model of ethnic enclaves (Shihadeh and Barranco 2010a). Following Feldmeyer (2009), this line of thinking is here referred to as the *community resource perspective*, since this term most fully encapsulates both the structural focus and the multifaceted linkages between immigrant communities and crime.

Scholarly research in a variety of fields has begun to offer support for the notion that increasing concentration of immigrants in an area is associated with a range of positive outcomes, including economic stimulation (Parrado and Kandel 2008; Portes and Rumbaut 2006; Reid, et al. 2005; Kotkin 2000; Portes and Zhou 1993), mortality rates (LeClere, Rogers, and Peters 1997), and reduced crime and violence (Shihadeh and Barranco 2010a; Desmond and Kubrin 2009; Feldmeyer 2009; Morenoff and Astor 2006; Lee, Martinez, and Rosenfeld 2001). These findings have led to the development of the concept of the Latino Paradox, which refers to the tendency of heavily Latino communities to have lower rates of crime and disorder, despite high levels of traditionally disorganizing factors, such as poverty, reduced education, and an abundance of low-skill workers (Burchfield and Silver 2013; Shihadeh and Barranco 2013; Stowell, et al. 2009; Sampson and Bean 2006). While the full range of mechanisms at work remain somewhat unclear, evidence points to a number of key factors, including the preservation of cultural norms, networks of information and social control, and employment opportunities.

Established immigrant communities can help to foster cultural norms based on shared heritage and traditions that bond members together. Successive waves of immigrants refresh and reconnect community members to that shared heritage, again reinforcing traditional norms and strengthening cohesion among community members (Feldmeyer 2009; Martinez 2002; Martinez, Stowell, and Cancino 2008). Immigrant concentration has also been shown to strengthen norms underlying conventional institutions such as marriage, family, and work. Recent immigrants tend to have lower rates of divorce, greater tendency to live in extended family units, and greater attachment to the labor force, despite lower lifetime earnings, relative to their native-born counterparts. Research has shown that unacculturated Mexican immigrants have lower incidence of psychiatric disorders across the life course than their more acculturated Mexican-American counterparts (Portes and Rumbaut 2006; Escobar 1998). Finally, as others have noted, the benefits of cohesion are particularly helpful in reducing pressures on immigrant youth. Sutherland (1947) first pointed out the criminogenic "side effects" of the acculturation process for immigrant youth when exposed to the mainstream American culture. Portes and Rumbaut (2006) elaborate on this point in their discussion of "downward assimilation," whereby the pressures some youth face in their adopted schools and neighborhoods lead them to engage in drug use, participate in gangs, and drop out of school. According to those others, the cultural preservation offered by tight-knit immigrant communities can reinforce norms devaluing such behaviors, thereby buffering against peer group pressures.

Furthermore, concentrated immigration can foster tight-knit social networks that operate as sources of information, providing newcomers with information they can use to adjust to their new surroundings, such as local customs, language, and sources of aid. These networks also operate as sources of opportunity, connecting recent arrivals to sources of employment and income, thereby mediating the potential effects of poverty and unemployment. Such networks can also operate as sources of child care, enabling parents to maintain employment and ensuring children are supervised by community members, a key component of collective efficacy, which can help mediate the link between structural disadvantage and crime (Burchfield and Silver 2013). Portes and Stepick (1993) note the beneficial effects of immigration in stabilizing and revitalizing the local economy in Miami, as well as contributing to greater informal social control within the area.

Concentrated immigration also provides an important source of employment, particularly for those whose skills may be undervalued by the host culture. Desmond and Kubrin (2009: 586) note that "the enclave in particular allows immigrants to find employment that yields better returns to their human capital than would be found in the secondary labor market outside of the area." Additionally, Portes and Rumbaut (2006) note that enclaves offer important opportunities for financing entrepreneurial businesses, which then generating further employment opportunities for local residents in a spin-off effect. These sources of employment may be key not only in warding off the criminogenic consequences of poverty, but also in strengthening social control. Card (1990) finds that the infusion of Mariel Cubans, expected by both Fidel Castro and the American public to be a major source of economic and social disruption, was far less problematic than anticipated. Existing immigrant businesses essentially absorbed the newcomers, providing them and their families with important sources of income to establish themselves in their new communities. As these studies have shown, there is good reason to suspect that among some communities, immigrant concentration is likely to have suppressive effects on crime, whether by reinforcing norms against it, strengthening community ties and informal social control, or providing opportunities that make crime a less attractive alternative. In the last two decades, a number of criminological studies have offered empirical support to these claims.

Recent Research and Hypotheses on the Immigration-Crime Link

Over the last ten years, a number of social scientists have begun to test the tenets of social disorganization theory and the community resource perspective on the experiences of and outcomes for today's immigrants at varying levels of aggregation. While several studies have found limited support for social disorganization theory, in the form of null effects of immigration or positive effects for specific crime types, the majority of studies have tended to find suppressive effects of immigration on crime, controlling for a host of relevant factors.

At the individual level, Kposowa, Adams, and Tsunokai (2009) find no effect of citizenship status on the occurrence of being arrested for violent crime, but a significant negative effect on other types of crime. Specifically, those authors find that non-citizens are less likely to be arrested for property crimes, drug offenses, and weapons offenses than U.S. citizens.[25] Similarly, Desmond & Kubrin (2009) find that immigrant concentration has a negative and significant effect on self-reporting delinquent behavior, an outcome firmly in line with the community resource perspective's view of the role of family and community in exerting social control on youth. Sampson, Morenoff, and Raudenbush (2005) find lower rates of violence among Mexican

---

[25] The only offense for which non-citizens are *more likely* to be arrested, according to the study by Kposowa, Adams, and Tsunokai (2009), is counterfeiting/forgery, an offense consistent with producing documentation of legal status.

Americans, compared to whites, a discrepancy they suggest is explained by the greater tendency for Mexican Americans to have married parents, live in a community with a high concentration of immigrants, and be an immigrant themselves. Their finding that rates of violence among first-generation Mexicans are lower than second-generation Mexican Americans, which are in turn lower than third-generation rates points to a process of downward assimilation, as outlined by segmented assimilation theory.

This effect of acculturation is highlighted by several more recent analyses. First, Peguero's (2011) study of school misbehavior indicates first-generation foreign-born youth are less likely to misbehave at school compared to their native-born counterparts, but through exposure to school social disorder, such as physical conflicts, crime, and alcohol use. Moreover, foreign-born youth are more likely to misbehave in schools with higher shares of native-born black and white youth. Similarly, Esbensen and Carson's (2012) study of youth gang-involvement suggests that foreign-born youth are less likely to be gang-involved at younger ages, but by their mid-teen years, these same youth constitute a disproportionate share of gang-affiliated young people. However, these authors note that even though foreign-born youth may be somewhat more likely to be involved in gangs, their rates of actual offending are significantly lower than those of native-born youth. Finally, Alvarez, Nobles, and Lersch (2013) analyze Latino arrest records in two southwestern cities, finding a consistent, significant, and positive effect of acculturation on criminal arrests. Taken together, these findings raise the question of whether immigrant youth learn to become more criminal from native-born youth. At the least, the results suggest that acculturating to American society does not always put the children of immigrants onto a trajectory toward middle-class success.

While individual-level analyses can address the question of whether immigrants are involved in crime to greater or lesser degrees than native-born Americans, aggregate level studies are required to address whether the *process* of immigration may be implicated as criminogenic. The last few years have seen an increase in these types of analyses. For example, an analysis of the effect of the percent foreign-born on the occurrence of homicide within census tracts reveals that increasing immigration has a depressive effect not only on foreign-born homicides, but also white and Latino homicides as well (Martinez, Stowell, and Lee 2010). Similarly, in a tract-level analysis of aggravated assault rates in Miami, Martinez, Rosenfeld, and Mares

(2008) find that measures of social disorganization all exert significant effects, though not all in the expected direction. While population instability and economic deprivation are both positively correlated with assault rates, population heterogeneity actually has a negative indirect effect; that is, a heterogeneous population reduces the likelihood of drug market activity, thereby reducing rates of aggravated assault. The pattern is similar for robbery with the exception of a nonsignificant effect of deprivation. Consistent with social disorganization theory, instability and deprivation have positive significant direct effects on aggravated assault. Instability has a limited indirect effect on assault rates through drug activity. Inconsistent with social disorganization theory, heterogeneity has no direct effect on aggravated assault rates, but has a negative indirect effect on them by suppressing drug activity.

The findings on heterogeneity suggest, "either that the nature of immigration and ethnic relations has changed or that population heterogeneity—as distinct from racial disadvantage and isolation—is simply not the 'disorganizing' social condition that generations of theorists have assumed it is" (Martinez, Rosenfeld, and Mares 2008: 868). Stowell, et al. (2009) reach a similar conclusion in their metropolitan level analysis, arguing that it is not that today's immigrants are different from those who came before, but that the immigration-crime link is, as Hagan and Palloni (1999) argue, a myth. Results of a time series analysis for 1994-2004 and a cross-sectional analysis for 2000 for metropolitan areas with a population of at least 500,000 suggest, respectively, that immigration either was responsible for broad reductions in violent crime, especially robbery, or had no effect on most categories of crime.

In a tract-level analysis using multiple ethnic groups, Martinez, Lee, and Nielsen (2004) investigate whether drug violence in Miami and San Diego is influenced by a community's ethnic composition or the presence of enclaves. In Miami, Cubans were more likely to live in non-drug areas than drug areas (as measured by the number of drug homicides) while Haitians were more likely to live in drug, rather than non-drug areas. However, controlling for other factors, the percent of the population that is Cuban, Haitian, or Central American was found to have no significant effect on drug homicides. Predictors of drug homicide included economic deprivation (positive and significant) and the percent of the immigrant population that arrived in the 1960s (negative and significant). The results for San Diego were somewhat different. There, Mexican Latinos, African Americans, Southeast Asians, recent immigrants and those who arrived during the 1970s were all more likely to live in drug, rather than non-drug, areas. Unlike Miami, the percent of the population that was African American and the percent Southeast Asian were positively correlated with drug homicides. Also distinct, areas with more recent immigrants were more likely to be drug areas, a finding consistent with social disorganization theory. Areas with both Mexican Latinos *and* low-skill workers were less likely to be drug areas, suggesting a surprising buffering effect of low-skill immigration, an outcome more consistent with the community resource perspective. As with Miami, economic deprivation had a positive and significant effect on the occurrence of drug homicides in San Diego neighborhoods.

The results suggest the importance of ethnic enclaves like those found throughout Miami for reducing crime. In either city, those living in barrios or enclaves were less likely to live in drug areas. While San Diego "offers a wider range of economic opportunities than does Miami, it also offers a limited immigrant opportunity to move up the socioeconomic ladder. One potential result is that immigrants and ethnic minorities are concentrated in areas where exposure to drugs is more routine" (Martinez, Lee and Nielsen 2004: 149). In general, the authors' findings support community resource view, with Miami serving as the exemplar of immigrant revitalization and ethnic enclaves, and San Diego serving as an example of downward assimilation and the type of community whose ability to aid immigrants' incorporation is limited. In Miami, well-connected and well-established enclaves provide opportunities for advancement of successive groups of immigrants, which helps explain Card's (1990) finding that the influx of Mariel Cubans had no effect on the employment of the existing workforce. In San Diego, a lack of well-defined enclaves leaves successive immigrants to follow the path of earlier immigrants to low-skill, low-paying jobs in disadvantaged and marginalized communities.

At the city-level, recent research findings have as well tended to present a challenge to the social disorganization view. Ousey and Lee (2007) find that homicide rates declined in cities that experienced population growth and in cities that saw growth in relative size of their Latino population. These findings are inconsistent with social disorganization, broadly conceived, which would predict increasing rates of crime in areas marked by increasing immigration. Research findings by Ousey and Kubrin (2009) that growth in rates of immigration from 1980-2000 were associated with overall reductions in violent crime over the same period are also at odds with traditional expectations. The authors suggest that the effect may be a product of immigration's tendency to strengthen families, relative to the native-born. Immigration is negatively correlated with both the incidence of divorce and the presence of single-parent headed households, each of which is positively correlated with violence. Also within cities, Martinez (2000) finds no significant effect of immigration variables on total homicides, but positive effects on felony homicides, and negative effects on homicides in which the offender knew the victim.

In a place-level study of 459 cities with population greater than 50,000, Wadsworth's (2010) change-over-time analysis indicates a significant negative effect of foreign-born concentration on overall robbery rates, and a significant negative effect of recent foreign-born concentration on homicide rates. Both findings lend support to the community resource view, suggesting that immigrant incorporation may not be the socially disorganizing or criminogenic force once thought. Also at the place level, Feldmeyer (2009) finds support for both social disorganization theory and the community resource perspective. Consistent with the former, areas with greater Latino immigrant concentration tend to have higher rates of residential mobility, language heterogeneity, and racial and ethnic population heterogeneity, each of which is found to directly increase rates of violence. Consistent with the latter, however, immigration is found to directly reduce the occurrence of Latino robbery and works to reduce specific and general rates of violence indirectly by strengthening social institutions such as the family and social support systems. The overall effects of immigration, according to Feldmeyer are small but inverse; as immigrant concentration increases, rates of violence, especially robbery, decline.

At somewhat larger aggregations, research has tended to offer more support for social disorganization theory, though the distinction is far from finite, and may depend more on the type of analysis and question at hand. In a cross-sectional county-level study, for example, Lee and Slack (2008) find that, consistent with social disorganization theory, violent crime is higher in more disadvantaged areas and where there is greater population turnover. Also consistent with social disorganization, violent crime is lower in homogenous counties and in communities where people either tend to work from home or work outside of their county of residence. Lastly, the authors find that employment in low hour or seasonal work is associated with reduced rates of violence, suggesting that "even partial labor force participation can contribute to the regulation of group behavior and interactions" (Lee and Slack 2008: 765). Within metropolitan areas, cross-sectional analyses have found no significant effects of immigration on either total or violent crime (Butcher and Piehl 1998). In contrast, change-over-time analyses looking only at within-unit effects have found significant negative effects of the recent foreign-born population on homicide (Reid, et al. 2005), and significant negative effects of the total foreign-born population on overall violent crime, and robbery and aggravated assault in particular. These latter findings are more in line with expectations of the community resource view of immigration and crime.

Immigration, Crime, and the Challenge of New Settlement Patterns

The dynamic spread of immigrants to new locations poses a number of challenges to researchers, policy-makers, service providers, and even local residents. Because many of the new locations to which today's immigrants are moving have at best a limited history in dealing with and incorporating disparate groups, it is unclear what the overall effects will be. With respect to crime, then, there are factors that theoretically should predispose immigrants and their offspring to engage in crime and factors that should act as buffers, keeping crime rates low.

Recent research by Donato, et al. (2008) buoys these points. Those authors investigate the changing socioeconomic and demographic factors of the foreign-born, and in particular the Mexican-born, across metropolitan and non-metropolitan counties, as well as within what the authors term *offset* metropolitan and non-metropolitan counties—places where the arrival of the foreign-born has prevented population decline—from 1990 to 2000. Their findings suggest that not only are the settlement destinations for immigrants changing, but immigrants themselves are also changing on a host of key demographic and socioeconomic factors. From 1990 to 2000, as the overall native U.S. population aged, the overall foreign-born population grew younger. Moreover, the foreign-born in 2000 reported fewer years of formal education and fewer high school graduates than in 1990, despite the fact that in 2000 the foreign-born were *less likely* than in 1990 to live in poverty. They were also less likely to speak English well or to speak it in the home in 2000 than in 1990.

Comparing immigrants in non-metropolitan counties to those in metropolitan ones yields some interesting differences as well. In the former, both the foreign-born and Mexican-born experienced significant declines in poverty, while those in metropolitan counties experienced only tiny declines. This difference suggests the boom economy of the 1990s yielded weaker returns for those in major urban areas, such that by 2000, compared to natives and their counterparts in non-metropolitan counties, the foreign-born and Mexican-born in metropolitan counties grew more disadvantaged in terms of income and education.

Also, both the foreign-born and Mexican-born in non-metropolitan counties were much less likely to become naturalized citizens in 2000 than in 1990; the foreign-born experienced a decline from 46.6 percent to 36.9 percent, while the Mexican-born declined from 28.7 percent to 23.6 percent (the declines were even greater for those in non-metropolitan *offset* counties). In contrast, rates of naturalization for those in metropolitan counties remained steady at approximately 40 percent of the foreign-born and 22 percent of the Mexican-born.

There were also important differences between those who moved into areas offsetting native population decline and those who didn't. Compared to all non-metropolitan counties, both the foreign-born and Mexican-born in non-metropolitan *offset* counties were more geographically mobile, being more likely to have arrived within the five years preceding the study and having fewer mean years of U.S. residence. They were also likely to have more children under age 18 and less likely to speak English well or speak it in the home. Taken together, these comparisons across national origin and U.S. residence indicate a trend whereby, beginning in the 1990s, as increasing numbers of immigrants entered the country, not only did many eschew traditional urban destinations in favor of new non-metropolitan areas, but those who did so tended to rate higher on a host of criminogenic factors.

Research is just beginning to address whether patterns of association between immigration and crime differ across areas depending on their history of immigrant reception. While only a few such analyses exist, their results are instructive. At the place level, Lichter, et al. (2010) find that Latinos experience greater segregation within new destinations than traditional areas and find greater difficulty in either structural or cultural assimilation. With regard to crime, at the county level, research by Shihadeh and colleagues suggests that while in traditional receiving areas, Latino communities provide a buffer between economic deprivation and violence, the same buffer is absent within new destinations (Shihadeh and Barranco 2013; Shihadeh and Winters 2010). These results suggest that the re-organizing effects of contemporary immigration highlighted by the community resource perspective may not be consistent features of the process within new destinations. Instead, there is greater reason to expect the process to be more traditionally disorganizing in new receiving areas, perhaps owing to the lack of established networks to aid immigrant incorporation. The analyses presented in Chapters 4 and 5 seek to provide insight into this issue by determining whether patterns of association between immigration and crime differ between traditional and emerging immigrant destinations. Should the analyses indicate differential effects of immigration on crime across types of receiving areas, the results might suggest the limits of the community resource perspective and the continued applicability of social disorganization theory.

Hypotheses on the Relationship between Immigration and Crime

Despite the recent growth in research on the immigration crime link, questions regarding the nature of the connection still exist. Several studies continue to find support for the traditional model of social disorganization, with some noting null effects of immigration on crime, others finding positive effects, and still others suggesting effects mediated by disadvantage. The majority of recent research, however, offers support for the community resource perspective: new waves of immigrants exert no effect on crime either directly or indirectly, and in many cases, may offer a suppressive effect, particularly in the case of violent crime. With these findings in mind, this research proceeds with a number of key hypotheses. Consistent with the community resource view and existing place-level research findings, I expect to find changes in the concentration of the total foreign-born are (1) negatively correlated with changes in rates of overall, violent, and property crime. Within the overall sample, I also expect to find (2) the patterns do not substantively differ whether the independent variable represents the concentration of total foreign-born or only those recently arrived.

In contrast, for the subset of new destinations, I expect to find stronger support for social disorganization theory. Given that new destinations very likely lack mechanisms by which to aid in the incorporation of newcomers, their arrival is likely to manifest as more of a traditionally disorganizing force. Moreover, given the current cultural context of opposition and research indicating greater marginalization of ethnic minorities within new destinations (Lichter, et al. 2010), it is likely that foreign-born in these areas may experience blocked economic and employment opportunities. Consequently, in these areas, I expect to find that (3) changes in the concentration of total immigrants are positively and significantly associated with changes in the rates of property and overall crime (with the former driving correlation to the latter), but (4) no effect on changes in the rate of violent crime. Finally, while I expect significant findings with regard to total immigrant concentration, I expect (5) the patterns to be heightened for changes in the concentration of the *recent* foreign-born, given as well research indicating their greater likelihood of being young, male, poorly-skilled and a visible minority (i.e. Latino as opposed to white European immigrants). These hypotheses are offered for the relationship between immigration and traditional crime. As the next section will show, there are good reasons to suspect the relationships will differ when the crime in question involves the victimization of newcomers.

IMMIGRANT VICTIMIZATION

Discussions of the immigration-crime link have almost universally accepted that, where it does exist, it's a one-way correlation: that immigration leads to higher crime rates *because* immigrants engage in more crime or displace vulnerable members of the local population. One of the peculiarities of this view is that engaging in crime doesn't make a lot of sense for immigrants, especially those who are without documentation. Given the overall unsympathetic stance at the state and federal levels and the increase in deportation as a solution to immigrant crime, the costs of crime would seem to far outweigh any benefits (Sayad 2004; Hagan et al. 2008).

What is at least theoretically more likely is that even documented immigrants, lacking a firm grasp of the language, knowledge of their rights, or methods of calling advocates or agents of social control to their aid, are prime targets for victimization (Hopkins 2010). Undocumented immigrants are especially vulnerable as any invocation of official agents is likely to jeopardize their continued stay. This line of reasoning parallels the routine activities approach, which suggests that the crime rate can go up without any increase in the number of offenders (Felson 1996; Osgood et al. 1996). Cohen and Felson's (1979) routine activities theory focuses on criminal incidents, rather than criminals, and suggests there are three minimal elements necessary for predatory offenses: (1) a likely offender, usually a young male; (2) a suitable target for crime, determined by the value, inertia, visibility, and access to the item; and (3) the absence of a capable guardian. Immigration may increase the pool of potential targets or victims, simply by increasing the overall population but more pointedly by bringing in a vulnerable population of people who may not know their legal rights, may not speak the native language, and who may be construed negatively by the native population. Additionally, the changing structure of local labor markets coupled with the cheap source of labor that immigrants often represent to employers can displace native workers, especially native-born minorities (Reid et al., 2005), who then may be cast into in the pool of likely offenders. Previous research indicates that employers often prefer immigrant workers over African Americans for sound business reasons—native-born workers command higher pay, better working conditions, and greater benefits—and more overtly racist ones as well—immigrants are perceived as hard-working while native-born Blacks are viewed as lazy and a liability in the workplace (Waldinger 1997, 1996; Beck 1996).[26]

According to the Leadership Conference on Civil Rights (2009), the annual number of hate crimes against Latinos increased 40 percent from 2003 to 2007. Though in a larger sense, immigrants are victimized by a variety of social actors at every point from the start of their journey through their settlement and employment in the U.S. As McDonald (1997: 4) notes,

> Guides and organized gangsters have robbed, raped and killed them; abandoned them in the desert; tossed them overboard at sea or out of speeding cars under hot pursuit; or forced them to work in sweatshops or prostitution rings to pay off the cost of

---

[26] Amazingly, Pager (2003) finds greater hiring discrimination against Blacks than against convicted felons.

the trip. Bandits prey upon them during their journeys. Xenophobes and hatemongers terrorize them. Some employers cheat them of their earnings. The fact that illegal immigration is a crime makes the immigrants particularly vulnerable because they are unlikely to seek the protection of the law.

All the while, the exploitation of immigrants is a lucrative business. By 1993, the market for smuggling Chinese immigrants into New York was an estimated $3.5 billion. Individual migrants were typically charged $1500 up front, with the rest of the debt amount vague and paid off via something akin to indentured servitude (McDonald 1997). By 1995, "Central America had become a free-trade zone in which government officials sold the visas and passports necessary to leave China via plane for $25,000 to $50,000 apiece" (McDonald 1997: 5).

At a more local level, a recent review of immigrant reception in Suffolk County in Long Island, New York by the Southern Poverty Law Center (SPLC 2009) highlights the potential for conflict between newcomers and the local population. As an exemplar of the violence that can occur, the authors of that report point to the November 8, 2008 murder of Marcelo Lucero, an Ecuadorian immigrant, in Patchogue, NY. The murder was committed by a group of local youth who referred to themselves as "the Caucasian Crew" and claimed to have targeted Latinos as "part of a sport they termed 'beaner-hopping' " (SPLC 2009: 5). According to the report, rather than an isolated incident, the attack on Lucero was part of a larger pattern rooted in a "climate of fear" developed out of anti-immigrant rhetoric and policy of political leaders.

Latino immigrants are drawn to Suffolk County in search of work in its wealthy seaside communities. Unable to afford residence in those same places, they settle in the area's more affordable inland towns, "alongside middle- and working-class American families who are more likely to view the brown-skinned newcomers as competitors for jobs than hired help" (SPLC 2009: 10). In less than two decades, some towns in Suffolk County have transitioned from homogenous white communities to 15 percent Latino; many of the newcomers are from Mexico and Central America. The pace of the change has been met with resistance. Latino immigrants report being regularly harassed, taunted, and attacked, typically by young white males, though incidents involving black males and white females have been reported as well. Interviews with immigrants suggest they are increasingly unlikely to report these attacks, believing law enforcement either indifferent or hostile. According to the SPLC, their fears may not be unwarranted. While Latinos make up 14 percent of Suffolk County's total population, they routinely make up roughly 50 percent of those charged in court for motor vehicle violations on any given day, and a review of police blotters suggests the same pattern for individuals fined for motor vehicle infractions (SPLC 2009).

Vocal opposition has come in particular from political leaders. For example, upon taking office, Suffolk County Executive Steve Levy proposed filing a Memorandum of Agreement with Immigrations and Customs Enforcement, which would empower Suffolk County police officers to detain Latinos they suspected of being undocumented immigrants and hand them over to the ICE for deportation.[27] Addressing day laborers, who congregate in public places waiting for work and thus constitute a very visible subset of the population, County Legislator Michael D'Andre of Smithtown, NY stated in August 2001, "We'll be up in arms; we'll be out with baseball bats" (quoted from SPLC 2009: 8). Of the same issue, County Legislator Elie Mystal stated in March 2007, " 'If I'm living in a neighborhood and people are gathering like that, I would load my gun and start shooting, period. Nobody will say it, but I'm going to say it'" (ibid.).

The opposition toward immigrants in Suffolk County coalesced in the form of the anti-immigrant activist group, Sachem Quality of Life (SQL), founded in 1998 and disbanded in 2004. Following the 2003 murder of two Mexican day laborers, Suffolk County legislator Paul Tonna held a rally for racial unity. In response, SQL held a rally outside Tonna's home, and "hurled racial slurs at his adopted children, four of whom are Mexican-American and one a Native American" (SPLC 2009: 13). Two weeks later, SQL held a "Day of Truth" rally, featuring speakers from several established hate groups. At the meeting, SQL members stated: "'Farmingville is a one-day job, that's Farmingville! If the INS wanted to do it, they'd come in the morning with buses, with document people, and remove them all, repatriate them. One-day job. Farmingville would be restored'" (ibid.).[28] A few

---

[27] The motion was ultimately quashed by police unions for fear that it would make victims and witnesses unlikely to comply with investigations.

[28] At the time of the meeting, Immigration and Naturalization Services (INS) no longer existed. As of March 1, 2003 its administration duties had been transferred to Customs and Immigration Services (CIS) and its enforcement

days later, on July 5, 2003, five local teenagers set fire to the home of a Latino family with firecrackers. When asked by the local District Attorney to explain their motives, one of the teens stated, "Mexicans live there" (ibid.).

Recent Research on Immigrant Victimization

While the situation in Suffolk County should not be taken as the norm, neither should it be discounted as an isolated incident. Valenzuela (2006) investigates the degree to which day laborers—the thousands of men and women, many of whom are immigrants, who congregate daily on street corners in major cities across the country looking for a day's work—in Los Angeles are victims of violence. Because of the scarcity of consistent work, competition among laborers is fierce and relationships with bosses tense (wages are often bartered for onsite). Valenzuela finds that day laborers are victimized by a variety of sources, including other day laborers, police, employers, local residents, and local merchants, and are victimized in a number of ways, ranging from hold-ups, to hate crimes, to death (cf. Pritchard 2004). Consistent with other research findings, they are vulnerable to violence because of language barriers, their immigration status, a fear of reporting, a lack of knowledge of their rights, and the cash-only nature of their employment (see Hendricks et al. [2007] for how these same factors affect victimization and perception of bias in Arab-American communities). Similarly, in her study of Latino migrants in post-Katrina New Orleans, Fussell (2011) finds that day laborers are at increased risk of experiencing wage theft, relative to other types of workers, while Latino migrant laborers in particular are also at risk for robbery and physical assault. Drawing from laborers' physical appearance, language use, and job-seeking behavior, employers and street criminals are able to identify laborers as likely undocumented and so easy targets. The abuses committed against laborers may go unnoticed as they lack documents or a formal relationship with their employer, they work "under the table," and may be unfamiliar with their rights. Fussell terms this condition the *deportation threat dynamic*, "a highly exploitative interpersonal dynamic between targeted

---

powers, to which the speaker quoted appears to refer, transferred to Immigration and Customs Enforcement (ICE), under the DHS restructuring.

migrants and those who seek to take advantage of them" (Fussell 2011: 594), which is fueled by two key conditions: the high and steady demand for cheap migrant labor and the continued enforcement of harsh migration policies, largely in the form of deportations.

This dynamic highlights what researchers have alternately referred to as state-sponsored violence, legal violence, or symbolic violence (cf. Aliverti 2012; Menjívar and Abrego 2012; Hagan, Levi, and Dinovitzer 2008; Hagan and Palloni 1999; for a discussion of the use of symbolic politics in the 2008 Presidential election, see Marion and Oliver 2012), a condition whereby the state uses existing—and, where necessary, creates new—laws to apply harsh punishment and enforce exceedingly strict requirements on the conduct and presence of immigrants. The actions of the state then serve to signal to its citizens that immigrants are unwelcome and worthy of harsh penalties. In analyzing the role of criminal law, Aliverti (2012) finds that it serves as much as a symbolic instrument as a protective one. She notes that passing anti-immigrant legislation is relatively easy and allows the state to 'do something' about the 'immigration problem.' whether the policies are enforced or not, and whether the flow of immigrants is stemmed or not are relatively extraneous; what matters is that something has 'been done.' But as others have pointed out, this symbolic effect can have important consequences on those it identifies as problematic. According to Menjívar and Abrego,

> legal violence is rooted in the legal system that purports to protect the nation but, instead produces spaces and the possibility for material, emotional, and psychological injurious actions that target an entire group of people with a particular set of shared social characteristics (2012: 1413-14).

As Fussell notes, when the economic demands of a capitalist system interact with the legal violence of the state, the result is a sort of carte blanche for employers and criminals to victimize newcomers. One of the ironies of this dynamic is that violence against day laborers may actually engender violence *by them* as well, as they may perceive few other alternatives for recourse (Valenzuela 2006).

While day laborers tend to occupy the lower echelons of the class hierarchy, upward mobility does not necessarily reduce the likelihood of victimization. Miller (2007) finds that contrary to popular belief, increasing acculturation results in more complex victimization that is often more difficult to uncover. Even those who possess greater human and financial capital have been victims of housing scams, education scams, workplace abuse, and so on. What may change with increasing mobility and acculturation is the predominance of violence by the victimizers, rather than the overall victimization.

Research by Biafora and Warheit (2007) provides insight into the complexity of the issue of immigrant victimization. Comparing victimization histories not only across the Latino-White-Black continuum, but also within the Latino group, disaggregating by immigrant status, those authors find that immigrant status had no effect on the likelihood of being a victim of violence among young adults in Miami-Dade County, Florida. Consistent with previous research, African Americans were more likely than Latinos or native whites to experience *vicarious victimization* (i.e., witnessing violence happen to another person) and males were more likely to be victims of street violence than females, regardless of race/ethnicity or immigrant status. Somewhat inconsistent with the literature, the authors find no effect of immigrant status or race on *personal exposure* to violence, nor a significant difference between the lifetime victimization rates for foreign-born and native-born Latinos. The lack of a finding is attributed to "the unique social environment awaiting Hispanic immigrants arriving in Miami-Dade county" (Biafora and Warheit 2007: 45); that is, a welcoming reception from a well-established immigrant community with available political power. The emergence of ethnic strongholds like Miami leads the authors to suggest that "we might be witnessing a trend towards more stable residency among inner city immigrant areas due to a composite of economic, political and culturally enhanced opportunities" (Biafora and Warheit 2007: 51). An implication of this research is that the context of immigrant reception, and thus the potential for victimization, likely varies geographically.

So while scholars are beginning to address the victimization of immigrants (see Cuevas, Sabina, and Milloshi 2012; McDonald and Erez 2007; Valenzuela 2006; Reid et al. 2005; Levin and Rabrenovic 2004; Levin and McDevitt 2002), to date there have been few large-scale studies focused specifically on rates of victimization of immigrants.[29] Several research pieces have relied on victimization rates as proxy measures for *offending rates* (Martinez and Nielsen 2006; Nielsen and Martinez 2006; Lee, Martinez and Rosenfeld 2001), yet their overall focus has been on connecting that victimization to crime *committed by immigrants*. Further, these studies have tended to focus on a limited number of immigrant groups and locations, typically those cities that have traditionally been points of entry or destination. The problem with regard to studying victimization in such places is that they have long histories of interactions between natives and non-natives, which may potentially make those interactions routinized, thereby reducing the likelihood of victimization (cf. Shihadeh and Barranco 2013).

Immigration and the Place of Victimization

As with traditional forms of crime, the geographic diversification of immigration raises questions as to the likelihood of immigrant victimization within new destinations. As political rhetoric has appeared to "prime" residents of such areas to view newcomers as threats, it is likely that many will be met with opposition and that such opposition may crystallize into anti-immigrant collective action (Olzak 1992). There is potential for many to be victims of unfair housing practices, and to have difficulty procuring legitimate employment. The children of immigrants are likely to face significant pressure in school, particularly to the degree that they stand out socially, culturally, or phenotypically. That pressure can manifest itself in a number of ways, most prominently in either outperforming native-born peers or rejecting the school system. Attacks on immigrants are another potential outcome. Previous research has shown that "at the local level, hate crimes directed at Asians and Latinos have been found to increase when these groups move into traditionally white neighborhoods" (Citrin et al. 1997: 877).

Shihadeh and Winters (2010) are among the first to investigate victimization across types of settlement destinations. Their research finds that Latinos are more likely to be victims of crime, homicide in particular, in new destinations than in traditional settlement areas. The

---

[29] A search of the *Sociological Abstracts* database for the terms "'immigra*' and 'hate crime' " yielded not a single quantitative research item as of February 11, 2011.

implication of these findings is that minority group movement into primarily dominant group areas leaves the newcomers without the support of an established community that can "compensate for poverty, unemployment, and other factors known to elevate crime" (Shihadeh and Winters 2010: 645). More recent research supports these findings. According to Shihadeh and Barranco (2013), Latinos are at increased risk of being the victims of homicide in new destinations, but not in traditional receiving areas. Moreover, in new destinations, victimization in general increases with Latino immigration, an effect found only for recent foreign-born, those entering after 1990. Consistent with Social Disorganization theory, Latino socioeconomic deprivation is associated with increased victimization only in new destinations, not in traditional receiving areas. This finding suggests a "clear duality in the experience of U.S. Latinos" (Shihadeh and Barranco 2012: 96), whereby those newcomers who settle in traditional receiving areas benefit from a social organization that provides a buffer against victimization, while those who settle in new destinations, places lacking in protective social organization, are more likely to experience criminal victimization. It would appear that the link between immigration and crime long ago predicted by social disorganization theory, may again be at work in new destinations.

Consequently, at least in the case of Latinos, the newcomers are at heightened risk of violent victimization. While Latinos make up the lion's share of contemporary immigrants, Shihadeh and colleagues' research captures both native- and foreign-born Latinos, and it remains to be seen whether the pattern holds for immigrants specifically. There is good reason to believe that as immigration spreads to ever newer and previously homogenous areas of the country, conflict will ensue in some of those areas and sometimes become violent, particularly where the incoming group is perceived by the majority as posing a threat and where local leaders benefit from potential conflict (Levin and Rabrenovic 2004; Rabrenovic 2007). Adequately addressing the issue requires attention to *demographic change* as a predictor of biased crime, a focus largely absent in the existing literature. Consequently, inferences about the effect of population shifts on the occurrences of biased crime must be culled from cognate research on racial attitudes.

Cognitive/Attitudinal Research and Hypotheses on Anti-Immigrant Crime

Insight into the native-born response to increases in local immigration can be drawn from the body of work on group threat theory.[30] Traditionally, this research has been applied to categories of race generally, and the black-white dichotomy in particular, as a way of interpreting reactions to increasing settlement of African Americans in predominantly white areas (Blumer 1958; King and Wheelock 2007). Recently, researchers have begun extending this line of thinking to other subordinated groups, including Latinos and Asians (Green, Strolovich, and Wong 1998) and the foreign-born (Vallas, Zimmerman, and Davis 2009; Semyonov, Raijman, and Gorodzeisky 2006; Quillian 1995).

In its traditional form, group threat theory suggests that prejudice toward immigrants is a function of the perceived—rather than the actual—size of the population of newcomers, relative to the dominant group and economic conditions (Wang 2012; Welch, et al. 2011). An analysis of attitudes toward immigrants across twelve European countries finds that indicators of threat—subordinate group size and economic conditions—explain most of the variation in levels of prejudice across the sample (Quillian 1995). A more recent extension of that research comes to virtually identical conclusions, stating that growth in the size of the immigrant population translates to "greater competition for rewards and resources and greater challenge to the actual interests and prerogatives of the dominant population" (Semyonov, Raijman, and Gorodzeisky 2006: 428). Research by Welch, et al. finds that "the rapidly growing U.S. Hispanic population represents a compelling crime threat, at least perceptually, which fosters consistent and strong support for punitive crime control" (2011: 832-33). Importantly, the authors also find that the effect is heightened in states where there is actually a smaller percentage of Latino immigrants, suggesting that native-born Americans' fear is strongest

---

[30] Here, *group-threat theory* denotes the broad category of research including that theory in its original formulation (Blumer 1958; Blalock 1957; Quillian 1995) and its variants: realistic group conflict theory (Bobo 1988), the power-threat hypothesis (Tolnay, Beck, and Massey 1989), the power-differential hypothesis (Levine and Campbell 1972), and the defended neighborhoods thesis (Green, Strolovich, and Wong 1989).

where the 'threat' is least, a finding that is consistent with the "clear duality of experience" identified by Shihadeh and Barranco (2013) between traditional receiving areas and new destinations.

Regarding economic conditions, research has tended to find opposition to out-groups is greatest in times of economic recession (Burns and Gimpel 2000), and greatest when the national, rather than individual, economic outlook is dim (Espenshade and Hempstead 1996). This pattern results from dominant group members' either blaming the subordinate group for the poor economic circumstances, or their perception of competition with the subordinate group for resources, such that "the greater the sense of threat to their prerogatives, the more likely are members of the dominant group to express prejudice against threatening outsiders" (Quillian 1995: 588). Accordingly, Wang (2012) finds that the level of unemployment in an area strongly predicts native-born Americans' perceptions of the undocumented as a criminal threat, more so than the actual size of the population, supporting the notion that the native-born "are not simply concerned about the actual size of the immigrant population, but instead, they are concerned about economic competition for limited economic resources and opportunities, especially job opportunities" (Wang 2012: 764).

While group threat theory offers expectations for and explanations of the link between increasing immigration and oppositional attitudes among the members of locally dominant groups, it does not specify the manner or mechanisms by which prejudice may manifest as biased crime. Subsequent variations of the theory have sought to address this aspect, though as Green, Strolovich, and Wong (1998) note, with conflicting hypotheses. For example, realistic group threat theory predicts that attacks on immigrants would be more common in places where their numbers are very large (Bobo 1988). The power-threat hypothesis suggests that immigrant victimization would be at its peak where size of the group is just large enough to present a challenge to the social, economic, political standing of whites (Tolnay, Beck, and Massey 1989), though it is unclear what that threshold would be and whether it is dependent on spatially or temporally variant factors. Alternatively, the power-differential hypothesis suggests that anti-minority crimes should be greatest when numbers of the minority group are small. In this situation, members of the dominant group "may be emboldened to attack by the perception that law enforcement officials and the majority of those living in the neighborhood are unsympathetic to the victim group. By the same token, where minorities are few in number, perpetrators have less to fear by way of reprisal" (Green, Strolovich, and Wong 1998: 375). Finally, research on the defended neighborhoods thesis indicates that anti-immigrant acts of intimidation will diminish once a critical mass establishes residence. Until that point, however, the influx of minorities "represents a catalyst for action among those who seek to preserve racial homogeneity" (ibid: 376). According to this perspective, increasing numbers of minority group members, including immigrants, function as a force of social disorganization, disrupting preexisting social networks which, among other effects, "foster whites' sentimental attachment to a racially homogenous image of the community" (ibid). The disruption of these networks, and presumably the larger socially disorganizing outcomes, provide the motivation for attacks against the newcomers by community members who feel most threatened and who are the most aggressive.

Despite the relatively limited research findings specific to immigrant reception to date, key hypotheses can be drawn from the existing literature. I expect that (1) across the sample as a whole, there will be no significant effect of changes in immigration—either total foreign-born or the recently arrived—on the occurrence of anti-immigrant hate crime, once controlling for relevant factors. This expectation is consistent with group threat theory's two key postulates, population size and economic conditions. First, in the majority of places sampled immigrants have had a consistent presence, such that changes in their numbers would be perceived as less threatening.[31] Second, the period under study—2000 to 2007—can be characterized generally as one of economic vitality, ending just prior to the onset of the global recession. However, within the new destination places— places to which immigrants have only arrived within the last 10 years— I expect that (2) changes in the shares of total foreign-born will be positively and significantly associated with changes in the occurrence of anti-immigrant hate crime. Further, (3) the effects within new destinations will be heightened for changes in the shares of the recently

---

[31] This expectation is offered with the place-level unit of analysis in mind. At smaller aggregations, such as census tracts, even relatively small changes in immigrant population may be perceptible to neighborhood residents, and thus the expectation may more accurately be a positive correlation.

arrived foreign-born. Within new destinations, the arrival of even small numbers of foreign-born is likely to be noticed, and growth in their numbers may be viewed as more threatening.

CONCLUSIONS

Theories on the connection between immigration and crime are fundamentally rooted in the dominant views of the process of immigrant incorporation. Social disorganization theory, long held as the definitive model of immigration and crime, is rooted in the traditional assimilation view that immigration disrupts social cohesion and that once settled, immigrants experience social and economic marginalization and disadvantage that leads to criminal involvement. In contrast, the community resource perspective, rooted in the segmented assimilation perspective, suggests that immigrant status alone will not predict increased criminal activity. Rather, it is the complex interplay among a variety of factors—the range of human and social capital contemporary immigrants bring, their increased likelihood to settle away from impoverished urban enclaves, their specific historical experiences, and the context of reception received upon arrival—that will determine which *groups* of immigrants may be more likely to engage in crime. Moreover, this perspective, unlike social disorganization theory, can capture and explain recent findings of significant negative effects of immigration on crime.

Neither of these theories incorporates a focus on immigrant victimization; guidance for this how that phenomenon may play out can be found in the body of work known as group threat theory. While the existing group threat literature with respect to immigrants is still limited, it suggests that attacks on immigrants are a function of both increases in population size and economic conditions. As discussed, there are competing hypotheses about the nature of the linkages population size and victimization, specifically, the requisite size of the subordinate group to elicit violence from members of the dominant population. While several notable studies have investigated the causes and consequences of immigrant victimization, few studies have systematically addressed the effect of demographic change—in the form of increasing immigration—on the likelihood of victimization.

From the extant literature, this chapter has drawn a set of hypotheses to be tested in the chapters that follow. These include: (1)

changes in the concentration of the total foreign-born are negatively correlated with changes in rates of overall, violent, and property crime; (2) within the overall sample, the patterns do not substantively differ whether the independent variable represents the concentration of total foreign-born or only those recently arrived; (3) in contrast, for the subset of new destinations, changes in the concentration of total immigrants are positively and significantly associated with changes in the rates of property and overall crime, but (4) no effect on changes in the rate of violent crime; (5) the patterns to be heightened for changes in the concentration of the *recent* foreign-born. With regard to the analysis of immigration and hate crime, and consistent with research on group threat theory, I offer three additional hypotheses: (6) across the sample as a whole, there will be no significant effect of changes in immigration—either total foreign-born or the recently arrived—on the occurrence of anti-immigrant hate crime; within the new destination sub-sample, (7) changes in the shares of total foreign-born will be positively and significantly associated with changes in the occurrence of anti-immigrant hate crime; and (8) the effects within new destinations will be heightened for changes in the shares of the recently arrived foreign-born. These hypotheses will be systematically tested in the analyses presented in Chapters 4 and 5. In preparation, the next chapter outlines the methodology employed in those analyses, including the sources of data, variables to be analyzed, and the analytical techniques employed.

CHAPTER 3

Framing the Immigration-Crime Question

INTRODUCTION

This research is focused on the broad question of the extent to which immigration contributes to the occurrence of crime. I deconstruct the question into two of its component parts: (1) to what extent does immigration contribute to the occurrence of crime through the supply of perpetrators[32] and (2) to what extent does it contribute through the supply of victims? Underlying these general questions is a more specific one: do the effects of immigration vary by "immigration history"? That is, do places which have experienced major influxes of immigrants in only the last few years and places with long histories of receiving foreign-born newcomers experience differing effects on crime, net of other factors? This question develops out of the recent interest in and research on what Singer and colleagues have termed "new gateways" (Lichter, et al. 2010; Donato, et al. 2008; Price and Singer 2008; Singer 2008). Recent research has begun to investigate whether the conceptual distinction between new and traditional settlement locales bears out an empirical one as well.

To address these questions, I conduct an analysis of change over time in the rates of crime and immigration at the place level. This

---

[32] As has been discussed, this increase can theoretically occur either as a product of immigrants' involvement in crime or as a product of their displacing native workers, who might then be more prone to engage in crime for economic gain.

requires a multi-pronged approach. In effect, the sub-questions require their own data sets, one for the commission of crime and one for the victimization. The reason for this is a product of the manner in which official data are recorded for the unit of analysis in question. Data for the overall occurrence of crime are typically gathered from the Federal Bureau of Investigation's (FBI) Uniform Crime Reports (UCR), which are monthly totals for all crime types reported to the FBI by the individual agencies in whose jurisdiction the crime occurred. Unfortunately, the UCR do not report significant details for crimes that take place, most notably for the purposes herein, relevant socioeconomic and sociodemographic characteristics of the either the perpetrators or victims involved.[33] To get at those characteristics, many researchers often rely on the National Crime Victimization Survey (NCVS), which reports the results of telephone surveys of persons who have been victimized by crime. While NCVS data do offer increased detail on relevant social characteristics, they do not allow the researcher to determine whether that victimization is a consequence of those characteristics. An alternative is found in the FBI's *Hate Crime in the United States*, which records the occurrence of biased crime on an incident basis.

Data Description

Sociodemographic data for this research are drawn from two sources, the 2000 decennial census and the 2005-2007 American Community Survey (ACS) three-year product. The 2000 decennial census (hereafter, "the Census") provides a wealth of data on population demographics and allows the researcher to break down the block group "immigrant" by, for example, race/ethnicity and length of stay, allowing for comparisons both across and within immigrant groups.

---

[33] This is a shortcoming that is being addressed by the National Incident-Based Report System (NIBRS), though according to the FBI's website, there is no timetable for full compliance with NIBRS reporting. Rather, its implementation "is occurring at a pace commensurate with the resources, abilities, and limitations of the contributing law enforcement agencies" (http://www2.fbi.gov/ucr/faqs.htm). As of June 2012, 43 percent of law enforcement agencies participated in NIBRS, representing 29 percent of the nation's population and 27 percent of the nation's crime, making it unattractive for a study seeking to provide generalizable results at an aggregate level.

The ACS provides much of the same information as the Census (in most cases the wording of questions asked is identical), the major differences being that the ACS is conducted in 1-, 3-, and 5-year "waves" and is extrapolated from a sample of the population, as opposed to the counts offered by the Census. Though few studies have used the ACS to date, there are several reasons to do so. First, because it is conducted yearly, the ACS provides some of the most recent data available on demographic and economic characteristics for the nation's population. Second, the ACS offers data products in 1-, 3-, and 5-year forms, with each increase in the number of years corresponding to a smaller population threshold for inclusion, essentially allowing researchers the option of choosing between increased data currency or heightened stability.[34] Third, in contrast to a point-in-time survey such as the decennial census, wherein data are tied to a specific date, ACS data represent the *average* of any given characteristic over a twelve, thirty-six, or sixty month period.[35] Lastly, the ACS has been designed to replace the decennial census long form, making it likely that the ACS will soon become one of the major sources of demographic and economic data used by social researchers, as the decennial census has been for decades.

This research relies on the ACS 3-year estimate for 2005-2007. Though doing so does not allow it to comment on the most recent

---

[34] The 1-year product presents the most up-to-date social and demographic data for areas with a population of 65,000 or greater. The 3-year products offer data on areas with populations as small as 20,000 and while they lack currency—in that the data are essentially averages of characteristics over a given three year period—they offer more data stability and do so for many more geographic areas. Lastly, the 5-year data (averages of characteristics across a 5-year span) present highly stable data on every geographic area, down to the tract level, though with less currency than either the 1- or 3-year products; the first set of 5-year data, covering 2005-2009, was released in 2010.

[35] In theory, decennial census data are anchored to April 1st of each survey year. In practice however, data are spread over closer to a six month period, due to follow-up questionnaires typically mailed in June and July to those who failed to respond in April and May. Because of its rolling reporting nature, the ACS offers a much more accurate view of social and economic characteristics of the population across 1-, 3-, and 5-year periods.

trends in population migration, this data source offers much more stability than the 1-year product at a smaller unit of analysis. Further, the 3-year data allow the inclusion of many more "places" in this study.[36] Lastly, relying on the 2005-2007 product eliminates a potentially confounding variable: the global economic crisis that began in earnest in 2008. While it is still too early to fully comprehend the effects of the recession, it is clear that there have been profound effects on immigration. From 2007 to 2008, for the first time in nearly four decades, the rate of immigration to the U.S. held steady (U.S. Census Bureau 2009; see also Frey 2009), perhaps signaling that in the midst of an economic downturn, the U.S. had lost some luster as a settlement destination, or perhaps signaling that the global movement of people was put on hold, as belts were tightened around the world. Whatever the reason, the result has been a fairly dynamic change to immigration patterns that had held on an incline virtually since the passage of the Hart-Cellar Reform Act of 1965.

The third source of data is the aforementioned Uniform Crime Reports. The UCR provide yearly reports on the specific incidence of inter-personal and property crimes in communities across the country. The reports are compiled by the individual agencies in which the crimes occurred and typically, though not always, supplied monthly to the FBI. The UCR violent and property crime data allow this research to determine whether rates of crime are influenced by rates of immigration for places with populations greater than 20,000.

The final source of data is the FBI's annual report, *Hate Crime in the United States*, which presents data "regarding incidents, offenses, victims, and offenders in reported crimes that were motivated in whole or in part by a bias against the victim's perceived race, religion, ethnicity, sexual orientation, or disability" (US Dept. of Justice 2009). The incorporation of hate crime data allows this research to determine whether an influx of immigrants results in increased crime against minority group members, thereby contributing to the literature on group threat theory.

---

[36] The 3-year product includes roughly four times the number of places as the 1-year estimates; generally, $n_{3yr} \sim 2000$ while $n_{1yr} \sim 500$.

Unit of Analysis

While much recent research has focused on the metropolitan statistical area (Butcher and Piehl 1998; Reid, et al. 2005; Stowell, et al. 2010), that level of analysis is too broad for the purposes of this research. The MSA level includes not only major central cities, but many satellite cities that could be destinations for recent immigrants as well. This analysis focuses on large and medium-sized U.S. cities and towns for the period 2000-2007. I include places with a minimum population of 20,000 individuals in 2007. While 2,065 cities and towns meet this criterion, missing data effectively reduce the number of useable locations to 1,252. By looking at the place level, this analysis will be able to focus more squarely on those smaller cities and towns.

Data Compilation

Construction of the data set for use in the final analyses began by downloading all relevant variables for all places listed in the 2000 decennial census (n=25,150, after removing places in Puerto Rico) and the 2005-2007 ACS (n=2,065, after removing Puerto Rico).[37] Using the unique geographic identifier supplied by and constant across both data sources, I combined the two data sets to create a third set of "base cities" that were common between the 2005-2007 ACS and 2000 decennial Census, which resulted in an 'n' of 2,052. This merger revealed 18 places that experienced some type of official change between the two periods; that is, their unique identifiers did not match up. In six cases the changes were technical; there was no geographical change but a Federal Information Processing Standards (FIPS) change. Typically these changes occur when an entity modifies its name. For five of these six cases, I merely recoded the geographic identifier (and place name where applicable) in the Census dataset to comply with the ACS data. The change for the sixth case, 'Louisville/Jefferson County Metro Government,' involved not only a technical change, but a geographical one as well, making the two units uneven across years in

---

[37] The data were "cleaned" in MS Excel: variable names were reformatted and certain variables were combined to create conceptually relevant measures. All subsequent data manipulation and analyses were performed using SAS version 9.2 (with all available hot fixes installed).

terms of geographical space and thus the populations contained therein. Consequently, it was dropped from the analyses. Ten of the remaining cases involved the creation of a new 'place' either from the incorporation of previously unincorporated places or, more often, the merger of two or more existing places. As with Louisville/Jefferson County, the resultant entities for the ACS were not comparable with those from the earlier Census and were thus excluded from the analyses. Finally, for two cases I could find no information via the Census Bureau explaining the type of change that took place but the populations for each were small (n<26,000) and their exclusion is not anticipated to significantly alter the results. From these population data, then, the maximum size of the sample could be no larger than n=2,052, based on places available from the ACS 2005-07 and in common with the 2000 Census.

I next began to compile the violent and property crime data from the FBI's UCR program. To strengthen the data against the effects of any single-year anomalies in crime rates, three years of crime data were selected for each of the two time periods covered by the population data, 2000 and 2005-2007. For the first time period, crime data were combined for the years 1999, 2000, and 2001. For the second time period, data were combined for the years 2005, 2006, and 2007. While the FBI does well to provide the data on its website in aggregated yearly form, the data lack a unique identifying variable for each agency, such as an Originating Agency Identifier (ORI) code, making it exceedingly difficult to merge across the three years and virtually impossible to merge with the Census or ACS data. Fortunately, the data were available with ORI codes—in raw monthly form—from the Interuniversity Consortium for Political and Social Research (ICPSR). These data were aggregated into yearly reports by summing individual counts of each crime type across the twelve months for each agency and each year. I then combined the six yearly data sets into two "period" sets, again, 1999-2001 (n=22,226) and 2005-2007 (n=22,755). As the raw data are available by agency, rather than place, I removed (1) all agencies that were not either Municipal or Township police departments (e.g. University police departments, Fire Departments, Drug Task Forces, State Police, Tribal Police, etc.) as well as (2) any agencies that failed to report in at least two of the three years in each time period (i.e. a minimum reporting of four out of the six years covered), leaving n=12,402 for 1999-2001 and n=14,193 for 2005-

2007. If a department failed to report data for all twelve months in a given year, the entire year was coded as missing.[38]

While the population and crime datasets each had unique identifying variables, the former used FIPS codes and the latter ORI codes. To merge the sets required a single variable common to all cases. This was made possible through the application of the 2005 Law Enforcement Crosswalk file, also available from ICPSR, which contained both ORI and FIPS codes. The Crosswalk file was merged with the crime data using the common ORI code and then subsequently merged with the population data using the FIPS state and lace codes. A check of the data merger revealed approximately 100 places which should have been included in the final set (i.e. both the population and crime data were available and met the minimum reporting requirements and population threshold) but were being excluded due to a coding error in the Crosswalk file.[39] For these locales, almost exclusively Census Designated Places (CDPs), the Crosswalk file (and thus the merged crime data) contained a FIPS County Subdivision (CoSub) Code, rather than a FIPS Place code, which the population data contained. Within each crime type—violent/property and hate crime— cases were matched using the existing FIPS state and County Subdivision code. Those that were not present in both time periods were discarded. The remaining cases were then matched to the set of base cities common in both the 2005-2007 ACS and 2000 Census. Because there was no unique identifier common to all cases, the selection criteria for inclusion were several and conservative: a combination of an identical FIPS state code, an approximate "name" match, an approximate population size, and an established link between the FIPS CoSub and place codes. The latter criterion was made possible via the Census Bureau's 1% Public Use Microdata Sample Equivalency

---

[38] The departments did not have to submit a report *in* each month, but had to submit a report *for* each month. For example, an agency could submit data for both January and February in February.

[39] There were in total 746 of these "No Matches" in the UCR 1999-2001 data, 330 in the UCR 2005-2007, 257 for the hate crime 1999-2001 data, and 109 for the hate crime 2005-2007. The reason for the much larger numbers for the first time period is that the decennial Census includes all places in the country, while the ACS 3-year product has a minimum population threshold of 20,000.

(PUMEQ1) file.[40] In sum, 83 places were found to be miscoded but for which all data were available and all requirements for inclusion met.[41] Each of the erroneous FIPS codes was recoded in the original Crosswalk file and the data mergers redone.

Once the two crime data sets were complete, I merged each with its corresponding population data set, which left a total matched set of n=1,252 places for each time point. In sum, from the base of 2,052 I effectively lost 1,000 cases for each time period. Table 3.1 presents the coverage of key explanatory variables for each time point. In most instances, the places that did not make the cut were ones which failed to comply with either UCR reporting guidelines (e.g. submitting incomplete data, or making errors in the coding of certain types of crime) or the minimum requirements for inclusion in the study (i.e., reporting fewer than two full years of data for each of the two time periods). In the vast majority of cases, police departments reported either one year or not at all. Because the error in reporting was uneven across years (i.e. locales had data for one time point, but not the other), additional "single year" cases were removed, leaving only those places for which compliant data was available at both time points.[42]

I repeated much of this process for the Hate Crime data, also drawn from ICPSR, with a few crucial differences. First, these data were available in yearly, rather than monthly form, such that no

Table 3.1 Place Level Population Coverage by Time Period and Data Set, Traditional Crime

	2000		2005-2007	
	Census 2000 (Place Level)	Sample (Population 20k or Higher)	ACS 2005-2007 (Place Level)	Sample (Population 20k or Higher)
Total Population	206,468,617	119,021,134	154,241,294	125,935,932
	(73.37)	(42.29)	(51.63)	(42.15)
Foreign-Born Population	27,790,726	20,426,813	27,698,485	23,575,195
	(89.34)	(65.66)	(74.39)	(63.31)
Recent Foreign-Born Population	6,840,189	5,088,015	7,027,245	6,070,925
	(90.49)	(67.11)	(74.30)	(64.19)
	n = 25,150	*n = 1,252*	*n = 2,065*	*n = 1,252*

*numbers in parentheses represent percentages of national totals

[40] Available at http://www2.census.gov/census_2000/datasets/PUMS/

[41] There were a total of 36 cases from the hate crime dataset and 18 which were also present among those from the violent/property crime dataset.

[42] See Tables A1a and A1b in Appendix A for detailed explanation of case exclusions from analyses of traditional crime.

summing across months was required. Second, because both data sets were 'case-based' rather than 'place-based' (as is the case with the UCR violent and property crime data), individual incidents needed to be aggregated into counts for each place in which they occurred. As with the UCR data, three years of hate crime and supplementary homicide data were averaged around each of the two time periods. Unlike violent/property crime, the hate crime data were left as counts, rather than being converted into rates, because the incidence of these types of crime are so low as to produce dramatically skewed rates if calculated per 100,000 in population. The full hate crime data set covers 1,276 jurisdictions in which at least one biased crime was reported in two of the three years of the first time period, with 1,361 jurisdictions covered for the second.[43] After removing all agencies that were neither municipal nor township[44] and matching with the "base-city" data set, the final hate crime data set contains 423 matched total cases. Table 3.2 presents the sample coverage for places included in the hate crime analysis.[45]

Table 3.2 Place Level Population Coverage by Time Period and Data Set, Hate Crime

	2000		2005-2007	
	Universe	Sample	Universe	Sample
Total Place-Level Population wherein a Hate Crime Occurred	82,511,078	70,079,393	91,077,851	73,393,367
	(100.00)	(84.93)[1]	(100.00)	(80.58)[1]
Foreign-Born Population	16,346,761	14,572,126	18,502,284	16,271,748
	(52.55)[2]	(46.84)[3]	(49.69)[2]	(43.70)[3]
Recent Foreign-Born Population	4,005,975	3,549,638	4,630,114	4,040,998
	(52.84)[2]	(46.82)[3]	(48.96)[2]	(42.73)[3]
Percent of Nation's Population Covered	29.32	24.90	30.49	24.57
	n = 642	n = 423	n = 700	n = 423

*numbers in parentheses represent percentages

[1] Indicates the percentage of the total U.S. population living in places wherein a hate crime occurred that is included in the data set

[2] Indicates the percentage of the U.S. population living in places wherein a hate crime occurred

[3] Indicates the percentage of the U.S. population included in the universe data set

[43] The slightly larger number of places in the Time 2 data set is more likely a product of greater reporting compliance, than increased incidence of offense.

[44] This criterion had a greater impact on the size of the hate crime dataset, as places like college campuses—where large numbers of hate crimes tend to be reported—were excluded from the analysis.

[45] See Tables A2a and A2b in Appendix A for exclusion details.

Dependent Variables

The dependent variables analyzed are the logged rates of overall, violent, and property crime. Much research on immigration and crime has tended to focus on violent crime, and to a lesser extent, property crime (Martinez and Nielsen 2006; Sampson et al. 2005; Lee et al. 2001). Following that previous research, I examine an index of violent crime, created by summing the average yearly counts of murder, robbery, and aggravated assault, and dividing by 100,000 to create a standard rate (per 100,000 of population). I examine as well an index measure of property crime created from the summed average yearly counts of burglary, larceny-theft, and motor vehicle theft. These two indices are summed to create a third, overall crime index. In all cases I employ the natural log of the crime rate to correct for hetero-skedasticity.

To date, few studies have systematically investigated the effect of change in immigration on hate crime, the result being that much of the research on immigration and crime has tended to address the relationship from only one direction: whether immigrants or immigration increase crime via the supply of offenders. Incorporating data on hate crime allows this research to investigate whether, group threat theory suggests, immigration might increase rates of crime by providing a larger pool of potential victims. Unfortunately, FBI data offer a limited range of hate crime motivations and no measurement of victim's immigrant status as a motivating factor. Essentially, the data allow for only one category of ethnicity, anti-Hispanic, lumping all other ethnically-motivated hate crime into a catch-all category of "anti-Other Ethnicity/National Origin." While this is admittedly an unfortunate limitation, several categories offered can be used as rough proxies. Specifically, the categories of "anti-Asian" and the aforementioned "anti-Other Ethnicity" measure crime committed against individuals in racial or ethnic minority groups. Additionally, the anti-Islamic category offers an opportunity to capture transplanted Middle Easterners, among others. None of these measures is ideal, in that each covers both native- and foreign-born individuals, and perhaps across several generations of U.S. nativity. For readers, however, there must remain the question of whether proxy measures of racial and ethnic minority status can serve also as proxies for immigrant status. There is no easy answer.

United States hate crime law is predicated on the intent of the offenders to engage in the commission of a crime against a person or persons based on certain recognized characteristics of the victims. The categories covered are race, religion, sexual orientation, ethnicity, national origin (either Hispanic or 'Other"), and disability. As yet, immigrant status is not a recognized category of biased crime victimization. This omission may be read simply as a product of the natural evolution of democratic law, or conversely as exemplifying structural opposition to immigrants (cf. Hagan and Palloni 1999). Regardless of the interpretation, the result is to prevent crimes committed against immigrants *because of their being foreign-born* from being recorded as biased crimes, and necessitating the use of proxy measures of immigrant status.

While the use of proxies is not ideal, it does raise the issue of whether the *actual* immigrant status of hate crime victims matters as much on face value as one might think. To clarify: what may matter most in the commission of an anti-immigrant hate crime is the offender's *perception* that the victim is an immigrant, irrespective of whether that is truly the case. Thus, a likely target of hate crime victimization is one who resembles the socially constructed image of "immigrant." A number of news reports indicate that offenders often yell anti-immigrant or anti-ethnic epithets during the commission of the act, and that often those epithets do not "fit" with the ethnicity or national origin of the victim (Akam 2009; Fahim 2009; Planer 2009; Sacchetti 2009; Southern Poverty Law Center 2009).

If the reader accepts the general use of proxies as stand-ins for immigrant status, the next question is whether the specific proxies used herein are valid. The measure of anti-immigrant hate crime is constructed by summing the counts of anti-Asian, anti-Islamic, anti-Hispanic, and anti-other ethnicity hate crimes, as reported by the FBI. The summed counts are produced for each of the years under study and pooled across each of the two three-year time periods. Virtually all of the constituent "parts" of the anti-immigrant measure (1) include both native- and foreign-born and (2) encompass broad subcategories of the populations. For example, the anti-Asian variable includes a variety of ethnic and national origin groups with varying levels of human and social capital. The anti-Islamic variable is a measure of religious persecution, rather than ethnicity, and as such includes people from any racial or ethnic background (cf. Hendricks, et al. [2007] for precedent in this measure's use).

Ultimately, as researchers, we are often forced to work with what we have, and must do our best, when faced with data limitations, to ensure findings are interpreted cautiously, within the scope afforded by the data. The hate crime portion of this research is, in effect, exploratory; no studies to date have systematically investigated the place-level relationship between immigration and biased crime.[46] This research can help to establish a baseline, one from which future research can expound.

Explanatory Variables

Immigrant Concentration
To measure immigrant concentration, I employ an index created from the summed z-scores of the percent of the population that is foreign-born and the percent Latino (cf. Ousey and Kubrin 2009; Stowell, et al. 2009).[47] Because much research and popular discussion has centered on *recent* immigrants, I construct a secondary index wherein the z-score for percent foreign-born is replaced b the z-score for percent recent foreign-born, measured as the percentage of the foreign-born population that entered the U.S. in the previous five years.[48]

---

[46] The reason is more likely due to other researchers' recognition of porous data, than this researcher's insight but there remains a need, given increased immigration and concomitant opposition in certain places to which immigrants have been drawn.

[47] It was hoped that this index would also include the z-score for the percent of the population that speaks English less than very well, capturing variations in human capital. However, given the extent of missing values on that measure, as drawn from the ACS 2005-07, it was excluded to preserve sample size.

[48] For the first time period, recent immigrants are those who arrived between 1995 and March 2000; for the second time period, those who arrived between 2000 and the average of 2005-2007. While not an ideal comparison in that the number of years included in the measures are not identical, because the ACS data are essentially averaged across the period and growth in immigration began to slow from 2006-2007 (before declining from 2007-2008), the total number of recent foreign-born drawn from the data set most closely resembles the total from 2006, effectively adding only one additional year's worth of immigrants. So while imperfect the measure is a more accurate representation

Immigration History

In recent years, considerable academic interest has developed around the concept of the "new gateway," a term coined and a concept delineated in the work of Singer and colleagues (cf. Oberle and Li 2008; Price and Singer 2008; Singer 2008). Conceptually, "new gateway" refers to an immigrant settlement destination that has only recently become so. It contrasts with traditional gateways, such as New York, Chicago, and other major urban centers of the northeast, which have experienced inflows of migrants at a fairly constant, and high, rate for decades. Singer (2008) outlines a multipart typology of gateways, of which "new gateway" is but one. Other gateway types may include *former*, places like Boston and Cleveland, which saw high rates of immigration through 1930, followed by declines through the year 2000; *continuous*, places like the aforementioned New York and Chicago, which have received numbers of immigrants above the national average every decade from 1900-2000; *post-World War II*, places like Los Angeles, which experienced increases in immigration after 1950 and sustained through 2000; *emerging*, which had lower than average rates of immigration until 1980, after which rates surpassed the national average; *re-emerging*, which saw high rates of immigration from 1900-1930, followed by a decline until 1980, and then a resurgence from 1980 to present; and finally *pre-emerging*, which have only begun attracting large numbers of immigrants since 1990.

The typology is an excellent heuristic for understanding changes in the geographic patterns of immigrant settlement and it conceptually underscores the structural differences across settlement destinations that might help or hinder successful immigrant incorporation. Practically, however, the model proves difficult to emulate, often producing anomalies when hard delineations are calculated.[49] Still, those structural differences are potentially key in understanding both the link between immigration and crime as well as the potential for immigrant victimization. Places wherein immigration has a long history

---

than would be available alternatives, which, due to data constrictions, were to use the number arriving from 1990-2000 versus 2000 to the 2005-2007 average (yielding a four year difference) or to exclude the measure entirely.

[49] For example, a firm application of Singer's definition consistently returned the city of Chicago as a *new gateway*.

are likely to have developed mechanisms that aid in immigrants' successful incorporation. Moreover, residents of such places have likely come to define immigrants as part of the local fabric. Conversely, places to which immigration is something new may lack the means to successfully incorporate newcomers, and residents of such places may be more likely to view them as threats to shared resources (Blumer 1958; Quillian 1995).

To capture the potential differing effect of immigration across new and traditional destinations, I operationalize "new destinations" as places wherein the number of foreign-born has increased greater than 50 percent since 1990 (cf. Shihadeh and Winters 2010). This measure results in 573 new destination places for the traditional crime data set and 173 for the hate crime data set. This operationalization essentially aggregates Singer's six-part typology into a dichotomy: *new gateways*, composed of emerging, re-emerging, and pre-emerging; and *traditional gateways*, made up of former, continuous, and post-WWII gateways. Implicit in my use of the concept is a modification of its traditional operationalization. As Singer (2008: 24, n.17) notes, the term "gateway" typically refers to a metropolitan area with a population over one million. This research, however, is focused on the place-level, not the metropolitan statistical area. Consequently, I refer to such places as either new settlement destinations, or simply new destinations. The destinations included here are conceptually very similar to those in previous research, following essentially the same trends, only at the place level. The theoretical concern is whether cities with histories of immigration—and thus established mechanisms of immigrant incorporation—experience similar rates of crime, all else being equal, to cities with only recent exposure to immigration. Incorporating a measure of new settlement destinations enables this analysis to integrate research and test hypotheses related to theories of group threat.

Socioeconomic Disadvantage

Previous research has indicated that disadvantage is associated with crime (Agnew, et al. 2002; Kovandzic, Vieraitis, and Yeisley 1998; Merton 1938). Consistent with the literature, I control for socioeconomic disadvantage using a scale composed of the summed z-scores for the natural log of the median family income (in 2009 inflation-adjusted dollars), the percentage of families living below the poverty line, the percentage of households headed by single females living with their own children under age 18, and the percentage of the population age 15 and older who are unemployed (cf. Ousey and Kubrin 2009; Morenoff, Sampson, and Raudenbush 2001; see Stowell, et al. 2009 for an inverse representation measuring resource, rather than disadvantage).

Residential Stability

I include a second index of control variables designed to measure the effect of residential stability. Previous research has consistently indicated a link between the incidence of crime—particularly violence—and the degree of population turnover (Martinez, Rosenfeld, and Mares 2008; Sampson, et al. 2005; Lee, et al. 2001; Sampson, et al. 1999). Areas wherein residents are able to "set down roots" tend to have lower rates of crime, net of other factors, while areas marked by a steady stream of residents "passing through" tend to experience higher incidence of crime. Consistent with previous immigration-crime research, I control for residential stability using an index composed of the summed z-scores for the percentage of households that are owner occupied and the percentage of households occupied for two years or more (Stowell; et al. 2009; Sampson, et al. 2005; Morenoff, et al. 2001; see also Lee, et al. 2001 for a similar measure of residential *in*stability).[50]

---

[50] For this research, the decision to use "two years" as the measure of stability is entirely data-driven, as appears to be the case for other researchers. The decennial census specifically asks whether householders have resided in the same place for at least the last five years, while the ACS asks only whether residence has been continuous since the previous year. Such a disparity is unacceptable. Fortunately, each data set also includes a variable reporting when the householder moved into the home, coded in 5-year blocks. As a result, the stability variable incorporated here from the ACS measures the percentage of householders who moved in prior to 2004, two years from the median time point of the data set, while the decennial census variable measures the percentage of the population who moved in prior to 1998, approximately two years prior to the decennial census.

Of larger concern, perhaps, is the substantive question of just what constitutes "stability." Certainly there is a temporal aspect, though this begs the question of "how long" is enough? Some families and individuals might ingrain

<u>Employment Structure</u>

Recent research has suggested that the type of employment predominant in an area also has an effect on crime; Sampson, et al. (2005) find that the presence of managerial positions in a community has a depressive effect on African American crime rates (see also Alaniz, Cartmill, and Parker 1998). The dampening effect of employment type is conceptually related to both Merton's and Agnew's strain theories (1938 and 1992, respectively), in that a greater availability of white collar work could be indicative of an open opportunity structure, while the absence of white collar jobs—in an increasingly service-oriented national economy—might be an indication of blocked opportunity. The effect is also implicated in Sutherland's (1947) differential association theory: when children and young people are surrounded by adults working in relatively high skilled, high status positions, they are likely to aspire to those same positions, model the methods used to achieve them (education, hard work, delayed rewards, etc.), and likely eschew alternative illegitimate means. To control for labor market characteristics, I include a measure of the percentage of the population employed in management and professional occupations.

I also include a second measure of employment structure, though one focused more squarely on immigrants: the availability of seasonal work. In previous research, Lee and Slack (2008) find a significant negative effect of seasonal employment on crime, suggesting that even short-term work may structure time and buffer against involvement in criminal activity. While such a finding offers reason to suspect that places with increased opportunity for seasonal work should have lower rates of crime, there are as well reasons to suspect that such places may have higher rates of biased crime *against* immigrants. In a study of violence against person involved in day labor—employment similar to seasonal work in a number of aspects—Valenzuela (2006) finds that because of the scarcity of consistent work, competition among laborers

---

themselves in the community fairly quickly—within a year, perhaps—while others may take many years and some may never fully incorporate themselves. To date, research has tended to err on the side of caution and, where possible use a base of 5-years of residence, though as discussed above, that option is not always available. Most researchers are agreed on the importance of it, though the concept requires further fleshing out. In the meantime, we rely on a fuzzy proxy, admittedly askew, regrettably accepted.

is fierce and relationships with bosses tense. These workers are susceptible to violent victimization by other day laborers, employers, local residents, and local merchants. In contrast, Shihadeh and Barranco (2010b) find that shifts of low-skill work to predominantly Latino laborers in rural counties is associated with increases in non-Latino white homicide, perhaps evidencing a displacement effect. To capture this aspect of the labor structure, I include a measure of the percentage of the population aged 15 and over employed in seasonal work.

Population Structure

Social Disorganization theory suggests that as the size and heterogeneity of a community increase, crime will increase as well. This implies an *absolute* increase in overall crime rates. Moreover, urbanization theory suggests that as the size of a community increases, there should be greater reliance on agents of formal control, thereby increasing the *official* rates of crime in a given area (Schulenberg 2003). To account for the effect of population structure, I use the natural log of population size.

The presence of youth and young adults is also conceptually connected to crime. Research has consistently shown crime to be perpetrated by the young, and that crime, over the life course, corresponds to a normal curve, increasing as the individual approaches the teenage years and petering out as he or she approaches adulthood (Agnew 2001; Sampson and Laub 1993; Hirschi and Gottfredson 1983). Moreover, research on recent immigration indicates that the majority of newcomers from Latin America tend to be young males (Donato, et al. 2009). I control for age using the percentage of the population who are male aged 15-29.

Finally, following recent research I control for the ratio of adults to children in the population (Martinez, et al. 2010; Stowell, et al. 2009; Martinez, et al. 2008; see also Feldmeyer 2009 for a variant incorporating the elderly as well). The higher the ratio, the greater is the number of adults, and the fewer the number of children. One implication is that places with extremely high ratios would be less likely to be populated by families. Another implication is that places with high ratios of adults to children should be more likely to also have high rates of crime—a consequence of having a greater number of potential adult offenders.[51] Table 3.3 presents a statistical profile of the places both included in and excluded from the analyses.

Additional Measures Employed in Hate Crime Analyses

The analyses of hate crime data differ slightly from the analyses of traditional crime. First, because the concern is with the impact of immigrants on anti-immigrant victimization, the index measures of foreign-born concentration (which include the percent of the population that is Latino) are eschewed in favor of percentages of the population who are foreign-born, and who are foreign-born arrived within the previous five years. Second, the correlates of hate crime incidence are not assumed to be the same as for traditional crime. Drawing from the literature on group threat theory, dominant group membership is likely to exert a positive effect on biased crime. To account for this, I employ a measure of the percent of the population that is non-Hispanic white. Also, while generalized disadvantaged has been shown to be a consistent and significant predictor of traditional crime, it is unlikely to have a similar effect on crimes motivated by bias or hate. Hate crimes are very much political statements—whether intended or not—perpetrated by a person or persons who perceive *themselves* as representative of the in-group and perceive their *victims* as representative of an out-group, and very likely as embodiments of threat. While group threat theory acknowledges the importance of economic conditions on biased crime, the confluence of race and class in this country leads traditional measures of disadvantage to include large numbers of subordinate group members, immigrants as well. What is needed is a measure of the economic conditions among dominant group members. To account for this, I employ an inverse measure of disadvantage among whites, specifically, the percent of non-Hispanic white households with incomes greater than $100,000. Table 3.4 presents a profile of places included in and excluded from the hate crime analyses.

---

[51] This is not to say that children (i.e. individuals under age 18) don't engage in criminal activity. Certainly large numbers do, but only in extreme cases is their activity likely to enter into official rates of crime.

Table 3.3 Statistical Profile of Places Included in and Excluded from Traditional Crime Analyses.

	Included				Excluded			
	2000		2005-2007		2000		2005-2007	
	Mean	Std Dev	Mean	Std Dev	Mean	Std Dev	Mean	Std Dev
Total Population	95,065	292,335	100,588	298,625	31,621	23,151	34,816	30,252
Percent Foreign-Born	13.29	11.30	15.29	11.58	11.51	12.29	13.25	12.75
Percent Recent Foreign-Born	3.32	2.79	4.02	3.06	2.75	3.29	4.29	3.89
Percent Latino	15.02	17.60	17.68	18.63	12.18	19.19	16.08	20.96
Percent Male Aged 15-29	11.16	3.73	11.48	3.80	10.47	3.90	10.86	4.00
Adult-Child Ratio	3.12	1.12	3.25	1.11	4.08	23.83	3.27	3.13
Socioeconomic Disadvantage								
Percent Less than High School	17.95	10.33	15.00	8.88	17.30	11.37	14.43	9.76
Percent SFHH	7.39	2.99	13.98	7.52	7.10	3.54	12.73	9.24
Median Household Income	60,072	21,532	56,580	21,031	64,204	24,578	60,671	24,939
Pct of Households in Poverty	11.30	6.77	12.52	6.93	9.99	7.78	11.33	8.14
Pct Unemployed	5.81	2.90	6.64	2.52	5.41	3.26	6.76	3.37
Residential Stability								
Pct of Households Owner-Occupied	61.42	13.94	62.33	13.40	68.24	15.21	69.17	14.56
Pct of Households Occupied 2 years or more	76.91	6.60	76.88	6.65	79.33	7.38	79.27	7.34
Pct Management/Professional Occupations	35.05	10.77	35.12	11.06	34.33	12.17	35.94	11.98
Percent Seasonal Occupations	0.55	1.69	0.52	1.83	0.53	2.25	0.22	0.47
Overall Crime Rate[1]	5,770.86	3,095.34	5,482.78	2,879.07	3,599	3,777	3,822	3,669
Violent Crime Rate[1]	1,575.53	1,114.89	1,589.59	1,135.08	1,033	1,320	1,141	1,316
Property Crime Rate[1]	4,195.33	2,180.94	3,893.19	1,946.65	2,566	2,628	2,681	2,502
	n = 1,252		n = 1,252		n = 813		n = 813	

[1] Rate calculated as number of offenses per population of 100,000

Table 3.4 Statistical Profile of Places Included in and Excluded from Hate Crime Analyses.

	Included				Excluded			
	2000		2005-2007		2000		2005-2007	
	Mean	*Std Dev*	*Mean*	*Std Dev*	*Mean*	*Std Dev*	*Mean*	*Std Dev*
Total Population	165,672	484,953	173,507	496,032	45,564.45	56,576.80	49,237.47	57,416.53
Percent Foreign-Born	15.96	11.40	17.93	11.68	11.73	11.65	13.60	12.04
Percent Recent Foreign-Born	3.84	2.73	4.54	2.87	2.90	3.05	3.97	3.46
Percent White	63.88	21.64	59.73	21.94	69.10	24.33	64.97	23.21
Percent Male Aged 15-29	11.47	3.32	11.64	3.33	10.74	3.91	11.13	4.01
Adult-Child Ratio	3.21	1.17	3.34	1.05	3.57	16.73	3.24	2.34
Residential Stability	0.00	1.74	0.00	1.77				
Pct of Households Owner-Occupied	59.13	13.58	60.35	12.98	65.37	14.87	66.22	14.33
Pct of Households Occupied 2 years or more	76.97	6.28	76.99	6.39	78.08	7.18	78.03	7.16
Percent of White Households with Income	16.38	9.97	24.92	12.41	15.17	11.54	23.25	14.36
Percent Seasonal Occupations	0.41	1.07	0.41	1.27	0.57	2.09	0.42	1.58
Total Count of Anti-Immigrant Offenses	7.17	26.64	4.41	11.22	0.94	1.87	1.00	2.27
	n = 423		*n = 423*		*n = 1,642*		*n = 1,642*	

Analytical Techniques

Because the data on traditional crime and biased crime are structured differently—the former as rates, the latter as counts—they require different methods of analysis. I review the technique applied to traditional crime first.

Violent and Property Crime

Generally, there is no singly agreed upon technique for a cross-sectional analysis of immigration and crime data, nor for a repeated cross-sectional testing change-over-time. Recent studies have tended to employ one of a few alternatives, including random effects models (Stowell, et al. 2009), fixed-effects models (Ousey and Kubrin 2009), or structural equation models (Feldmeyer 2009). Each is preferred over Ordinary Least Squares (OLS) analyses, given the potential for heteroskedasticity. Following Ousey and Kubrin (2009: 460), I employ a fixed-effects model because it "focuses solely on the within-unit variation...[and] controls for the influence of *all* time-invariant factors," which the random-effects and structural equation models do not. Consequently, whereas with OLS one must specify all relevant control variables, a fixed effects regression controls for the effects of all unspecified variables, provided those variables are stable over time. As Allison notes, "the essence of a fixed effects method is captured by saying that each individual serves as his or her own control. That is accomplished by making comparisons *within* individuals...and then averaging those comparisons across all the individuals in the sample" (2005: 3; emphasis in original). Of course, rather than individual persons, this analysis relies on data from individual *places*. The model employed is as follows:

$$y_{it} = \mu_t + \beta x_{it} + \alpha_{it} + \varepsilon_{it}$$

where *i* refers to the various places (*i*= 1...n), *t* refers to the different time points (*t* = 1, 2), and α_i refers to a set of fixed parameters.

To confirm the fit of a fixed effects model over a random effects one, I performed a centered scores test. For this approach, two new variables are created for each predictor in the model—one for the mean and one for the deviation (the actual score minus the mean score). A model is then run contrasting the mean and deviance variables. If the random effects model were a better fit, then the coefficients for each should be the same, indicating that the time-variant predictor variables are not correlated with place-specific fixed-effects. If the coefficients are significantly different, a fixed effects approach is warranted. Table 3.5 presents the results of the centered scores test. Results from the contrast statements indicate we must reject the null hypothesis that the mean coefficients are the same as the deviation ones. The results suggest that the random effect is in fact correlated with the measured predictor variables, warranting the use of a fixed effects model.

Hate Crime

Analysis of the hate crime data require a different approach than that used for the violent and property crime data because the occurrence of biased crime is a much rarer event.[52] Once again, Ordinary Least Squares (OLS) regression is not an ideal method of analysis because the rarity of hate crime occurrence results in a highly skewed distribution, even at the place level and even once log-transformed, and would consequently violate the OLS assumption of a normal distribution. To deal with the scarcity of occurrence, I follow the criminological literature on neighborhood-level crime (Nielsen and Martinez 2006; Lee, et al. 2001), and employ a fixed-effects negative binomial technique with an overdispersion correction. As with the violent and property crime analyses, this technique controls for all unmeasured, time invariant characteristics. While several researchers have used Poisson regression for count data (Lee, et al. 2001; Osgood 2000; Sampson, Raudenbush, and Earls 1997), one concern with Poisson is the tendency to run into overdispersion (Allison 2005). The benefit of negative binomial regression is that it directly accounts for overdispersion, with the result that "estimated regression coefficients might be more efficient (in the statistical sense), and the standard errors and test statistics might be more accurate" (Allison 2005: 93).[53] The formula for the negative binomial analysis of hate crime data is:

$$\Pr(y_{it} = r) = \frac{\Gamma(\theta+r)}{\Gamma(\theta)\Gamma(r+1)} \left(\frac{\lambda_{it}}{\lambda_{it}+\theta} \right)^r \left(\frac{\theta}{\lambda_{it}+\theta} \right)^\theta$$

---

[52] Only 642 places in the U.S. with a population greater than 20,000 even reported the occurrence of hate crime for the first time period; that number increased only slightly in the second period to 700.

[53] Allison (2005) notes that Poisson can be regarded as a specialized case of negative binomial, and vice versa, that negative binomial regression can be viewed as a generalization of Poisson for count data.

Table 3.5. Centered Scores Regression Models Predicting Overall Crime Rate (log-transformed), 2000-2007

	Full Sample	New Destinations
Predictors		
Immigration Index	-.013	-.001
	(.021)	(.034)
City/Town Population (logged)	-.252***	-.389***
	(.043)	(.072)
Males Aged 15-29 (logged)	.069	.034
	(.055)	(.102)
Adult-Child Ratio (logged)	.157*	.139
	(.074)	(.136)
Disadvantage Index	.023***	.017†
	(.006)	(.010)
Residential Stability	-.007	-.010
	(.011)	(.019)
Managerial/Professional	.000	.000
	(.002)	(.004)
Seasonal	-.014	-.016
	(.011)	(.017)
Difference in time	.031***	-.028*
	(.008)	(.013)
Constant	8.466	8.804
Contrasts (F Value) [1]		
All	26.48***	13.46***
Immigration Index	15.82***	8.28**
City/Town Population	71.74***	51.37***
Males Aged 15-29	22.79***	11.24***
Adult-Child Ratio	52.70***	17.27***
Disadvantage Index	33.32***	16.92***
Residential Stability	0.28	0.03
Managerial/Professional	46.12***	25.19***
Seasonal	2.49	1.45
Model Summary Information		
Covariance Parameter		
Intercept (Geography)	.112	.106
	(.005)	(.007)
Residual	.026	.031
	(.001)	(.002)
-2 Res Log Likelihood	907.5	541.4
Total Number of Observations ($N \times T$)	2,504	1,146
Total Number of Cities/Towns (N)	1252	573

$^\dagger p<.10$, $*p<.05$, $**p<.01$, $***p<.001$

[1] The Contrasts provide another test of the Fixed Effects vs. Random Effects models by testing the null hypothesis that deviation coefficients are the same as mean coefficients. In other words, a test of whether the random effect of geography is uncorrelated with the measured predictor variables. A significant finding indicates that the random effects model should be rejected in favor of a fixed effects approach. Readers will note, however, that the results offered above are nearly identical to those offered for the fixed effects analyses presented in chapter 4.

CONCLUSIONS

The purpose of this research is to provide a full investigation of the contemporary relationship between immigration and crime at the place-level. In doing so, it seeks to offer a more comprehensive analysis of that relationship by focusing on rates of overall, violent, property, and hate crime. The fixed-effects approach allows this research to investigate whether the large numbers of foreign-born arriving in the last decade exerted a significant effect on the occurrence of crime in the places in which these newcomers settled. In doing so it provides a test of whether the process of immigration brings with it a socially disorganizing effect, which would theoretically result in higher rates of crime among cities experiencing the greatest increase in shares of foreign-born.

This research extends beyond the extant literature in two key ways. First, by incorporating a measure of the concept of *new destinations*, it controls for the effect of a city or town's immigration history in the occurrence of crime. To date, while researchers have begun to focus on the differing outcomes of immigration to places with previously few immigrants, there is little research on the likelihood of criminal involvement in such places. Second, this research addresses whether increased immigration results in increased crime against persons who ostensibly *appear* foreign-born. Existing research has tended to tackle the immigration-crime relationship from only one direction: whether or not immigrants (or immigration) increase rates of crime via the supply of offenders. This research addresses that question and incorporates its mirror: whether immigration increases rates of crime via the supply of victims, in the form of biased, or hate, crimes. The hate crime aspect of the immigration-crime nexus is one that as yet has not been elucidated.

CHAPTER 4

Are New Americans Really New Criminals? The Relationship Between Crime and Immigration

INTRODUCTION

The goal of this chapter is to examine whether changes in rates of immigration within American cities and towns are significantly correlated with changes in rates of crime within those same places, controlling for relevant factors. The primary analytical technique employed is fixed effects regression. As discussed, by testing only *within* units, rather than *within and between*, as is the case with traditional regression analyses, this method essentially controls for any unmeasured *time-invariant* effects. As a consequence, however, the results of a fixed-effects analysis are valid only for the units covered by the sample. That is, they are not generalizable. For this analysis then, the results of the fixed effects analyses described below are applicable only to the 1,252 places included in the sample. This limitation underscores the importance of employing a sample that is both large and diverse.

The central hypotheses tested in this chapter are that, at the place-level, (1) changes in the concentration of the total foreign-born are negatively correlated with changes in rates of overall, violent, and property crime; (2) within the overall sample, the patterns do not substantively differ whether the independent variable represents the concentration of total foreign-born or only those recently arrived; (3) in contrast, for the subset of new destinations, changes in the concentration of total immigrants are positively and significantly associated with changes in the rates of property and overall crime, but (4) no effect on changes in the rate of violent crime; (5) the patterns to be heightened for changes in the concentration of the *recent* foreign-born. These hypotheses are tested primarily by conducting fixed effects regressions of the change in immigration on the log-transformed rates of overall, violent, and property crime, for both the overall sample and the sub-sample of places categorized as new settlement destinations. The results of these analyses and several secondary ones are presented in the pages that follow.

THE IMPACT OF CHANGES IN IMMIGRATION ON CHANGES IN CRIME

Univariate Results

We begin by looking at the results of univariate analyses for the total sample. Table 4.1 presents the means and standard deviations for each of the variables included in the analysis. The first two panels of the table offer the sample mean scores and standard deviations for the year 2000 and the 2005-2007 period, respectively. The third panel offers the average within unit change for the 1,252 places included in the sample. In general, while mean scores on a number of key variables changed very little, others changed quite a bit, despite the relatively short period under study.

Looking first at the measures of population structure, we see that places with populations of at least twenty thousand (at the time of the ACS 2005-2007) saw their populations increase over the period, on average by roughly five and a half thousand. At the same time, the percent of males aged 15-29 and the ratio of adults-to-children in these areas remained relatively unchanged. There was an overall increase in the percent of the population that is foreign-born from 13.3 percent in Time 1 to 15.3 percent in Time 2. There were as well accompanying increases in the percent of the population that is recently-arrived foreign-born, from 3.3 percent to 4 percent, and in the percent Latino, from 15 to 17.7 percent. Both increases are consistent with rising immigration generally over the last decade and among immigrants from Mexico in particular, and consistent with those who have noted that immigration has increased precisely while national crime rates have declined (Wadsworth 2010; Stowell, et al. 2009; Sampson and Bean

Table 4.1 Profile of Places Included in UCR Analyses

	2000		2005-2007		Within-Place Change	
	Mean	Std Dev	Mean	Std Dev	Mean[1]	Std Dev
Total Population	95,065	292,335	100,588	298,625	5,523	16,880
Foreign-Born Index	0.00	1.83	0.00	1.81	0.00	0.33
Recent Foreign-Born Index	0.00	1.73	0.00	1.71	0.00	0.53
Percent Foreign-Born	13.29	11.30	15.29	11.58	2.00	2.46
Percent Recent Foreign-Born	3.32	2.79	4.02	3.06	0.71	1.36
Percent Latino	15.02	17.60	17.68	18.63	2.66	3.12
Percent Male Aged 15-29	11.16	3.73	11.48	3.80	0.32	1.41
Adult-Child Ratio	3.12	1.12	3.25	1.11	0.13	0.36
Socioeconomic Disadvantage	0.00	2.73	0.00	2.62	0.00	1.12
Percent Less than High School	17.95	10.33	15.00	8.88	-2.95	2.88
Percent SFHH	7.39	2.99	13.98	7.52	6.59	5.11
Median Household Income	60,072	21,532	56,580	21,031	-3,492	4,839
Pct of Households in Poverty	11.30	6.77	12.52	6.93	1.22	2.44
Pct Unemployed	5.81	2.90	6.64	2.52	0.82	2.29
Residential Stability	0.00	1.74	0.00	1.77	0.00	0.59
Pct of Households Owner-Occupied	61.42	13.94	62.33	13.40	0.91	3.07
Pct of Households Occupied 2 years or more	76.91	6.60	76.88	6.65	-0.03	3.19
Pct Management/Professional Occupations	35.05	10.77	35.12	11.06	0.07	2.77
Percent Seasonal Occupations	0.55	1.69	0.52	1.83	-0.03	0.58
Overall Crime Rate[2]	5,771	3,095	5,483	2,879	-288	1,332
Violent Crime Rate[2]	1,576	1,115	1,590	1,135	14	542
Property Crime Rate[2]	4,195	2,181	3,893	1,947	-302	1,001
	n = 1,252		*n = 1,252*		*n = 1,252*	

[1] Within-place change is calculated by subtracting the value for Time 1 (2000) from the value for Time 2 (2005-2007) for each place and then averaging the differences across the sample. As such, a negative value indicates, on average, a
[2] Rate calculated as number of offenses per population of 100,000.

2006). Readers will note that the mean scores for the index measures over the full sample are all very close to zero. This is to be expected, given that the variables are constructed from standardized scores for their component parts. They are included here primarily for juxtaposition with their values for the subset of new settlement destinations, to be discussed shortly.

Economically, on average places in the study became more disadvantaged over the period. While the share of those failing to graduate high school fell approximately 3 percent, indicating a slight increase in educational attainment, median household income (in 2009 U.S. dollars) also declined, roughly three and a half thousand dollars, as did the share of single-female headed-households increased (6 percent), while the ratio of households in poverty at any point in the 12 months prior to each survey and the unemployment rate remained each increased about 1 percent over the period. Perhaps surprisingly, at the same time, measures of residential stability remained about the same; the percent of households that were owner-occupied increased less than one percent, while the percent of households occupied two years or more remained effectively unchanged. Similarly, employment structure remained fairly stable; the period saw no real change in either the share of seasonal workers or the share of managerial positions

Finally, places included in the sample, on average, experienced declines in the overall crime rate from Time 1 to Time 2, of approximately 288 crimes per 100,000 of population. This decline appears driven entirely by rather large decreases in nonviolent property offenses. In sum, across the last decade and on average, places included in the full sample experienced a surge in population growth coupled with declines in overall crime. At the same time, measures of socioeconomic well-being either declined slightly or remained stable, on the whole. A look at whether these patterns hold for the subset of new settlement destinations is instructive.

Table 4.2 presents the means and standard deviations for the 573 cities and towns categorized as new settlement destinations. The increase in population size observed in the overall sample is virtually identical within new destinations. As with the full sample, the ratio of adults-to-children and the share of the population that is male aged 15-29 remained fairly stable. It is worth noting that the mean value for the logged variable measure (not shown) in both time periods indicates these places had slightly higher shares of this age group than the overall sample, which may be due in part to the immigration of young men (Donato, et al. 2008).

As expected, for these places, we see an increase in their shares of foreign-born. Unlike with the full sample, the scores for the index measures in the new destination subset are instructive. The negative mean scores indicate that at both Time 1 and Time 2, new gateways had lower than average shares of foreign-born, recent foreign-born, and Latinos. What makes these places significant is not so much the raw numbers of foreign-born (or even the percent of the population that is foreign-born), but the change in those numbers over time. While a cross-sectional look shows that at each time point these places had below average foreign-born population concentrations, across the time period, these places saw greater increases in their shares of foreign-born than the sample as a whole. These places saw their shares of foreign- born increase on average from 10.55 percent in 2000 to 13.3 percent during 2005-2007. As with the full sample, these increases are accompanied by increases in the share of the population that is Latino, pointing generally toward greater immigrant concentration.

Finally, the recent foreign-born in new destinations increased a little less than a one percent from Time 1 to Time 2. The greater increase in overall foreign-born populations, compared to the recent foreign-born, may point to the effects of intranational population shifts, due both to labor market forces and state and local level policy enactments (cf. Massey and Capoferro 2008).

The value of the disadvantage index indicates that in both time periods, new settlement places experienced higher levels of social and

Table 4.2 Profile of New Destinations Included in UCR Analyses

	2000		2005-2007		Within-Place Change	
	Mean	Std Dev	Mean	Std Dev	Mean[1]	Std Dev
Total Population	95,558	166,076	101,121	170,035	5,563	14,942
Foreign-Born Index	-0.52	1.29	-0.45	1.38	0.07	0.33
Recent Foreign-Born Index	-0.15	1.52	-0.05	1.57	0.10	0.60
Percent Foreign-Born	10.32	8.41	12.82	9.33	2.50	2.48
Percent Recent Foreign-Born	3.61	2.91	4.57	3.25	0.97	1.59
Percent Latino	10.55	11.82	13.34	13.31	2.79	3.13
Percent Male Aged 15-29	12.44	4.51	12.57	4.66	0.12	1.38
Adult-Child Ratio	3.25	1.20	3.35	1.24	0.10	0.33
Socioeconomic Disadvantage	0.13	2.61	0.22	2.55	0.09	1.14
Percent Less than High School	17.74	9.00	14.95	7.77	-2.80	2.92
Percent SFHH	7.84	3.06	15.09	7.53	7.25	5.07
Median Household Income	54,048	17,391	49,914	16,607	-4,134	4,395
Pct of Households in Poverty	12.99	7.17	14.63	7.11	1.64	2.48
Pct Unemployed	5.93	2.77	6.90	2.53	0.97	2.25
Residential Stability	-0.66	1.63	-0.69	1.64	-0.03	0.61
Pct of Households Owner-Occupied	57.77	12.66	58.76	12.21	0.99	3.18
Pct of Households Occupied 2 years or more	74.30	6.53	74.08	6.21	-0.21	3.24
Pct Management/Professional Occupations	34.32	9.79	34.26	10.17	-0.06	2.84
Percent Seasonal Occupations	0.52	1.50	0.53	1.68	0.01	0.64
Overall Crime Rate[2]	6,768.15	3,339.99	6,338.31	3,080.05	-429.84	1,547.22
Violent Crime Rate[2]	1,858.25	1,235.05	1,886.33	1,242.17	28.08	627.94
Property Crime Rate[2]	4,909.91	2,341.31	4,451.98	2,068.32	-457.92	1,137.78
	n = 573		*n = 573*		*n = 573*	

[1] Within-place change is calculated by subtracting the value for Time 1 (2000) from the value for Time 2 (2005-2007) for each place and then averaging the differences across the sample. As such, a negative value indicates, on average, a decline over time.

[2] Rate calculated as number of offenses per population of 100,000.

economic disparity. Relative to the entire sample, these areas had lower median incomes, higher rates of poverty and unemployment, and higher shares of single female headed households, which in particular increased from roughly 8 percent to 15 percent of all households. These places also experienced less residential stability, though as with the full sample, the value of this measure remained fairly stable over time. New destination places experienced a similar employment structure in terms of managerial and seasonal work, and similar stability in that structure over time. In both the overall sample and sub-sample, slightly more than one third of workers were employed in managerial or professional jobs at each time point.

We again see declines in overall crime across the years of study, but the decline is greater, on average, within new destinations. Whereas places in the full sample experienced declines of roughly 288 crimes per 100,000, in the new destinations sampled, the decline on average is 43 crimes per 100,000. And again, the result appears largely due to declines in property crime.

To highlight differences in changes over time between the two samples, Table 4.3 presents the difference in means scores between the new destination subset and the full sample. It is important to note that the data here presented are merely for heuristic purposes. No controls are imposed and as such the values for a given variable may not be directly comparable. Nonetheless, Table 4.3 underscores some key differences that are consistent with previous research.

As discussed, new destinations tend to have slightly higher than average populations, suggesting that while immigrants may be slowly moving away from *traditional* urban hubs, they continue to settle in fairly large cities and towns. New destinations tend also to have fewer total immigrants, but on average, slightly higher shares of recent immigrants, and the shares of total immigrants appear to be growing faster in these areas than in the larger sample, offering an implicit test of the validity of the measure of "new destination" here employed. On the whole, these places also tend to rank higher on measures of socioeconomic disadvantage, having lower median household income, a greater percentage of households in poverty, and a greater percentage of households headed by single mothers. Not surprisingly, they also tend to be less residentially stable, with fewer households that are owner-occupied, and fewer households occupied two years or more.

Table 4.3 Difference in Means Between New Destination and Overall Samples

	2000	2005-2007	Within-Place Change
	Mean Difference[1]	Mean Difference[1]	Mean Difference[1]
Total Population	493	533	40
Foreign-Born Index	-0.52	-0.45	0.07
Recent Foreign-Born Index	-0.15	-0.05	0.10
Percent Foreign-Born	-2.98	-2.48	0.50
Percent Recent Foreign-Born	0.29	0.55	0.26
Percent Latino	-4.47	-4.34	0.13
Percent Male Aged 15-29	1.28	1.09	-0.20
Adult-Child Ratio	0.13	0.10	-0.03
Socioeconomic Disadvantage	0.13	0.22	0.09
Percent Less than High School	-0.20	-0.05	0.15
Percent SFHH	0.45	1.11	0.66
Median Household Income	-6,024	-6,666	-642
Pct of Households in Poverty	1.69	2.10	0.42
Pct Unemployed	0.11	0.26	0.15
Residential Stability	-0.66	-0.69	-0.03
Pct of Households Owner-Occupied	-3.65	-3.57	0.08
Pct of Households Occupied 2 years or more	-2.61	-2.79	-0.18
Pct Management/Professional Occupations	-0.73	-0.86	-0.14
Percent Seasonal Occupations	-0.03	0.01	0.03
Overall Crime Rate[2]	997.29	855.53	-141.76
Violent Crime Rate[2]	282.72	296.74	14.02
Property Crime Rate[2]	714.58	558.79	-155.78

[1] Difference is calculated by subtracting the mean value for the overall sample from the mean value for the new destination subsample. As such, negative values indicate, on average and relative to the overall sample, a smaller share of a given variable within new destinations

[2] Rate calculated as number of offenses per population of 100,000.

Multivariate Results

To review, multivariate analyses were conducted on six types of crime: three violent criminal acts (murder, robbery, and assault) and three typically nonviolent, or property, offenses (burglary, larceny, and motor vehicle theft). For each of the six individual crimes, the actual counts, drawn from the FBI's UCR, were calculated as rates per hundred thousand of population. Rates for the three violent criminal acts were then aggregated into a violent crime index, while the three nonviolent acts were aggregated into a property crime index. These two indices were themselves aggregated into a third, *overall crime* index. Because of significant kurtosis and heteroskedasticity, each of the indices was log-transformed prior to analysis. For sake of brevity, only the analyses of the three index measures of crime are presented here.[54] The analyses proceed in a stepwise fashion, with each of four models adding an additional component conceptually related to the interaction between immigration and crime. The first model regresses only change in the foreign-born index on the dependent variable. The second model adds controls for population structure, namely, the natural log of the size of the total population, the percent of the population that is male aged 15-29, and the ratio of adults to children. The third model incorporates two index measures controlling for place-level socioeconomic conditions: disadvantage and population stability. The fourth and final model adds controls for employment structure using the percentages of the population age 15 and older employed in either seasonal work or management or professional positions.

As a starting point for the multivariate analyses, analysis begins by estimating cross-sectional OLS regressions for each time period. The model specified is essentially the same as the full model employed in subsequent fixed effects regressions; the primary difference between this approach and those to come is that traditional OLS controls for variation both within and between places, while the fixed-effects approach controls only for within-unit variation. Models were estimated for the overall rate of crime, as well as for the sub-indices for violent and property crime. Table 4.4 presents the results.

---

[54] Additional analyses were also run on each type of crime for each time period, for a total of 12 additional models, all of which are substantively similar to the ones presented here. They are available upon request from the author.

Table 4.4 OLS Regression Models Predicting Selected Crime Rates (log-transformed), 2000 and 2005-2007

Predictors	Overall Crime		Violent Crime		Property Crime	
	2000	2005-2007	2000	2005-2007	2000	2005-2007
Immigration Index	-.096***	-.101***	-.104***	-.123***	-.090***	-.090***
	(.007)	(.006)	(.009)	(.009)	(.008)	(.007)
City/Town Population (logged)	.129***	.122***	.150***	.149***	.125***	.118***
	(.014)	(.014)	(.018)	(.019)	(.015)	(.014)
Males Aged 15-29 (logged)	-.319***	-.348***	-.394***	-.365***	-.288***	-.336***
	(.064)	(.052)	(.082)	(.072)	(.067)	(.054)
Adult-Child Ratio (logged)	.202***	.212***	.232***	.305***	.198***	.178***
	(.049)	(.045)	(.062)	(.062)	(.050)	(.047)
Disadvantage Index	.064***	.060***	.107***	.097***	.046***	.043***
	(.007)	(.006)	(.008)	(.008)	(.007)	(.006)
Residential Stability	-.108***	-.105***	-.117***	-.117***	-.106***	-.103***
	(.011)	(.008)	(.014)	(.012)	(.011)	(.009)
Managerial/Professional	-.019***	-.019***	-.028***	-.028***	-.016***	-.016***
	(.001)	(.001)	(.002)	(.002)	(.001)	(.001)
Seasonal	.007	.006	-.018	-.013	.016*	.013*
	(.007)	(.006)	(.009)	(.008)	(.008)	(.006)
Constant	8.297	8.402	7.142	7.005	7.865	8.022
	(.220)	(.201)	(.282)	(.280)	(.229)	(.211)
Model Summary Information						
R^2 (Adj R^2)	.496 (.492)	.552 (.549)	.545 (.542)	.557 (.554)	.411 (.407)	.457 (.453)
Total Number of Obs (N)	1,252	1,252	1,252	1,252	1,252	1,252

*p<.05, **p<.01, ***p<.001

For overall crime, each of the predictor variables, with the exception of the percent of the population employed in seasonal work, exerts a highly significant effect at both time points. Most notably, the index measure of immigration, composed of the percent foreign-born and the percent Latino, is negatively correlated with crime, such that as rates of immigration increase, this model suggests that rates of crime would decrease, net of other factors. The effects of traditional criminogenic factors such as population size and socioeconomic disadvantage are positive and significant. Similarly, as the ratio of adults to children increases, results indicate a concomitant increase in rates of overall crime. The interpretation of the relationship between this variable and crime is two-fold. First, a high ratio of adults to children indicates a general movement away from families and toward a greater number of single unattached adults. This latter population is more likely to be engaged in crime, and perhaps more likely to be victimized. The traditional crime inhibiting factors of residential stability and primary-sector employment here exert a significant negative effect.

The models for overall crime explain approximately 49- and 55 percent of the variation in crime for 2000 and 2005-2007, respectively. The results of the models for violent and property crime are almost identical, with a slightly better fit for violent crime than for property crime. The major difference across the models is the effect of seasonal work, which in the overall crime models is nonsignificant. However, for the violent crime models, the effect is negative and significant at the $p<.05$ level, while for the property crime models, the effect is positive and significant. The results suggest a differential effect of seasonal work, whereby it is at once associated with reduced levels of interpersonal violence and increased levels of crime for economic gain.

The high significance levels found in the models are a product of its measuring both within and between unit variations. There are important concerns with this approach. First, OLS requires in effect a fully specified model, that is, that all relevant factors are explicitly included in the model. This requirement in practice is notoriously difficult to achieve. Second, because the findings include between unit variations, some of the correlations may be spurious. The variations between places are very likely influenced by local characteristics associated with crime, and it would be virtually impossible to account for all such correlates. A fixed-effects approach can address these concerns, essentially by using each place as its own control. This is done by comparing *within* places, and averaging the differences over time across all places sampled. As Allison (2005: 3) notes, by focusing only on within-unit change, a fixed effects approach offers the ability to "control for all stable characteristics of the individuals in the study, thereby eliminating potentially large sources of bias."

Table 4.5 presents the results of the fixed-effects regression of changes in the logged rate of overall crime on changes in measures of immigration and key socioeconomic and demographic factors. The first panel presents the regression on only change in the immigration index. As we see in this base model, the effect of the immigration index on overall crime is negative and nonsignificant.[55] As indicated by the base

---

[55] The minimum number of foreign-born population of any place in either the overall sample or the new destination subset is 226. Additional analyses (not shown) were run with minimum foreign-born thresholds of 300 (n=1,250 places for the overall sample, n=572 for the subset) and 500 (n=1,235 for the

Table 4.5 Fixed Effects (Within-City) Regression Models Predicting Overall Crime Rate (log-transformed), 2000-2007

	Model 1	Model 2	Model 3	Model 4
Predictors				
Immigration Index	-.013	.002	-.015	-.013
	(.020)	(.020)	(.021)	(.021)
City/Town Population (logged)		-.267***	-.247***	-.252***
		(.042)	(.042)	(.043)
Males Aged 15-29 (logged)		.084	.071	.069
		(.054)	(.055)	(.055)
Adult-Child Ratio (logged)		.101	.154*	.157*
		(.074)	(.074)	(.074)
Disadvantage Index			.023***	.023***
			(.006)	(.006)
Residential Stability			-.007	-.007
			(.011)	(.011)
Managerial/Professional				.000
				(.002)
Seasonal				-.014
				(.011)
Intercept	-.044	-.027	-.031	-.031
	(.007)	(.008)	(.008)	(.008)
Model Summary Information				
Between-Unit Variation	.952	.952	.952	.952
R^2 (Adj R^2)	.0003 (.000)	.040 (.037)	.052 (.047)	.053 (.047)
Total Number of Observations ($N \times T$)	2,504	2,504	2,504	2,504
Total Number of Cities/Towns (N)	1,252	1,252	1,252	1,252

† $p<.10$, * $p<.05$, ** $p<.01$, *** $p<.001$

model's associated R-square value, controlling for immigrant concentration alone explains virtually none of the within-unit change in crime across the time under study.

Model 2 incorporates controls for population structure, specifically: population size, the percentage of the population comprised by males age15-29, and the ratio of adults to children.[56]

---

overall, n=566 for the subset), the idea being that there may be a "tipping point" at which the number of foreign-born in an area exhibits an effect. At neither threshold did the results differ substantively from those presented here.

[56] For both the overall sample and the new gateway subset, models were also run including interaction effects for each of the predictor variables with the time variable, to determine if any effects varied significantly across the two time periods. In neither of the analyses were the main effects of a variable and its interaction term significantly correlated with any of the three crime indices;

Previous research suggests that rates of crime will tend to increase as population size increases, a product in part of the heightened tendency to rely on official agents of social control (Schulenberg 2003). Research also suggests that crime is skewed in terms of both the age and gender of offenders, with males being more likely to offend than females and young adults more likely to offend than either the middle-aged or elderly (Sampson and Laub 2003, 1993). Finally, the literature has suggested the need to control for the ratio of adults to children (Martinez, et al. 2010; Stowell, et al. 2009). Interpreting an effect of the adult-child ratio is two-fold. First, the higher the ratio, the greater is the number of adults and simply, the greater the number of potential adult offenders and victims. Second, a high ratio of adults to children might indicate the presence of large numbers of single adults, or at least, a small share of families. Research suggests the former would be more likely to engage in crime, while members of the latter less so (Anderson 1999; Messner and Rosenfeld 2001). After introducing these controls the effect of immigration remains nonsignificant though its direction has reversed, indicating that perhaps the share of males or presence of single adults controls for some aspects of immigration.

Looking at the effects of the controls themselves, results indicate that the log-transformed measure of population size is strongly and negatively correlated with the log-transformed rate of overall crime. For every one unit increase in the log of the total population, there is a corresponding decrease in the logged crime rate of .267, significant at the $p<.001$ level. The finding is in direct opposition to that found in the traditional OLS analyses, which again account for both within and between-unit variation. Together, the results suggest that while places with greater population experience greater crime than those with smaller population, positive *change* in population (i.e. increases) are associated with negative *change* in crime (i.e. decreases). This finding is consonant with recent research noting that the continuing decline of U.S. crime rates has been greatest in our larger cities. The effect of the percent male aged 15-29 and adult-child ratio are both positive, but nonsignificant. We see an increase in the adjusted R-square value to 4.1 percent of the within-unit variation. While the value here appears quite low, it actually represents the majority of within-unit variation. The nature of a fixed-effects analysis is to essentially difference out the

---

consequently, interaction models were abandoned in favor of ones incorporating only main effects.

between-unit variation and measure effects only on *within-unit* variation. In the sample under study, approximately 95 percent of the total variation is between units (a product of a large sample size and a relatively short time period of 7 years), leaving approximately 5 percent of the total variation that is within-units, such that the 4 percent of variation explained by Model 2 in effect represents roughly 80 percent of the total within-unit variation.

Building on the first two models, Model 3 incorporates additional controls for socioeconomic conditions. Results suggest that, as expected, changes in the disadvantage index are strongly and positively correlated with changes in the rate of overall crime.[57] For every one unit increase in the disadvantage index from Time 1 to Time 2, the logged rate of crime increases .023, significant at the *p<.001* level. Residential stability, as expected, is negatively correlated with crime, though its effect is far from significant. Once these socioeconomic factors are controlled, the effect of the immigration index, while still nonsignificant, is again negative in direction, suggesting that the effect measure is in part working through socioeconomic disadvantage, a finding that would be consistent with social disorganization theory. The log-transformed population variable remains significant, though

---

[57] As mentioned, the disadvantage index is comprised of the z-scores for the percent of the population with less than a high school education, the percent of female headed households with children under 18, the log of the median household income, the percent of households in poverty in the preceding 12 months, and the percent of the population age 15 and over who are unemployed. Some may question the omission of a measure of the percent non-Hispanic black. The analyses were re-run (not shown here) with a disadvantage index containing the percent of the population that is non-Hispanic black, in addition to those mentioned above, and a third time with the NH Black measure included as its own predictor, with no substantive differences to the results discussed here. The only considerable effect of the measure's inclusion was to reduce the overall sample size by approximately 60 cases, due to missing data from the ACS. As (1) the purpose of this analysis is to investigate the effects of *immigration* on crime, rather than correlates of crime generally, and (2) the results of a fixed-effects analysis are not generalizable beyond the sample under study, the decision was made to omit the measure, thereby retaining as many cases as possible.

slightly mediated. The effect of the adult-child ratio becomes significant at the $p<.05$ level. For every one unit increase in the logged ratio of adults to children, the logged rate of crime increased by .154. The emergence of a significant effect in model may suggest that the measure's effect is masked in part by residential stability, such that in stable areas, the presence of large numbers of adults may not exert an effect on crime.

Finally, Model 4 incorporates controls for place-level employment structure. Neither the percent of the population employed in management/professional occupations nor the percent employed in season work exerts a significant effect on overall crime. While the effect of seasonal work on crime is negative, it is far from significant. The large standard deviation may be an indication that there were too few data on seasonal workers in the sample. Despite the inclusion of more than 1,200 U.S. cities and towns with population minimums of 20 thousand, the numbers of seasonal workers was still quite small. And given the nature of the work, it is likely a population for which accurate data is difficult to obtain.

Ultimately, the inclusion of these measures does little to alter the results obtained in Model 3. Changes in the log-transformed population count remain significantly negatively correlated with crime, while the effects of changes in the adult-child ratio and disadvantage index remain positively and significantly correlated with crime. The effect of the immigration index on crime remains nonsignificant. Readers will note however, that with each successive model, the effect of the index is weakened, perhaps providing support for traditional social disorganization theory's notion that any seemingly direct effect of immigration is mediated once social structural controls are imposed. As the model summary information indicates, roughly 95 percent of the sample variation in the overall crime index is between units, with the remaining roughly five percent within units.[58] Thus the adjusted R-squared in Model 4 of .047 indicates that the fully specified model explains virtually all of the within-unit change in place-level crime from 2000-2007.

The analyses of the violent and property crime indices reveal distinct patterns of association, indicating that while explanations for

---

[58] The between unit variation is calculated by dividing the Type I Sum of Squares for the variable containing the geographic identifier by the model's corrected total Sum of Squares (see Allison 2005).

the two share similarities, there are also key differences. We begin with a review of findings of the analysis of the violent crime index. As the base model shows in Table 4.6, as with overall crime, changes in the effect of the immigration index are not significantly correlated with changes in the log-transformed violent crime rate. The second model, with controls for population structure, indicates that as the size of a given place increased from Time 1 to Time 2, there was a corresponding decrease in the occurrence of violent crime. Specifically, for every one unit increase in the log-transformed population, the logged rate of violent crime declined .418, significant at the $p<.001$ level. The effect of the immigration index increases from Model 1 to Model 2, but does not approach significance.

Table 4.6 Fixed Effects (Within-City) Regression Models Predicting Violent Crime Rate (log-transformed), 2000-2007

	Model 1	Model 2	Model 3	Model 4
Predictors				
Immigration Index	.006	.021	-.004	-.007
	(.028)	(.029)	(.029)	(.030)
City/Town Population (logged)		-.418***	-.387***	-.382***
		(.059)	(.059)	(.060)
Males Aged 15-29 (logged)		.110	.082	.076
		(.076)	(.078)	(.078)
Adult-Child Ratio (logged)		-.099	-.025	-.025
		(.104)	(.105)	(.106)
Disadvantage Index			.032***	.031***
			(.009)	(.009)
Residential Stability			-.020	-.020
			(.016)	(.016)
Managerial/Professional				-.002
				(.003)
Seasonal				-.004
				(.016)
Intercept	.006	.044	.039	.039
	(.009)	(.012)	(.012)	(.012)
Model Summary Information				
Between-Unit Variation	.951	.951	.951	.951
R^2 (Adj R^2)	.000 (.000)	.039 (.036)	.052 (.047)	.052 (.046)
Total Number of Observations ($N \times T$)	2,504	2,504	2,504	2,504
Total Number of Cities/Towns (N)	1,252	1,252	1,252	1,252

† $p<.10$, *$p<.05$, **$p<.01$, ***$p<.001$

Model 3, which again incorporates controls for socioeconomic conditions, reveals that changes in disadvantage are strongly and positively correlated with changes in the rate of violence. A one unit increase in disadvantage from Time 1 to Time 2 is associated with an increase the logged rate of violent crime of .032, significant at the $p<.001$ level. The inclusion of the measure of disadvantage reduces and reverses the effect of the immigration index from .021 to -.004, again providing support for the notion that any impact of immigration is largely a product of disadvantage. There is no significant effect of residential stability on violence.

Finally, results of the fully specified model, which includes controls for employment structure, indicates that changes in the number and types of jobs available neither exert a significant effect on violent crime nor mediate the effects of any of the other control variables. With only 4.9 percent within-unit variation, the adjusted R-squared of .046 indicates that roughly 95 percent of the total within-unit variation in change in violent crime is explained by the full model. It would appear that the model is a slightly stronger predictor of violent crime, than of overall crime or, as we will see, of property crime.

The analyses of the third crime type are presented next and suggest that at the place level, while the correlates of the two broad types of crime share some commonalities, they have some interesting differences. As we see from the base model in Table 4.7, the immigration index exerts no significant effect on property crime at the place level between the two time periods, though unlike the previous two analyses, the base-model effect is negative. As controls for population structure are introduced in Model 2, we again see a significant negative correlation between population size and the logged crime rate, indicating that large cities experienced a greater decline in property crime (and violent crime) across the period. Results also show that the ratio of adults to children is positively and significantly correlated with property crime, a finding inconsistent with the analysis of violent crime. For every one unit increase in the logged ratio of adults to children from Time 1 to Time 2, there is a corresponding increase in the logged rate of property crime of .159. It would appear that the greater the number of unattached adults, the more likely is the occurrence of property crime. Alternatively, it may be that a large adult-child ratio indicates the presence of more potential offenders; may also indicate the presence of more potential victims.

Table 4.7 Fixed Effects (Within-City) Regression Models Predicting Property Crime Rate (log-transformed), 2000-2007

Predictors	Model 1	Model 2	Model 3	Model 4
Immigration Index	-.022	-.007	-.022	-.019
	(.020)	(.021)	(.021)	(.022)
City/Town Population (logged)		-.210***	-.194***	-.199***
		(.043)	(.043)	(.044)
Males Aged 15-29 (logged)		.067	.064	.062
		(.056)	(.057)	(.057)
Adult-Child Ratio (logged)		.159*	.206**	.210**
		(.076)	(.077)	(.077)
Disadvantage Index			.021**	.021**
			(.006)	(.006)
Residential Stability			.001	.001
			(.012)	(.012)
Managerial/Professional				.000
				(.003)
Seasonal				-.015
				(.012)
Intercept	-.064	-.055	-.058	-.058
	(.007)	(.008)	(.009)	(.009)
Model Summary Information				
Between-Unit Variation	.943	.943	.943	.943
R^2 (Adj R^2)	.0009 (.000)	.029 (.026)	.038 (.033)	.039 (.033)
Total Number of Observations ($N \times T$)	2,504	2,504	2,504	2,504
Total Number of Cities/Towns (N)	1,252	1,252	1,252	1,252

[†] $p<.10$, *$p<.05$, **$p<.01$, ***$p<.001$

The addition of controls for socioeconomic conditions in Model 3 does not fundamentally alter any of the correlations from the previous model. Correlations between population size and the adult-child ratio remain significant. Additionally, results show that, while changes in residential stability are uncorrelated with changes in property crime, the index measure for disadvantage is positively associated with the logged rate of property crime, such that for every one unit increase in disadvantage from Time 1 to Time 2, there is, on average, a .021 increase in the logged rate of property crime, significant at the $p<.01$ level. Results are consistent with a wealth of criminological research indicating that the occurrence of crime-for-gain is in part a product of deprivation (Agnew, et al. 2002; Merton 1938).

Finally, results from the fully specified model indicate that controlling for employment structure does not fundamentally change the patterns of correlation observed in the previous models. Neither measure of employment structure exerts an effect on property crime that approaches significance. It is worth underscoring two findings with regard to the immigration index. First, while the effect of changes in immigration appeared to work through changes in disadvantage for overall and violent crime, the mediatory effect is largely absent for property crime. Second, and most notably for this study, changes in the index measure of immigration exert no significant effect, either alone (i.e. in the base model) or once controlling for a range of demographic, social, and economic factors, on changes in any of the crime indices. Generally, the stepwise inclusion of additional and traditional explanatory variables serves to systematically reduce any correlation between the index measure and crime. Moreover, additional models (not shown) wherein the index measure is replaced by its constituent parts find *even less* of an effect exhibited by either the percent foreign-born or the percent Latino alone.

Recent Immigration and Crime
As research suggests recent immigrants may rank higher on traditional criminogenic factors than those who came in earlier waves, analyses were also conducted using an index measure of the *recent foreign-born*, composed similarly of the standardized z-scores for percent Latino as well as the percent of immigrants arriving in the previous five years. Table 4.8 presents the results of the fixed-effects regression of the recent foreign-born index on overall crime.[59]

Despite a number of reasons to expect increased involvement in crime—not only the aforementioned criminogenic factors, but also the heightened public awareness of and political hostility toward immigrants, which in particular may negatively impact employment opportunities—results are virtually identical to those found by models for the overall foreign-born population for each of the three crime indices, even when the models were run with the difference in percent recent foreign-born in place of the index measure. The change in recent foreign-born exerts no differential effect on changes in crime than does the change in overall foreign-born, and neither appears to exert an independent significant effect on overall crime, violent crime, or property crime across the sample as a whole. The question remains as to whether changes in the foreign-born population have a differential

---

[59] To avoid redundancy, only the analysis of overall crime is presented here. Results for the analyses of violent and property crime can be found in Appendix B, Tables B1 and B2, respectively.

impact in places where their numbers have grown dramatically in recent years. The analysis turns now to the impact of the foreign-born in new settlement areas.

Table 4.8 Fixed Effects (Within-City) Regression Models Predicting Overall Crime Rate (log-transformed), 2000-2007, Recent Foreign-Born

	Model 1	Model 2	Model 3	Model 4
Predictors				
Recent Immigration Index	-.008	-.004	-.008	-.007
	(.013)	(.013)	(.013)	(.013)
City/Town Population (logged)		-.266***	-.248***	-.253***
		(.042)	(.042)	(.042)
Males Aged 15-29 (logged)		.089	.072	.069
		(.055)	(.056)	(.056)
Adult-Child Ratio (logged)		.097	.156*	.160*
		(.073)	(.074)	(.074)
Disadvantage Index			.022***	.022***
			(.006)	(.006)
Residential Stability			-.007	-.007
			(.011)	(.011)
Managerial/Professional				.000
				(.002)
Seasonal				-.014
				(.011)
Intercept	-.044	-.027	-.031	-.031
	(.007)	(.008)	(.008)	(.008)
Model Summary Information				
Between-Unit Variation	.952	.952	.952	.952
R^2 (Adj R^2)	.0003 (.000)	.040 (.037)	.052 (.047)	.053 (.047)
Total Number of Observations ($N \times T$)	2,504	2,504	2,504	2,504
Total Number of Cities/Towns (N)	1,252	1,252	1,252	1,252

$^\dagger p<.10$, $^*p<.05$, $^{**}p<.01$, $^{***}p<.001$

Immigration, Crime, and the New Settlement Destinations

As researchers have noted, there are reasons to expect that the impact of the foreign-born differs depending on the places in which they settle (Lichter et al. 2010; Donato, et al. 2008). Specifically, places with established histories of receiving waves of newcomers have mechanisms—social, economic, political—in place to ease their incorporation, whether structural, cultural, or both. In contrast, it is at least plausible that places with little or no history of receiving immigrants will lack those same mechanisms, and consequently the process of incorporation for the foreign-born will be more difficult in these areas, compared to those who settle in traditional areas. To address the question of whether immigration exerts a differential effect based on a history of immigrant reception, I conduct an analysis of a subset of places in the original sample, specifically, those wherein the percent of the population that is recent foreign-born increased by at least 50 percent from 2000 to the 2005-2007 period (for precedent see Shihadeh and Winters 2010). This results in a subset of n=573 places.[60] The results of the fixed effects analyses of overall crime within this sub-sample are shown in Table 4.9.[61]

As we see in the base model, with no additional controls imposed, the effect of changes in the immigration index is far from significant. Once controls for population structure are imposed in Model 2, we see that change in the logged population is negatively correlated with change in logged rate of overall crime, significant at the $p<.05$ level. For every one unit increase in population from Time 1 to Time 2, there is a corresponding decrease in the logged rate of overall crime of .413.

As with the analyses of the full sample, Model 3 incorporates controls for socioeconomic conditions. Unlike those analyses, however, the effect of the adult-child ratio is nonsignificant, and the effect of the disadvantage index is significant only at the $p<.10$ *level*. While the reduced effect of disadvantage may be somewhat surprising, univariate analyses have shown that relative to the full sample, new destinations experienced both heightened disadvantage and less crime at both time points, suggesting that while still an important indicator of crime, disadvantage exerts a spatially heterogeneous effect. Including measures of employment structure in Model 4 does not substantively alter the results from the previous model and in fact, as the adjusted R-

---

[60] Additional analyses (not shown) were run wherein new destinations were operationalized as (1) places whose recent foreign-born population increased by 100 percent (n=353) and (2) places wherein the percent of the population that were recent foreign-born at Time 2 are greater than or equal to one standard deviation above the mean for the entire sample (n=195). In neither case did the effect of changes in the immigration index significantly differ from what is resented here.

[61] Because the new destination variable is time-invariant (i.e. it either has a value of '1' at both time points or a value of '0'), its inclusion in the overall analysis would effectively yield no results. That is, because there is no change over time, it would be "differenced out" of the equation. Consequently, to test for new destination effects, it was necessary to construct a secondary sample.

Table 4.9 Fixed Effects (Within-City) Regression Models Predicting Overall Crime Rate (log-transformed) within New Destinations, 2000-2007

Predictors	Model 1	Model 2	Model 3	Model 4
Immigration Index	-.004	.010	-.003	-.001
	(.033)	(.032)	(.033)	(.034)
City/Town Population (logged)		-.413***	-.386***	-.389***
		(.068)	(.071)	(.072)
Males Aged 15-29		.046	.037	.034
		(.097)	(.101)	(.102)
Adult-Child Ratio		.099	.129	.139
		(.134)	(.135)	(.136)
Disadvantage Index			$.017^{\dagger}$	$.017^{\dagger}$
			(.009)	(.010)
Residential Stability			-.008	-.010
			(.019)	(.019)
Managerial/Professional				.000
				(.004)
Seasonal				-.016
				(.017)
Intercept	-.056	-.024	-.028	-.028
	(.011)	(.013)	(.013)	(.013)
Model Summary Information				
Between-Unit Variation	.937	.937	.937	.937
R^2 (Adj R^2)	.000 (.000)	.070 (.064)	.076 (.066)	.078 (.065)
Total Number of Observations ($N \times T$)	1,146	1,146	1,146	1,146
Total Number of Cities/Towns (N)	573	573	573	573

† $p<.10$, $*p<.05$, $**p<.01$, $***p<.001$

square for each model shows, their inclusion may weaken the explanatory power. It would appear that for the new settlement subset, the change in crime from 2000 to 2007 is largely a product of population shifts, with a minor effect of changes in disadvantage.

The same patterns found for overall crime within new settlement areas are present with respect to violent and property crime. As with the full sample, the change in immigration is negatively correlated with change in violent crime, though again results for none of the models approach significance (Table 4.10). In model 2, we see that the change in logged population exerts a strong negative effect on changes in violent crime, significant in at the $p<.01$ level. As with the analysis of overall crime, the controls imposed in Models 3 and 4 offer no additional findings of significance. Particularly surprising is the entire lack of effect of changes in disadvantage on changes in violent crime. It appears that the inclusion of employment conditions in Model 4 actually weakens the model's explanatory power, relative to model 3.

Table 4.10 Fixed Effects (Within-City) Regression Models Predicting Violent Crime Rate (log-transformed) within New Destinations, 2000-2007

Predictors	Model 1	Model 2	Model 3	Model 4
Predictors				
Immigration Index	-.043	-.033	-.048	-.052
	(.045)	(.045)	(.046)	(.047)
City/Town Population (logged)		-.535***	-.495***	-.488***
		(.093)	(.097)	(.099)
Males Aged 15-29		.140	.111	.102
		(.133)	(.139)	(.140)
Adult-Child Ratio		-.077	-.040	-.036
		(.185)	(.186)	(.187)
Disadvantage Index			.017	.017
			(.013)	(.013)
Residential Stability			-.022	-.023
			(.025)	(.026)
Managerial/Professional				-.002
				(.005)
Seasonal				-.009
				(.023)
Intercept	.029	.078	.072	.072
	(.015)	(.018)	(.019)	(.019)
Model Summary Information				
Between-Unit Variation	.943	.943	.943	.943
R^2 (Adj R^2)	.002 (.000)	.061 (.054)	.065 (.056)	.066 (.052)
Total Number of Observations ($N \times T$)	1,146	1,146	1,146	1,146
Total Number of Cities/Towns (N)	573	573	573	573

[†] $p<.10$, $*p<.05$, $**p<.01$, $***p<.001$

Table 4.11 Fixed Effects (Within-City) Regression Models Predicting Property Crime Rate (log-transformed) within New Destinations, 2000-2007

Predictors	Model 1	Model 2	Model 3	Model 4
Predictors				
Immigration Index	.005	.019	.006	.008
	(.033)	(.033)	(.034)	(.035)
City/Town Population (logged)		-.360***	-.336***	-.340***
		(.069)	(.072)	(.073)
Males Aged 15-29		.012	.008	.006
		(.098)	(.102)	(.103)
Adult-Child Ratio		.147	.176	.185
		(.136)	(.137)	(.137)
Disadvantage Index			.017[†]	.017[†]
			(.010)	(.010)
Residential Stability			-.005	-.006
			(.019)	(.019)
Managerial/Professional				.000
				(.004)
Seasonal				-.014
				(.017)
Intercept	-.088	-.061	-.065	-.065
	(.011)	(.013)	(.014)	(.014)
Model Summary Information				
Between-Unit Variation	.926	.926	.926	.926
R^2 (Adj R^2)	.000 (.000)	.056 (.049)	.062 (.052)	.063 (.049)
Total Number of Observations ($N \times T$)	1,146	1,146	1,146	1,146
Total Number of Cities/Towns (N)	573	573	573	573

[†] $p<.10$, $*p<.05$, $**p<.01$, $***p<.001$

The patterns observed thus far hold for change over time in the logged rates of property crime within the new settlement destinations (Table 4.11). Namely, the models show that the change in population is negatively correlated with change in property crime, significant at the *p<.10* level. As with the analysis of overall crime in the new destinations, the effect of disadvantage is marginally significant at the *p<.10* level. Model 3 is the strongest predictor of change in property crime. Finally, when the analyses were run with the immigration index measure replaced by its component parts, the changes in percent recent foreign-born exerted no significant effect on any of the crime indices. However, results (not shown) revealed that for the violent crime index, the change in percent Latino was negatively correlated, significant at the *p<.05* level.

Recent Immigration and Crime within New Destinations

As with the full sample, analyses of the impact of the changes in *recent* foreign-born within the new settlement areas are virtually the same as for the foreign-born as a whole (Table 4.12; for violent and property crime within new destinations, see tables B4 and B5 in Appendix B).

Table 4.12 Fixed Effects (Within-City) Regression Models Predicting Overall Crime Rate (log-transformed) within New Destinations for the Recent Foreign Born, 2000-2007

Predictors	Model 1	Model 2	Model 3	Model 4
Recent Immigration Index	.001	.004	.002	.003
	(.018)	(.018)	(.018)	(.019)
City/Town Population (logged)		-.412***	-.387***	-.390***
		(.068)	(.071)	(.072)
Males Aged 15-29 (logged)		.046	.033	.030
		(.100)	(.103)	(.104)
Adult-Child Ratio (logged)		.096	.131	.141
		(.134)	(.135)	(.135)
Disadvantage Index			.017†	.017†
			(.009)	(.009)
Residential Stability			-.008	-.010
			(.019)	(.019)
Managerial/Professional				.000
				(.004)
Seasonal				-.017
				(.017)
Intercept	-.057	-.023	-.028	-.028
	(.011)	(.013)	(.013)	(.013)
Model Summary Information				
Between-Unit Variation	.937	.937	.937	.937
R² (Adj R²)	.000 (.000)	.070 (.064)	.076 (.066)	.078 (.065)
Total Number of Observations (N x T)	1,146	1,146	1,146	1,146
Total Number of Cities/Towns (N)	573	573	573	573

† *p<.10* , *p<.05, **p<.01, ***p<.001*

And again, in neither case does the impact of change approach significance for any of the three indices of crime. Thus it would appear that changes in the foreign-born population, whether at large or among those arriving in the previous five years, and whether in the full sample or the subset of places which saw their immigrant populations increase the greatest from 2000 to 2007, fails to exert a significant effect on changes in crime, whether overall, violent, or property.

DISCUSSION AND CONCLUSIONS

This chapter has sought to address whether *change* in immigration exerts significant effects on *change* in rates of overall, violent, and property crime for 1,252 places over the years 2000-2007. Additionally, analyses were performed to determine whether outcomes differed (1) for immigrants arriving in the previous five years and (2) across places according to their history of immigrant reception. To test this last concern, analyses were performed on a sub-set of places wherein the share of foreign-born had increased by more than half since 1990. In general, the results offer somewhat of a mixed bag, consistent with some aspects of the hypotheses, and inconsistent with others.

Contrary to the expectation of a significant negative effect within the full sample of places, change in immigration exerted no significant effect on change in crime, whether violent, property, or total crime rates and whether the measure of immigrant concentration included the total foreign-born population or only those arriving in the last five years. The results offer a modicum of support for community resource view in that the incorporation of contemporary immigrants is neither a direct nor indirect criminogenic process and are consistent with the results of previous research (Feldmeyer 2009; Ousey and Kubrin 2009; Reid, et al. 2005; Butcher and Piehl 1998). More pointedly, the absence of a positive effect of immigration in either models 1 or 2, which did not include controls for socioeconomic disadvantage, for any of the analyses casts doubt on the social disorganization view of immigration. The results do not suggests that immigration contributes indirectly to higher rates of crime by contributing to traditional indicators of disorganization.

Within the 1,252 places comprising the total sample, the strongest predictors of crime were change in overall population size (negative and significant across all models and for all crime types), change in disadvantage (positive and significant except for the change in violent crime within new destinations), and the ratio of adults to children (positive and significant for overall and property crime within the full sample only). Results suggests also that while explanations for changes in the occurrence of violent and property crime within the samples under analysis share some important commonalities, there are also important differences across the time period studied. For both subcategories of crime, the strongest predictor variables were change in disadvantage and change in population size. The former was positively correlated with changes in crime, while the latter was negatively so. While violent crime tended to increase across the two time periods, property crime tended to decrease. Furthermore, the change in the ratio of adults to children significantly predicts changes in overall and property crime in the full sample, net of other factors, it is not a significant predictor of changes in violence nor is its effect spatially homogenous; that is the ratio of adults to children does not effect changes in crime within the new destination subset. Thus, for at least the overall sample, property crime appears to be a product generally of large numbers of adults. The finding might be pointing to the criminogenic outcomes of the presence of large numbers of single, unattached adults, though it is difficult to state for certain as the variable employed does not allow for disaggregating the adult population by either marital or coupling status. Alternatively, the results may point to the disinhibiting effect of families on crime (cf. Ousey and Kubrin 2009), though again, the measure does not disaggregate by family type.

It is worth comparing these results to those produced by traditional OLS and offered at the outset. While those analyses indicated virtually all control variables were significantly correlated with crime, those correlations are likely products of a cross-sectional view and between-unit correlations. In contrast, controlling for variation *across* geographies, within-unit *change* in crime is predicted by *changes* in population size and disadvantage, with no significant effect of change in immigration.

The results are virtually identical for the subset of new settlement destinations, findings wholly at odds with the stated hypotheses. The arrival of newcomers was expected to pose a disorganizing force in places with theoretically limited mechanisms to aid in incorporation, but the results suggest otherwise. That change in immigration exerts no effect on change in crime, directly or indirectly, even within places for which immigrant settlement is a new phenomenon, poses a firm challenge to the social disorganization view. Given the current cultural context of opposition and research indicating greater marginalization of ethnic minorities within new destinations (Lichter, et al. 2010), the findings are somewhat surprising and may suggest, as the community resource view predicts, that immigrants who settle in nontraditional areas may in many ways be distinct from their counterparts, highlighting the notion of immigrant "pioneers," whose distinct personality traits that buffer from criminal involvement (Portes and Rumbaut 2006). The non-finding may also point to the effect of network ties and the existence of pull factors, such as the availability of employment, that draw them to these new places and provide a buffer (Lee and Slack 2008; Parrado and Kandel 2008). Moreover, results give credence to the notion that immigrant communities are able to provide their members with support systems by which to manage the stressors of social, cultural, and economic marginalization (Smith and Furseth 2008).

Ultimately, the lack of a finding in places whose experience with immigration either had been dormant for decades or is entirely new is in itself an important finding. That changes in immigration exert no effect on changes in crime, whether overall, violent, or property; whether among immigrants arriving only within the previous five years or those who have been here for decades; and whether in places with established histories of immigrant reception or those whose histories are just beginning casts another boulder of doubt on the persistent perception of an immigration-crime link.

As results thus far have undermined the connection between immigration and crime commission, the analyses turn now to whether changes in immigration are correlated with changes in immigrant victimization, as measured by the occurrence of anti-immigrant biased crime.

CHAPTER 5

New Neighbors or New Targets?
Anti-Immigrant Hate Crime

INTRODUCTION

The previous chapter sought to address the question of whether changes in immigration from 2000-2007 significantly impacted changes in rates of overall, violent, and property crime over the same period for 1,252 places with population greater than twenty thousand. Consistent with previous research, results indicate no significant effect of immigration on crime, suggesting that the process of immigrant reception is not the criminogenic force some have suggested (MacDonald 2004a, 2004b). Further, the lack of a significant effect in any of the models, but especially models 1 and 2, wherein no controls for socioeconomic condition are imposed, casts doubt on traditional social disorganization theory's premise that immigration's effect on crime is mediated through disadvantage. Finally, the results cast doubt on the likelihood that immigration contributes to crime by displacing native-born workers, who, once dislodged from the employment ladder are thought to be more prone to criminal activity. So while changes in immigration are shown to exert no significant effect on three broad types of crime, there remains the question of whether such changes exert an effect on the occurrence of a more specific type: the victimization of immigrants.

To measure the effect of changes in immigration on changes in immigrant victimization, fixed effects regression analyses are conducted on a sample of the places wherein hate crimes occurred. The approach to uncovering effects of immigration on biased crime differs slightly from that employed for traditional crime. First, given the rarity of hate crime incidence, it would be inappropriate to calculate rates per population. Consequently the analyses proceed using event counts, which necessitates a method of analysis that can handle discrete variables. In this case, negative binomial regression analyses are employed (Allison 2005). Second, the socioeconomic (and sociopolitical) predictors of traditional and biased crime are not assumed to be the same. While generalized disadvantaged has been shown here and elsewhere (Agnew, et al. 2002; Kovandzic, et al. 1998; Merton 1938) to be a consistent and significant predictor of traditional crime, it is unlikely to have a similar effect on crimes motivated by bias or hate. With regard to biased crime, measures of economic conditions should also account for dominant group membership. This is accomplished in the models presented here by imposing controls for the percent of the population that is non-Hispanic white, and the percent of white households with income greater than $100,000.

Drawing from the literature on group threat theory, three key hypotheses are tested. First, (1) across the sample as a whole, I expect no significant effect of changes in immigration—either total foreign-born or the recently arrived—on the occurrence of anti-immigrant hate crime, once controlling for relevant factors. Second, I expect that within new destinations, (2) changes in the shares of total foreign-born will be positively and significantly associated with changes in the occurrence of anti-immigrant hate crime, and further, that the (3) effects will be heightened for changes in the shares of the recently arrived foreign-born. We begin by looking at the results of the univariate analyses.

THE IMPACT OF CHANGE IN IMMIGRATION ON CHANGE IN ANTI-IMMIGRANT HATE CRIME

Univariate Analyses

Table 5.1 presents the means and standard deviations of the key variables employed for all places included in the analysis. The places included in the sample tend, on average, to be quite large in terms of population (particularly when compared to the sample mean employed in the analyses of traditional crime types).[62] From 2000 to 2007, the places sampled increased in population an average of nearly 8,000 persons. As would be expected given the mean population size, the percent that is foreign-born is also quite large, nearly four percent higher, on average, than in the nation as a whole at Time 1, and it increased nearly two percentage points from Time 1 to Time 2. At the same time, these places are also predominantly white, though while the share of the population that is foreign-born increased over the period, the share that is non-Hispanic white declined nearly four percentage points. On average, roughly 11.5 percent of the population is male aged 15 to 29 and there are approximately three adults to every child under the age of 18. Measures of residential stability remained stable across the period and are quite similar to the values reported among the places included in the analyses on traditional crime. We see a dramatic increase in the percent of white households with income greater than $100 thousand, from roughly 16 percent at Time 1 to nearly one quarter of all white households at Time 2. Finally, on average, the places in the sample experienced roughly seven hate crimes from 1999-2001, and about four and a half from 2005-2007.[63] Of note here is that the reporting of hate crime incidence remains a very rare event, and one whose frequency declined across the period under study.[64]

As with the analysis of traditional crime, the analysis of hate crime is interested in potential differences between traditional receiving areas and new destinations. Table 5.2 offers the means and standard deviations for the subset of 173 new destinations for which hate crime data are available. The new destinations included in the analysis are on average smaller than those in the total sample, with as well a lower share of total foreign-born. As would be expected among new

---

[62] Whether this size discrepancy is a product of hate crime being more likely to occur, be reported by victims, or recorded by metropolitan police departments in large urban areas is unclear and beyond the scope of this analysis.

[63] Readers should bear in mind these are pooled totals, rather than single year counts or averages.

[64] It is perhaps worth mentioning that the comparatively "large" incidence of anti-immigrant hate crimes recorded for Time 1 is unlikely to be a product of backlash from the attacks of September 11th, as the data cover only the first three and half months of the post-9/11 era.

Table 5.1 Profile of Places Included in Hate Crime Analyses

	2000		2005-2007		Within-Place Change	
	Mean	Std Dev	Mean	Std Dev	Mean[1]	Std Dev
Total Population	165,672	484,953	173,507	496,032	7,834	23,146
Percent Foreign-Born	15.96	11.40	17.93	11.68	1.97	2.30
Percent Recent Foreign-Born	3.84	2.73	4.54	2.87	0.70	1.25
Percent White	63.88	21.64	59.73	21.94	-4.15	3.54
Percent Male Aged 15-29	11.47	3.32	11.64	3.33	0.17	1.31
Adult-Child Ratio	3.21	1.17	3.34	1.05	0.13	0.36
Residential Stability	0.00	1.74	0.00	1.77	0.00	0.52
Pct of Households Owner-Occupied	59.13	13.58	60.35	12.98	1.23	2.80
Pct of Households Occupied 2 years or more	76.97	6.28	76.99	6.39	0.02	2.64
Percent of White Households with Income Greater than $100k	16.38	9.97	24.92	12.41	8.55	4.12
Percent Seasonal Occupations	0.41	1.07	0.41	1.27	0.00	0.42
Total Count of Anti-Immigrant Offenses	7.17	26.64	4.41	11.22	-2.76	17.56
	n = 423		n = 423		n = 423	

[1] Within-place change is calculated by subtracting the mean value for Time 1 from the mean value for Time 2. As such, positive values indicate, on average, an increase over time while negative values represent a decrease.

Table 5.2 Profile of New Destinations Included in Hate Crime Analyses

	2000		2005-2007		Within-Place Change	
	Mean	Std Dev	Mean	Std Dev	Mean[1]	Std Dev
Total Population	160,198	255,210	168,380	263,837	8,181	21,287
Percent Foreign-Born	12.25	8.82	14.60	9.66	2.35	2.21
Percent Recent Foreign-Born	4.22	2.95	5.13	3.15	0.91	1.50
Percent White	67.80	19.44	64.11	19.74	-3.69	3.23
Percent Male Aged 15-29	13.00	3.99	12.93	4.14	-0.07	1.26
Adult-Child Ratio	3.36	0.97	3.49	0.98	0.12	0.31
Residential Stability	-0.83	1.55	-0.90	1.50	-0.07	0.54
Pct of Households Owner-Occupied	54.60	11.51	55.85	10.89	1.25	2.81
Pct of Households Occupied 2 years or more	73.87	6.19	73.47	5.84	-0.40	2.72
Percent of White Households with Income Greater than $100k	13.00	7.84	19.86	9.83	6.86	3.39
Percent Seasonal Occupations	0.37	0.72	0.41	1.16	0.04	0.51
Total Count of Anti-Immigrant Offenses	6.68	16.48	4.79	9.70	-1.89	9.58
	n = 173		n = 173		n = 173	

[1] Within-place change is calculated by subtracting the mean value for Time 1 from the mean value for Time 2. As such, positive values indicate, on average, an increase over time while negative values represent a decrease.

destinations. However, these places have higher shares of recent foreign-born. In terms of population structure, new destinations had a slightly higher shares of males between the ages of 15 and 29, lower rates of residential stability, and a smaller percentage of white households with income greater than $100 thousand, compared to the full sample. In both, there were about three adults to each child.

The differences between the two sets are further illustrated in Table 5.3, which presents the difference in means between the new destinations and the overall sample. While new destinations have, on average, at each time point smaller total populations and smaller shares of foreign-born, they saw greater increases in both across the period and have greater shares of both recent foreign-born and non-Hispanic white populations. And while the ratio of adults-to-children is about the same in each sample, new destination places have somewhat higher shares of males aged 15 to 29. Turning to economic indicators, new destinations have at each time point lower measures of residential stability, with lower shares of both owner-occupied housing units and units occupied for two years or more, with a larger decline for the latter across the period. From this table we see that not only did new destinations have fewer shares of white householders with incomes greater than $100 thousand at each point, but they also experienced less of an increase in these households across the period. Finally, turning to hate crime incidence, new destinations had slightly fewer hate crimes on average at Time 1, and a slightly higher incidence at Time 2, indicating a slightly greater overall growth in the phenomena within new destinations than the overall sample across the years of study. With a rough image of the places under study, the next section investigates the effects of these variables on changes in the occurrence of anti-immigrant hate crimes for the years 2000 to 2007.

Multivariate Analyses

Multivariate analyses were conducted using data on hate crime incidence for two time periods: 2000 and 2005-2007. As discussed in Chapter 3, the FBI records several types of bias motivation, not all of which are applicable to the line of inquiry taken here.[65] Unfortunately, the data do not account for biased crimes based on nativity status. To

---

[65] The broad categories of bias covered include race, religion, sexual orientation, ethnicity/national origin, and disability. Within each type are

Table 5.3 Difference in Means Between New Destination and Overall Samples

	2000	2005-2007	Within-Place Change
	Mean Difference[1]	Mean Difference[1]	Mean Difference[1]
Total Population	-5,474	-5,127	347
Percent Foreign-Born	-3.70	-3.32	0.38
Percent Recent Foreign-Born	0.38	0.59	0.21
Percent White	3.92	4.38	0.46
Percent Male Aged 15-29	1.53	1.29	-0.24
Adult-Child Ratio	0.15	0.15	-0.01
Residential Stability	-0.83	-0.90	-0.07
Pct of Households Owner-Occupied	-4.53	-4.51	0.02
Pct of Households Occupied 2 years or more	-3.09	-3.52	-0.42
Percent of White Households with Income Greater than $100k	-3.38	-5.06	-1.69
Percent Seasonal Occupations	-0.05	0.00	0.04
Total Count of Anti-Immigrant Offenses	-0.50	0.37	0.87

[1] Difference is calculated by subtracting the mean value for the overall sample from the mean value for the new destination subsample. As such, negative values indicate, on average and relative to the overall sample, a smaller share of a given variable within new destinations

address this shortcoming, several biased crime types were employed to create a rough proxy for immigrant status. These include: anti-Asian/Pacific Islander, Anti-Islamic, Anti-Hispanic, and Anti-Other Ethnicity/National Origin. To strengthen the data and eliminate potential bias from any single year anomalies, data were pooled for each time period, such that the count of anti-immigrant hate crimes represents the pooled total of biased crimes occurring from 1999 to 2001 for Time 1 and those occurring from 2005-2007 for Time 2. Additionally, to broaden the sample size, inclusion required a minimum of two years reporting in each period, resulting in a final sample size of

---

included several more specific bias motivations. For example, the religion category includes anti-Catholic, anti-Protestant, anti-Jewish, anti-Islamic, anti-Other religion, anti-Multiple religions, and anti-Atheist/Agnostic crimes.

423 places.[66] Because the occurrence and reporting of hate crime incidence are rare events, and their distributions across cities and towns highly skewed, it would be inappropriate to employ analytical models that assume normally distributed errors, such as Ordinary Least squares or even the fixed effects linear regression methods employed in the previous chapter. The analyses presented in this chapter rely on negative binomial regression models, which are explicitly designed to model count data.[67]

Table 5.4 presents the results of the fixed effects negative binomial regression of the change in the percent foreign-born for the full sample. As we see from the base model, with no additional controls imposed, the change in the percent of foreign-born exerts a significant negative effect on the change in the occurrence of hate crime. That is, an increase in the percent of foreign-born is associated with a decrease in the occurrence of anti-immigrant hate crime. The finding is somewhat surprising and at odds with the hypothesis of a null effect. One interpretation is that increasing immigration in a city or town may provide a buffer against hate crime victimization.

The second model incorporates controls for population structure, namely, the size of the population (log-transformed), the percent of the population that is male aged 15 to 29, the ratio of adults to children, and the percent of the population that is non-Hispanic white. We see that change in neither overall population size nor percent male aged 15 to 29 is significantly correlated with the change in anti-immigrant hate

---

[66] As readers will note, this potentially results in a comparison of uneven years, and thus, unbalanced counts. To mitigate, additional analyses were run with a measure of the *average yearly* number of hate crimes (rounded to the nearest whole number, to facilitate the negative binomial regression) in place of the pooled total count. The results of those analyses can be found in Tables B5a through B5d in Appendix B and, with respect to the relationship between immigration and hate crime incidence, do not substantively differ from the results presented here.

[67] The negative binomial distribution is essentially a generalization of the Poisson distribution with an added parameter that allows for overdispersion, in the form of unobserved heterogeneity that is specific to particular points in time. Readers will recall that while fixed effects model allow for heterogeneity across units, the variation is expected to be *across or between* units, rather than within units. Negative binomial essentially offers an additional parameter to control for within-unit heterogeneity.

Table 5.4 Fixed Effects (Within-City) Negative Binomial Regression Models Predicting the Incidence
of Anti-Immigrant Hate Crime, 2000-2007

	Model 1	Model 2	Model 3	Model 4
Predictors				
Percent Foreign-born	-.046***	-.018***	-.012**	-.011*
	(.004)	(.004)	(.005)	(.005)
City/Town Population (logged)		-.022	-.012	-.023
		(.040)	(.042)	(.042)
Males Aged 15-29		-.007	-.018	-.013
		(.013)	(.016)	(.016)
Adult-Child Ratio		.146**	.202***	.181***
		(.046)	(.050)	(.050)
Percent NH White		.025***	.026***	.026***
		(.003)	(.003)	(.003)
Residential Stability			.035	.032
			(.034)	(.034)
White Wealth			-.018***	-.019***
			(.004)	(.004)
Seasonal Work				-.094**
				(.036)
Intercept	-7.791***	-10.056***	-9.981***	-9.791***
	(.077)	(.578)	(.619)	(.622)
Model Summary Information				
Goodness of Fit (Value/DF)				
Deviance	1.101	1.099	1.104	1.105
Scaled Deviance	1.000	1.000	1.000	1.000
Pearson Chi-Square	1.540	1.362	1.351	1.327
Scaled Pearson X2	1.398	1.239	1.224	1.201
Total Number of Observations (*N* x *T*)	846	846	846	846
Total Number of Cities/Towns (*N*)	423	423	423	423

NOTE: Population neither non-Hispanic white nor non-Hispanic Black (log transformed) used as offset.

† $p<.10$, *$p<.05$, **$p<.01$, ***$p<.001$

crime. Change in the ratio of adults to children, however, is positively correlated with biased crime, indicating that as the number of adults increases, relative to the number of children, the occurrence of hate crime against immigrants increases as well. As with the analysis of traditional crime, there is a dual interpretation here. First, a higher ratio means a greater number of adult victims and adult offenders. Unlike with traditional crime, where there may be valid reasons for juvenile offenders to be excluded from official counts, theoretically at least, the hate crime designation should be applied without reference to age of offender (see Levin, et al. 2007 for public attitudes toward juvenile hate crime perpetrators). Alternatively, to the degree that the ratio is seen as an inverse measure of families, the finding may indicate that while families exert a downward effect on hate crime incidence, unattached adults exert an upward effect. Model 2 incorporates one additional measure of population structure that is theoretically related to the occurrence of hate crime, particularly those against immigrants: the percent of the population that is non-Hispanic white. The effect of changes in the percent white is positive and significant. By including this measure, the effect of change in percent foreign-born, while still significant and negative, is greatly reduced.

Model 3 attempts to capture changes in socioeconomic conditions by adding controls for residential stability and non-Hispanic white affluence (i.e. the percent of non-Hispanic white households with incomes greater than $100 thousand). We see that while changes in residential stability exert no effect on changes in anti-immigrant hate crime, changes in non-Hispanic white affluence exert a significant negative effect. All else equal, as the percent of white households with incomes greater than $100k increase, the occurrence of hate crime is likely to decrease. At the same time, we see that the effect of changes in the percent of the population that is white remains positive and significant. Taken together the findings suggest that the presence of dominant groups exert differential effects, and may depend on whether the dominance is social or economic. Changes in whiteness appear to increase the likelihood of anti-immigrant hate crime, only insofar as the changes are not among the very wealthy. It may be that the very wealthy live in places with relatively few immigrants or that wealth acts as a buffer against viewing newcomers as threats. Those lower on the economic ladder would thus be less insulated and potentially more likely to perceive immigrants as threatening.

The final model incorporates a measure for change in seasonal employment. As we see, change in seasonal work exerts a significant negative effect on changes in anti-immigrant hate crime. It is possible that seasonal work taps into immigrant concentration, and in this way provides an additional indicator and source of that buffering. The buffering effect of immigration remains across all five models for the overall sample, suggesting that at the place level for the cities and towns included in the sample, immigrant concentration provides a significant measure of protection against victimization. While contrary to the stated hypothesis, this finding is in line with literature on ethnic enclaves, which has tended to show residence therein is associated with reduced levels of violence generally (Sampson, Morenoff, and Raudenbush 2005) and reduced likelihood of violent victimization (Nielsen and Martinez 2006). The results suggest that the immigrant revitalization thesis, by which is meant that immigration encourages new types of social organization, strengthening neighborhood institutions and social ties, and potentially negating criminogenic conditions (Lee, et al. 2001), may be extended to include a physically protective component.

Recent Immigration and Victimization within New Destinations

Whether the buffering effect observed for change in the total foreign-born population is present among those recently arrived remains in question. Table 5.5 presents the results of the fixed effects negative binomial regression of the change in recent foreign-born and other key variables on the change in anti-immigrant hate crime. As with Table 5.4, the base model for change in recent immigrants again shows a significant negative effect on change in the occurrence of hate crime, which is stronger for the recent foreign-born than the total foreign-born population. The effect persists once controls for changes in population structure are imposed, though it is reduced by more than two-thirds. As with the previous analysis, the effect of change in population size and the percent of the population that is male aged 15-29 are not significant. Change in the ratio of adults to children is positive and significant, again indicating that hate crimes are more common in places with large numbers of adults and relatively fewer children. Change in the percent of the population that is non-Hispanic white is positively and significantly correlated with change in anti-immigrant hate crime.

In model 3 we see that changes in residential stability are not significantly correlated with changes in the occurrence of anti-immigrant hate crimes, while changes in non-Hispanic white affluence are positively and significantly so. Unlike the models for the total foreign-born population, however, including controls for changes in the percent of affluent white families reduces the effect of changes in recent foreign-born to nonsignificance. Model 4 incorporates the measure of change in seasonal work, negative and significant at the $p<.01$ level. Again, the results indicate a buffering effect of employment, consistent with research by Lee and Slack, who note that "even partial labor force participation can contribute to the regulation of group behavior and interactions" (2008: 765). This finding suggests perhaps that in places where seasonal work is common, residents may be less likely to view newcomers as threatening.

Table 5.5 Fixed Effects (Within-City) Negative Binomial Regression Models Predicting the Incidence of Anti-Immigrant Hate Crime, 2000-2007, Recent Foreign-Born

	Model 1	Model 2	Model 3	Model 4
Predictors				
Percent Recent Foreign-born	-.129***	-.039*	-.015	-.012
	(.015)	(.016)	(.017)	(.017)
City/Town Population (logged)		-.007	-.005	-.017
		(.041)	(.042)	(.042)
Males Aged 15-29		.007	-.012	-.008
		(.013)	(.016)	(.016)
Adult-Child Ratio		.122**	.180***	.158**
		(.046)	(.050)	(.049)
Percent NH White		.030***	.029***	.029***
		(.002)	(.002)	(.002)
Residential Stability			.030	.028
			(.035)	(.035)
White Wealth			-.020***	-.021***
			(.004)	(.004)
Seasonal Work				-.099**
				(.036)
Intercept	-7.995***	-10.735***	-10.405***	-10.184***
	(.083)	(.555)	(.609)	(.612)
Model Summary Information				
Goodness of Fit (Value/DF)				
Deviance	1.113	1.108	1.113	1.113
Scaled Deviance	1.000	1.000	1.000	1.000
Pearson Chi-Square	1.515	1.437	1.411	1.381
Scaled Pearson X2	1.361	1.297	1.268	1.241
Total Number of Observations ($N \times T$)	846	846	846	846
Total Number of Cities/Towns (N)	423	423	423	423

NOTE: Population neither non-Hispanic white nor non-Hispanic Black (log transformed) used as offset.

†$p<.10$, *$p<.05$, **$p<.01$, ***$p<.001$

It would appear that settlement in relatively affluent cities and towns provides a buffer against hate crime victimization and that the concentration of total foreign-born (which includes older and likely more socially and financially established immigrants) provides a buffer over and above that provided by white affluence. The concentration of recent-foreign-born, however, provides no such buffer, suggesting that recently arrived immigrants who settle in nontraditional areas lacking an established immigrant presence would be more susceptible to victimization than their counterparts in traditional settlement locales, all else being equal. Additionally, as the final three models show, the recent foreign-born are more susceptible to victimizations in places marked by large numbers of adults, relative to children. For change in the recent foreign-born population, results support the hypothesis of no effect on change in anti-immigrant hate crime. Given the results for the total foreign-born population, there is limited support for group threat theory.

Immigration and Victimization within New Destinations

To this point, the results have suggested that *established* immigration may provide a buffer against hate crime victimization. If this is the case, then we would expect that in places where the settlement of foreign-born is a new phenomenon, there should be no buffering effect, either among the recently arrived or the total foreign-born population. To address this question, additional fixed effects analyses were conducted on a subset of new destination places. Table 5.6 presents the results of those analyses for the total foreign-born population. As with the analyses of the full sample of places, the effect of change in immigration within new destinations is negative and significant in the base model, though far less pronounced. Adding controls for changes in population structure, we see a similar pattern as for the overall sample for total foreign-born: change in population size is nonsignificant; change in the adult-child ratio is positive and significant, and change in the percent of the population that is non-Hispanic white is positive and significant. Unlike with the full sample, the effect of change in percent male 15 to 29 is positive and significant. Further, there is no significant buffering effect of immigrant concentration within the new destinations sampled once population controls are imposed.

In model three, we see that change in non-Hispanic white affluence is negatively correlated, as was the case within the full sample. However, changes in residential stability are positively correlated with changes in anti-immigrant hate crimes within new destinations, an effect not present within the full sample. Adding this control reduces the effect of change in the young male population to nonsignificance, indicating that that population may be mobile and unlikely to have established roots in a particular place. It would appear that greater residential stability, typically associated with reductions in traditional forms of crime, is positively associated with biased or hate crime within places experiencing the relatively recent incorporation of immigrants. Consistent with group threat theory and the defended neighborhoods thesis in particular, a likely interpretation is that long-term residents are more invested in their community, with a sense that there is both more to protect and more to be threatened by the arrival of newcomers.

The results of model four do not differ substantively from model three. The effect of changes in seasonal work—negative and significant in the full sample for changes in both total immigrants and the recently arrived—is not significant within new destinations, a finding consistent with the lack of buffering effect associated with immigration in new destinations generally. In the fully specified model, change in anti-immigrant hate crime is predicted by changes in the ratio of adults to children, the percent non-Hispanic white, residential stability, and non-Hispanic white affluence.

To more accurately determine the underlying processes at work with respect to residential stability, the analyses were re-run using the index's constituent parts, percent of households owned and percent of households occupied two years or more. The results (not shown) indicate that it is change in duration of residence, rather than home ownership, that significantly impact the occurrence of anti-immigrant hate crime, suggesting that in new destinations, the recent arrival of immigrants may be a more disorganizing process than in traditional

Table 5.6 Fixed Effects (Within-City) Negative Binomial Regression Models Predicting the Incidence of Anti-Immigrant Hate Crime within New Destinations 2000-2007

Predictors	Model 1	Model 2	Model 3	Model 4
Percent Foreign-born	-.031***	-.009	.003	.003
	(.007)	(.007)	(.008)	(.008)
City/Town Population (logged)		-.078	-.034	-.052
		(.062)	(.063)	(.063)
Males Aged 15-29		-.042*	-.029	-.027
		(.019)	(.024)	(.024)
Adult-Child Ratio		.306***	.430***	.412***
		(.082)	(.087)	(.087)
Percent NH White		.023***	.019***	.019***
		(.004)	(.004)	(.004)
Residential Stability			.141*	.137*
			(.062)	(.063)
White Wealth			-.030***	-.031***
			(.008)	(.008)
Seasonal Work				-.110
				(.070)
Intercept	-7.869***	-9.361***	-9.806***	-9.508***
	(.122)	(.900)	(.913)	(.930)
Model Summary Information				
Goodness of Fit (Value/DF)				
Deviance	1.097	1.093	1.103	1.103
Scaled Deviance	1.000	1.000	1.000	1.000
Pearson Chi-Square	1.492	1.400	1.407	1.384
Scaled Pearson X2	1.360	1.281	1.276	1.255
Total Number of Observations ($N \times T$)	346	346	346	346
Total Number of Cities/Towns (N)	173	173	173	173

NOTE: Population neither non-Hispanic white nor non-Hispanic Black (log transformed) used as offset.

† $p<.10$, *$p<.05$, **$p<.01$, ***$p<.001$

receiving areas. Moreover, in new destinations, immigrants may be perceived by the local population as representing a threat, particularly among those who have resided in the community for a longer period of time, and who may be thought of as being more invested in the community, and thus more likely to perceive both risk and threat.

Finally, Table 5.7 presents the results for the change in recent foreign-born within the sub-sample of new destinations. With one exception, the pattern of results is virtually identical to those obtained for changes in the total foreign-born population. In model two, we see that change in the recent foreign-born population is moderately positive significant, indicating that—without controls for socioeconomic conditions or employment—increases in the recent foreign-born population are associated with increases in the occurrence of anti-immigrant hate crime, significant at the $p<.10$ level. Controlling for changes in residential stability and non-Hispanic white affluence,

Table 5.7   Fixed Effects (Within-City) Negative Binomial Regression Models Predicting the Incidence of Anti-Immigrant Hate Crime within New Destinations 2000-2007, Recent Foreign-Born

Predictors	Model 1	Model 2	Model 3	Model 4
Percent Recent Foreign-born	-.093***	.039†	.000	.001
	(.022)	(.022)	(.024)	(.024)
City/Town Population (logged)		-.081	-.036	-.053
		(.062)	(.063)	(.063)
Males Aged 15-29		-.038*	-.029	-.028
		(.019)	(.024)	(.024)
Adult-Child Ratio		.314***	.431***	.413***
		(.082)	(.087)	(.087)
Percent NH White		.022***	.019***	.019***
		(.004)	(.004)	(.004)
Residential Stability			.140*	.135*
			(.063)	(.063)
White Wealth			-.029***	-.030***
			(.008)	(.008)
Seasonal Work				-.109
				(.070)
Intercept	-7.856***	-9.301***	-9.724***	-9.421***
	(.127)	(.887)	(.903)	(.921)
Model Summary Information				
Goodness of Fit (Value/DF)				
Deviance	1.098	1.092	1.101	1.101
Scaled Deviance	1.000	1.000	1.000	1.000
Pearson Chi-Square	1.411	1.384	1.401	1.379
Scaled Pearson X2	1.285	1.268	1.273	1.253
Total Number of Observations (N x T)	346	346	346	346
Total Number of Cities/Towns (N)	173	173	173	173

NOTE: Population neither non-Hispanic white nor non-Hispanic Black (log transformed) used as offset.

† $p<.10$, *$p<.05$, **$p<.01$, ***$p<.001$

however, reduces the effect to almost nothing. Results of the fully specified model are virtually identical to those obtained for the total foreign-born population within new destinations. For both populations, the results do not conform to the hypothesis, which predicted positive and significant correlations between change in immigrant population and change in anti-immigrant hate crime.

The results thus far suggest somewhat divergent patterns for the effect of change in immigration, depending on whether the immigrants are recently arrived and on where they settle one here. Within the full sample, we see a buffering effect of change in total immigration on change in anti-immigrant hate crime victimization, but no such effect for change in recent immigration. The findings suggests that older and more established immigrants may provide a source of protection for new waves, perhaps by providing welcoming places in which to live and work, an idea consistent with research on ethnic enclaves (Portes and Zhou 1993; Sampson, Morenoff, and Raudenbush 2005; Sampson and Bean 2006; Velez 2006). Alternatively, the results could suggest that older immigrants may "pave the way" for new arrivals by, in a sense, "priming" native-born residents, such that new immigrants are perceived as less of a threat. Within the subset of new destinations, however, there is no buffering effect, either for changes in total immigration or the recently arrived. In areas where the presence of foreign-born is a new phenomenon, the occurrence of anti-immigrant hate crime is predicated largely upon change in the ratio of adults to children, and to a lesser degree, change in the presence of *socially* dominant group members.

A concern with the analyses presented to this point is in the effect of comparisons across uneven years and thus uneven pooled counts. As discussed, the preceding analyses were based upon a dataset construction that sought the largest sample possible, given the lack of generalizability inherent in fixed-effects regression techniques. While the results do not differ substantively whether a pooled total count or the yearly average of hate crime incidence is used as the dependent variable, further analyses were conducted using only the cases for which total crime data is available, that is, full hate crime reporting for the years 1999-2001 and 2005-2007. This additional restriction greatly reduces the sample sizes, essentially cutting them by half, leaving *n=205* for total places, and *n=72* for the new destination subset.[68]

As we see from the univariate results presented in Table 5.8, this second set of places for which full hate crime data are available tends to have, on average, cities and towns with larger populations, greater shares of total and recent foreign-born and slightly higher shares of non-Hispanic whites. They also experienced more hate crimes, on average. The results of Table 5.9 indicate that the differences between the two sets of new destinations are not as great, though again the places in this second set have, on average, about 20 thousand more residents.

Where this second set differs dramatically is in its coverage of the population groups at interest. As we see from Table 5.10, this second set contains roughly half the places of the first set, and with that, covers about half of each key demographic: the place-level population wherein a hate crime occurred, total and recent-foreign-born, and only a fraction of the total U.S. population. Particularly because a fixed effects analysis is not generalizable beyond the units under study, this lack of coverage is perhaps particularly troubling, and any interpretation of results from these analyses must be made with caution. That said, the issue at hand—a dearth of solid criminological data—is not new and should not prevent the careful and cautious analysis of the sound data that are available. In the presentation and interpretation of results to follow, however, readers should bear in mind these data limitations and be cautious to avoid interpolating to all other cities and towns.

Table 5.11 presents the results of the analysis of places with full data for the total foreign-born population. Similar to the analyses using imbalanced data, model one indicates a significant negative buffering effect of the change in percent foreign-born on change in anti-immigrant hate crime. However, once controlling for changes in population structure, and specifically the percent of the population that is non-Hispanic white, that buffering effect disappears. In model 3 we see that, as with broader sampling method, the effect of change in the adult-child ratio is positive and significant, while change in white affluence is negatively so. In model 4, change in seasonal work is not

---

[68] See Tables A4a and A4b in Appendix A for sample coverage and exclusions profiles.

Table 5.8 Profile of Places with Fully Compliant Data in Hate Crime Analyses

	2000		2005-2007		Within-Place Change	
	Mean	Std Dev	Mean	Std Dev	Mean[1]	Std Dev
Total Population	184,712	364,415	194,821	366,637	10,108	23,894
Percent Foreign-Born	16.73	11.39	18.45	11.45	1.72	2.19
Percent Recent Foreign-Born	4.01	2.74	4.61	2.81	0.60	1.13
Percent White	62.47	20.86	58.60	21.23	-3.87	3.52
Percent Male Aged 15-29	11.72	3.56	12.04	3.57	0.32	1.32
Adult-Child Ratio	3.24	1.38	3.40	1.22	0.16	0.42
Residential Stability	0.00	1.74	0.00	1.76	0.00	0.48
Pct of Households Owner-Occupied	58.72	13.17	59.77	12.55	1.05	2.71
Pct of Households Occupied 2 years or more	76.34	6.51	76.45	6.43	0.11	2.38
Percent of White Households with Income Greater than $100k	17.01	9.37	25.76	11.55	8.75	3.94
Percent Seasonal Occupations	0.36	0.61	0.34	0.69	-0.02	0.30
Total Count of Anti-Immigrant Offenses	9.90	35.28	6.10	14.63	-3.80	23.31
	n = 205		*n = 205*		*n = 205*	

[1] Within-place change is calculated by subtracting the mean value for Time 1 from the mean value for Time 2. As such, positive values indicate, on average, an increase over time while negative values represent a decrease.

Table 5.9 Profile of New Destinations with Fully Compliant Data Included in Hate Crime Analyses

	2000		2005-2007		Within-Place Change	
	Mean	Std Dev	Mean	Std Dev	Mean[1]	Std Dev
Total Population	174,696	179,183	187,553	191,159	12,857	20,906
Percent Foreign-Born	12.94	8.67	15.05	9.22	2.11	2.10
Percent Recent Foreign-Born	4.54	2.82	5.29	2.99	0.76	1.36
Percent White	67.49	18.52	64.24	18.87	-3.25	3.32
Percent Male Aged 15-29	13.96	4.76	13.99	4.84	0.03	1.22
Adult-Child Ratio	3.47	1.01	3.64	1.09	0.17	0.32
Residential Stability	-1.00	1.76	-1.05	1.66	-0.05	0.49
Pct of Households Owner-Occupied	53.49	11.87	54.56	11.05	1.07	2.78
Pct of Households Occupied 2 years or more	72.42	7.19	72.39	6.61	-0.03	2.36
Percent of White Households with Income Greater than $100k	13.43	6.76	20.57	8.44	7.14	3.15
Percent Seasonal Occupations	0.28	0.36	0.28	0.51	-0.01	0.25
Total Count of Anti-Immigrant Offenses	8.22	19.14	6.22	12.84	-2.00	8.82
	n = 72		n = 72		n = 72	

[1] Within-place change is calculated by subtracting the mean value for Time 1 from the mean value for Time 2. As such, positive values indicate, on average, an increase over time while negative values represent a decrease.

Table 5.10 Difference in Means Between New Destination and Overall Samples, Fully Compliant Data

	2000	2005-2007	Within-Place Change
	Mean Difference[1]	Mean Difference[1]	Mean Difference[1]
Total Population	-10,016	-7,268	2,748
Percent Foreign-Born	-3.79	-3.40	0.39
Percent Recent Foreign-Born	0.53	0.69	0.16
Percent White	5.02	5.64	0.62
Percent Male Aged 15-29	2.24	1.95	-0.29
Adult-Child Ratio	0.23	0.25	0.01
Residential Stability	-1.00	-1.05	-0.05
Pct of Households Owner-Occupied	-5.23	-5.21	0.02
Pct of Households Occupied 2 years or more	-3.93	-4.06	-0.14
Percent of White Households with Income Greater than $100k	-3.59	-5.20	-1.61
Percent Seasonal Occupations	-0.08	-0.06	0.02
Total Count of Anti-Immigrant Offenses	-1.68	0.12	1.80

[1] Difference is calculated by subtracting the mean value for the overall sample from the mean value for the new destination subsample. As such, negative values indicate, on average and relative to the overall sample, a smaller share of a given variable within new destinations

significant, nor does its inclusion substantively mediate any of the results obtained in the previous model. For places with fully specified data, the strongest significant predictor of anti-immigrant hate crime is change in the percent non-Hispanic white and the percent of white households with income greater than $100 thousand, with a moderately significant effect of change in the ratio of adults to children. The key difference here from the broader sample is the lack of a buffering effect of change in immigration on change in anti-immigrant hate crime.

Table 5.11 Fixed Effects (Within-City) Negative Binomial Regression Models Predicting the Incidence of Anti-Immigrant Hate Crime, 2000-2007, Full Data Compliance

Predictors	Model 1	Model 2	Model 3	Model 4
Percent Foreign-born	-.037***	-.001	.006	.007
	(.005)	(.006)	(.006)	(.006)
City/Town Population (logged)		-.022	-.011	-.024
		(.053)	(.056)	(.057)
Males Aged 15-29		-.002	-.009	-.008
		(.017)	(.021)	(.021)
Adult-Child Ratio		.059	.126*	.110†
		(.053)	(.061)	(.061)
Percent NH White		.034***	.034***	.033***
		(.004)	(.004)	(.004)
Residential Stability			.050	.043
			(.047)	(.047)
White Wealth			-.021***	-.022***
			(.005)	(.005)
Seasonal Work				-.103
				(.074)
Intercept	-7.856***	-10.541***	-10.495***	-10.250***
	(.109)	(.783)	(.879)	(.897)
Model Summary Information				
Goodness of Fit (Value/DF)				
Deviance	1.124	1.099	1.107	1.109
Scaled Deviance	1.000	1.000	1.000	1.000
Pearson Chi-Square	1.700	1.493	1.460	1.444
Scaled Pearson X2	1.512	1.359	1.320	1.302
Total Number of Observations (N x T)	410	410	410	410
Total Number of Cities/Towns (N)	205	205	205	205

NOTE: Population neither non-Hispanic white nor non-Hispanic Black (log transformed) used as offset.
† *p<.10 , *p<.05, **p<.01, ***p<.001*

When the models are run using change in the recent foreign-born population, rather than showing no effect, as with the analyses using the broader sample, the results presented in Table 5.12 indicate a moderately significant *positive* effect, at the *p<.10* level, of change in recent foreign-born on change in the occurrence of anti-immigrant hate crime, with the relationships between change in percent white, change in non-Hispanic white affluence, and change in the adult-child ratio remaining essentially unchanged from the results for the total foreign-born. The results here do not conform to the expectation of a null effect. With respect to group threat theory, a moderately positive effect for the recent foreign-born, coupled with a null effect for the total immigrant population may suggest that native-born residents are able to disaggregate the foreign-born. That is, older, more established immigrants may be less likely to be viewed as threatening, while those arriving most recently are more likely to be cast as threats and more ikely to be victimized for it.

Given the patterns observed in the analysis of the broader sample, the results here suggest that in new destinations, where total hate crime data are reported, we would expect to see a similarly positive effect of change in immigration—whether in total or among those recently arrived—on change in the occurrence of anti-immigrant hate crime.

Table 5.12 Fixed Effects (Within-City) Negative Binomial Regression Models Predicting the Incidence of Anti-Immigrant Hate Crime, 2000-2007, Recent Foreign-Born, Full Data Compliance

	Model 1	Model 2	Model 3	Model 4
Predictors				
Percent Recent Foreign-born	-.103***	.004	.039†	.039†
	(.021)	(.021)	(.023)	(.023)
City/Town Population (logged)		-.020	-.009	-.022
		(.053)	(.056)	(.057)
Males Aged 15-29		-.002	-.013	-.012
		(.016)	(.021)	(.021)
Adult-Child Ratio		.053	.130*	.115†
		(.052)	(.060)	(.060)
Percent NH White		.034***	.033***	.033***
		(.003)	(.003)	(.003)
Residential Stability			.069	.062
			(.049)	(.049)
White Wealth			-.023***	-.024***
			(.006)	(.006)
Seasonal Work				-0.1004
				(.074)
Intercept	-8.037***	-10.637***	-10.508***	-10.255***
	(.116)	(.734)	(.850)	(.871)
Model Summary Information				
Goodness of Fit (Value/DF)				
Deviance	1.141	1.100	1.106	1.109
Scaled Deviance	1.000	1.000	1.000	1.000
Pearson Chi-Square	1.769	1.512	1.445	1.426
Scaled Pearson X2	1.551	1.374	1.306	1.286
Total Number of Observations ($N \times T$)	410	410	410	410
Total Number of Cities/Towns (N)	205	205	205	205

NOTE: Population neither non-Hispanic white nor non-Hispanic Black (log transformed) used as offset.

$^\dagger p<.10$, *$p<.05$, **$p<.01$, ***$p<.001$

Table 5.13 offers the results of the fixed effects negative binomial regression analysis of new destinations with full data for total foreign-born. In model one, without controls for change in the population structure, the effect of change in the percent foreign-born is nonsignificant. Once such controls are imposed, we see that change in foreign-born is moderately and positively significant at the $p<.10$ level in model two and at the $p<.05$ level in model four. Moreover, while the suppressive effect of change in non-Hispanic white affluence is still significant within new destinations, it is slightly mediated. Within this smaller set of new destinations, it appears that increases in the foreign-born population results in increases in the incidence of anti-immigrant hate crime, controlling for relevant factors. The results here are consistent with the guiding hypothesis and offer support to theories of group threat in their explanation for violent victimization of minority groups.

Table 5.13 Fixed Effects (Within-City) Negative Binomial Regression Models Predicting the Incidence of Anti-Immigrant Hate Crime within New Destinations 2000-2007, Full Data Compliance

	Model 1	Model 2	Model 3	Model 4
Predictors				
Percent Foreign-born	-.019	.019[†]	.028*	.028*
	(.012)	(.012)	(.013)	(.013)
City/Town Population (logged)		-.021	.018	.004
		(.109)	(.112)	(.114)
Males Aged 15-29		-.028	-.011	-.012
		(.031)	(.042)	(.042)
Adult-Child Ratio		.218	.400**	.391*
		(.136)	(.155)	(.156)
Percent NH White		.039***	.032***	.032***
		(.007)	(.007)	(.007)
Residential Stability			.161	.150
			(.106)	(.108)
White Wealth			-.030*	-.031*
			(.014)	(.014)
Seasonal Work				-.142
				(.218)
Intercept	-7.919***	-11.32***	-11.668***	-11.441***
	(.205)	(1.696)	(1.805)	(1.845)
Model Summary Information				
Goodness of Fit (Value/DF)				
Deviance	1.145	1.127	1.161	1.170
Scaled Deviance	1.000	1.000	1.000	1.000
Pearson Chi-Square	1.654	1.370	1.604	1.611
Scaled Pearson X2	1.445	1.215	1.381	1.377
Total Number of Observations ($N \times T$)	144	144	144	144
Total Number of Cities/Towns (N)	72	72	72	72

NOTE: Population neither non-Hispanic white nor non-Hispanic Black (log transformed) used as offset.
[†] $p<.10$, *$p<.05$, **$p<.01$, ***$p<.001$

Finally, looking at the effect of change in the recent foreign-born population (Table 5.14), we see a similar pattern whereby, once controlling for change in population structure, namely the ratio of adults to children and the non-Hispanic white population, and change in socioeconomic conditions, the effect of change in the recent foreign-born is positive and moderately significant. The findings for this limited sample are somewhat consistent with theoretical expectations. Further, comparing the results for new destinations to the 205 places for which full data are available seems to suggest that while in the larger sample, residents may be able to make distinctions between new and established immigrants, within new destinations, no such distinctions are made, as the change within each group of immigrants is positively correlated with the occurrence of anti-immigrant hate crime.

Table 5.14 Fixed Effects (Within-City) Negative Binomial Regression Models Predicting the Incidence of Anti-Immigrant Hate Crime within New Destinations 2000-2007, Recent Foreign-Born, Full Data Compliance

	Model 1	Model 2	Model 3	Model 4
Predictors				
Percent Recent Foreign-born	-.062	.052	.083*	.082†
	(.038)	(.038)	(.042)	(.042)
City/Town Population (logged)		-.027	.014	-.001
		(.109)	(.112)	(.114)
Males Aged 15-29		-.038	-.025	-.025
		(.031)	(.043)	(.043)
Adult-Child Ratio		.228†	.414**	.404*
		(.135)	(.155)	(.157)
Percent NH White		.037***	.031***	.031***
		(.007)	(.007)	(.007)
Residential Stability			.164	.152
			(.106)	(.108)
White Wealth			-.030*	-.030*
			(.014)	(.014)
Seasonal Work				-.158
				(.219)
Intercept	-7.889***	-11.029***	-11.398***	-11.159***
	(.224)	(1.671)	(1.780)	(1.817)
Model Summary Information				
Goodness of Fit (Value/DF)				
Deviance	1.145	1.124	1.153	1.162
Scaled Deviance	1.000	1.000	1.000	1.000
Pearson Chi-Square	1.588	1.377	1.553	1.561
Scaled Pearson X2	1.387	1.226	1.347	1.344
Total Number of Observations ($N \times T$)	144	144	144	144
Total Number of Cities/Towns (N)	72	72	72	72

NOTE: Population neither non-Hispanic white nor non-Hispanic Black (log transformed) used as offset.

† *p<.10*, *p<.05*, **p<.01*, ***p<.001*

DISCUSSION AND CONCLUSIONS

This chapter has sought to contribute to the discussion of immigrant victimization by providing a systematic analysis of the effect of changes in immigration on the occurrence of anti-immigrant hate crime. In doing so, the research helps to clarify the extension of group threat theory to the minority group, "immigrant," by addressing the question of whether change in immigrant population size translates to change in immigrant victimization. Analyses were conducted for the total and recent foreign-born populations within a broad sample of places and a subset of new destinations. To avoid methodological concerns and compensate for questionable data, these analyses were repeated on smaller samples for which full hate crime data were available. For the period under study, 2000-2007, results conservatively indicate that changes in immigration exert no effect on the occurrence of immigrant hate crime victimization, and suggest that increasing immigration may in fact contribute to increased victimization.

The results of the primary analyses, using broader inclusion criterion, suggest divergent patterns for the effect of changes in immigration, depending on whether the immigrants are recently arrived and on where they settle one here. The finding of a buffering effect for change in the foreign-born population within the total sample, but not for change in the recent foreign-born, and not within new destinations suggest that older and more established immigrant settlement areas provide a source of protection for new waves, perhaps by providing welcoming places in which to live and work, an idea consistent with research on ethnic enclaves (Sampson and Bean 2006; Velez 2006; Sampson, Morenoff, and Raudenbush 2005; Portes and Zhou 1993). Alternatively, the results could suggest that older immigrants may "pave the way" for new arrivals by, in a sense, "priming" native-born residents, such that new immigrants are perceived as less of a threat. Within the subset of new destinations, however, there is no buffering effect, either for changes in total immigration or the recently arrived. These results provide limited support for group threat theory, and suggest that the arrival of foreign-born may not pose quite the threat to the native-born population as was hypothesized, at least not at the level of city and town.

Given the sampling criteria, however, the results of the primary analyses are in a sense more conservative in their findings and applicability. In contrast, the results of the second analysis, while perhaps more striking, are based upon a small sample of places and arrived at by statistical analyses that cautions against generalizing to the broader universe of places. The results obtained using full data conform to theoretical expectations and provide evidence in support of group threat theory. While the samples are small and fundamentally not generalizable, the results suggest that increasing immigration to the places covered contributes to increased immigrant victimization when the immigrant population is recent and when immigrants—new and established—settle in nontraditional destinations. These results are consistent with the limited extant research investigating the effect of internal minority group population shifts on victimization (Shihadeh and Barranco 2013; Shihadeh and Winters 2010) and consistent with research on group threat theory that suggests a positive link (Green Strolovich and Wong 1998; King and Wheelock 2007; Semyonov, Raijman, and Gorodzeisky 2006).

Ultimately, what we can say conservatively is that within the majority of places wherein a hate crime occurred between 1999 and 2007, increasing immigration presented a buffer to hate crime victimization, a buffer that was absent among the recent foreign-born and absent as well within places where immigrant settlement is a new phenomenon. More simply perhaps, the change in foreign-born at best provides a buffer against anti-immigrant hate crime, and at worst exerts no effect. These results are in line with research on immigration and crime generally. As that research has tended to show either a null or suppressive effect of immigration on crime, these analyses have merely extended those results in a somewhat unexpected direction. More provocatively, the results have shown that in a subset of those places— the ones for which complete hate crime data are available for the six years of pooled data—the change in foreign-born at best exerts no effect, and at worst results in increased anti-immigrant hate crimes.

Finally, the conflicting results regarding changes in percent white and non-Hispanic white affluence warrant discussion. In areas where the presence of foreign-born is a new phenomenon, the occurrence of anti-immigrant hate crime is predicated upon change in the presence of *socially* dominant group members. Given the negative correlation between white affluence and hate crime incidence, however, the findings are somewhat complex and require a degree of deconstructing what is meant by *dominance*. In their work on social dominance theory (SDT), Sidanius and Pratto (1999) suggest that group-based social hierarchies are stratified according to three primary systems: age, gender, and what the authors call the *arbitrary-set* system.[69] While the first two systems tend to be fairly universal in their presence both geographically and historically, the characteristics contained within the arbitrary-set system are far more variable, depending on societal histories, cultures, and available resources, among other factors. Within U.S. society, the ideal type dominant group member for many might be a wealthy white male. While such a person may be thought of as embodying dominance, it is important to note that his dominance is predicated on the possession of three distinct characteristics, each of which operates within its own socially constructed hierarchy: whiteness, financial wealth, and male gender.

To the degree that immigrants possess characteristics ranking them lower within these social hierarchies, they may be perceived as threats. With regard to anti-immigrant hate crime, the results suggest that membership and location within the racial and financial hierarchies exert differential effects. While whiteness alone is associated with increased anti-immigrant hate crime, white affluence is associated with reductions in such crimes. It may be that wealth provides insulation from perceptions of immigrants as threats. Financial security may prevent persons from direct competition with the majority of immigrants, and thus the threat to jobs and income would be reduced. Alternatively, financial security may provide a geographical barrier to direct interaction with the majority of immigrants, such that the threat is never really perceptible at all. Finally, there may be a sort of additive effect of multiple dominant group membership, such that while wealthy whites could be threatened in terms of racial dominance, they feel a sense of protected position owing to financial security. In contrast, whites lacking the same financial security have only their dominance within the racial hierarchy, to which the presence of immigrants—to the degree that they are nonwhite—would perhaps pose a more visible and direct threat.

---

[69] According to the authors, the characteristics that can be found in the arbitrary set include, "clan, ethnicity, estate, nation, race, caste, social class, religious sect, regional grouping, or any other socially relevant group distinction that the human imagination is capable of constructing" (Sidanius and Pratto 1999: 33).

Rather than answers borne out by data, the notorious holes on those data have left us with more questions. Is the positive effect of change in immigration a product of the types of places from which full data is available? Are the police departments in these places more likely to record hate crimes and then report their records to the FBI? Is it a product of the larger population size—in the form of a greater mix of diverse peoples, or perhaps more diverse police forces? The well-known issues surrounding data on crime are perhaps exacerbated when it comes to hate crime. With traditional crime, the so-called holes in the data are often due to a lack of reporting on behalf of the victim, for fear of retribution, a lack of awareness of rights or the process of making complaints, a sense that such efforts would be futile, or a mistrust of law enforcement. When the criminal act is actually reported, the legal definitions are such that there is relatively little ambiguity in determining *which type* of crime has occurred. What remains is whether or not the reporting process will accurately be relayed up the law enforcement hierarchy. With hate crime, however, while the same issues regarding failure to report are still present—and given the nature of the crime, particularly against immigrants, the concerns are somewhat intensified—there are additional concerns as well. Despite existing legal statutes, there remain both ambiguity and subjectivity as to whether a particular crime was—in the eyes of law enforcement and, in turn, the courts—in fact motivated by a sense of bias or hate on the part of the perpetrator. Furthermore, the categories into which a particular hate crime may be sorted are still somewhat limited. While strides have been made in recent years, certainly with the inclusion of biases against sexual orientation, the presence of only one category of national origin, Hispanic, with all other such offenses lumped into a generalized "other" category, is troubling. Implications of these questions and the findings presented throughout are discussed in greater details in the next chapter.

CHAPTER 6

Conclusions

OVERVIEW

The preceding chapters have sought to address the broad question of whether immigration exerts a significant effect on crime. As has been discussed, the topic of immigration has received considerable attention over the last few decades, among academic researchers, politicians, and the general public. The opening chapter sought to distill dominant themes in the discourse surrounding immigration. Most notably, evidence was offered to suggest that for many Americans, the contemporary process of immigration is conceptually tied to fears over native-born job loss, an undermining of traditional ways of life, and in particular, threats of crime and violence. The conceptual linking of immigration to these social ills has in large measure contributed to the passage of a series of restrictionist immigration policies over the last two decades. In the most ironic of twists, researchers have suggested that the outcome of such policies—rather than the curbing of immigrant inflows—has been to catalyze its dispersion from regional concern to national phenomenon.

A second consequence has been the nullification or marginalization of the findings of social research. As Chapter 2 sought to show, over the last two decades, scientific analyses of the link between immigration and crime have largely failed to demonstrate a positive correlation and have often indeed found a suppressive effect of the former on the latter. At the individual level, studies have consistently found immigrants and their and second generation American children—to be less likely to engage in crime than their native-born counterparts. At aggregate levels, research has tended to show that the process of immigration does not significantly result in increased rates of crime, casting a seed of doubt on the disorganizing qualities of mass migration. Yet the perception that immigration begets crime remains a salient feature of political and public discourse. It is out of this contradiction that the current research has developed.

The literature on immigration and crime has grown rather dramatically in recent years, yet there remain a number of substantive questions regarding the nature of the relationship. This research has sought to both refine and extend our understanding of it. The analyses presented in Chapter 4 were designed to test whether the patterns observed in existing research at either the neighborhood or metropolitan level were similar to those at the place level for traditional forms of crime. Additionally, by focusing on change over time, these analyses could more accurately isolate potential effects of immigration on crime. While these results offer a refinement of knowledge, the analysis of the effect of immigration on hate crime, presented in Chapter 5, and the analysis of the effects within new destinations, presented in both Chapters 4 and 5, sought to extend the discussion and in particular establish new lines of inquiry.

This final chapter will provide a review of the major analytical findings offered in the preceding pages. It will highlight the key contributions this study offers to the larger bodies of research, and discuss the implications these findings have for the study of immigration and theories of social disorganization, community resource, and group threat. Following this review, a number of empirical and conceptual limitations of the current study will be discussed. As these limitations offer fertile ground for continued investigation, recommendations will be offered for avenues of future research. Finally, this chapter will put results of this work into context by discussing the broader implications the findings may have for the larger immigration-crime debate.

Review of Research Findings

Much research has developed in recent years around the topic of immigration and crime; this study sought to build on that work in three key areas. First, the analyses sought to refine our understanding of the effect of immigration on traditional crime. This was done by extending analysis to the place-level and by focusing on change-over-time. Second, the analyses sought to bring into the discussion the issue of crime against immigrants, a focus underrepresented in the criminological literature, by testing for effects of change in immigration on change in anti-immigrant hate crime. Finally, this work sought to incorporate recent research on new destinations, by testing whether the effect of immigration on crime varies by a place's history of immigrant reception. In the following discussion, the major findings of each of these areas are reviewed.

<u>Immigration and Traditional Crime</u>
To date, studies of the connection between immigration and crime have tended to focus on either the neighborhood level or the metropolitan statistical area. Important contributions have come from each approach, but neither is without its limitations. While neighborhood level research can far more accurately account for the variations and complexities within both the foreign-born population and rates of crime, its view can also sometimes miss the larger structural forces, such as labor market conditions, impinging on both. Similarly, while analyses of metropolitan areas are more capable of capturing the effects of large-scale social processes, they tend to subsume important demographic, economic, and criminological variations, at times making too homogenous areas that may very well be distinct. This research sought a middle ground of sorts: the place level. By looking at cities and towns, rather than metro areas or neighborhoods, this research is able to capture important aspects of each view and provide additional insight into the role of place.

In addition to focusing on the place level, this study drew from an under-utilized source of demographic data: the American Community Survey, specifically its 2005-2007 three-year product. In general, the benefit of this relatively new data source is that it essentially provides the breadth of decennial census data at far more frequent intervals. In particular, the 2005-2007 three year product has the added benefit of largely precluding the mediating forces of the global economic crisis, to which subsequent versions, and even the 2010 decennial census to a degree, would be prone.

Lastly, this study sought to refine our understanding of immigration and traditional crime by analyzing within-unit change-over-time, a method which in many ways allows the analysis of non-experimental data to achieve some of the virtues of experimental designs. Particularly because this analysis is conducted at the city or town level for a national sample of places, the ability to control for unmeasured time-invariant differences between the units is key. Rates of immigration and crime vary geographically and are differentially impacted by federal, state, and local policies, employment structures, and economic conditions, which themselves vary geographically. Within units, however, such sociopolitical determinants are likely to be much more uniform, particularly in the relatively brief period under study, allowing this research to more accurately isolate the potential effects of immigration on crime.

The analyses presented in Chapter 4 sought to address whether *change* in immigration exerts significant effects on *change* in rates of overall, violent, and property crime for 1,252 places over the years 2000-2007. Drawing from the existing literature, it was hypothesized that change in immigration would exert a significant negative effect within the full sample of places. In contrast, however, results indicate no significant effect of change in immigration on change in rates of crime, whether violent, property, or total. Further, results indicate that duration of U.S. residence as well exerts no significant effects; neither change in the total foreign-born population nor change in the subset of those arriving in the previous five years was significantly correlated with change in crime.

The results of the analyses of traditional crime do not conform to expectations laid out by social disorganization theory. While they also failed to conform to the stated hypotheses, they are consistent with the results of previous research (Feldmeyer 2009; Ousey and Kubrin 2009; Reid, et al. 2005; Butcher and Piehl 1998) and demonstrate support for the community resource perspective.

With respect to the total foreign-born population, the analyses of overall, violent, and property crime rates (Tables 4.5-4.7, respectively) failed to show a significant effect of change in immigrant concentration, whether direct—nonsignificant despite controlling for additional key factors—or indirect—nonsignificant once additional controls were added to the models. This lack of effect, particularly through socioeconomic disadvantage or residential stability, is at odds with the traditional view of immigration as disorganizing. According to social disorganization theory, growth in a community's population of persons speaking different languages, holding different traditions and cultural norms, and possessing varied human and social capitals should operate as a locally disorganizing force, undermining the existing informal mechanisms by which social behavior is regulated.

The strongest predictors of change in crime among the total foreign-born population were change in disadvantage (positive and significant) and change in population size (negative and significant), with a slight positive effect of the change in the ratio of adults to children on change in overall and property crime rates. This pattern is virtually identical to those obtained when change in the recent foreign-born population is the independent variable.

The results thus offer a modicum of support for the community resource perspective. According to this view, increasing immigration to an area can provide newcomers with a range of benefits to mediate against negative socioeconomic and sociopolitical forces, such as poverty, lack of opportunity, blocked opportunity, undervalued skills, and racism. For the most recent arrivals, as well as those already established in the community, immigrant concentration can reinforce traditional cultural norms, strengthen family and kinship ties, operate as a source of information to help orient new arrivals and direct them toward resources such as housing, employment, education, and social aid.

The perspective also acknowledges that not all immigrant communities are able to so assist their members, and those that can do so to varying degrees. Thus the finding of no effect of change in immigration on any of the three crime rates may be interpreted as immigrant concentration simply providing a buffer against traditionally criminogenic forces, enabling residents to be no more criminally active than their native-born counterparts. Alternatively, as the nature of the fixed effects analytical technique is to average within-unit differences across the entire sample, we may interpret these findings as a sort of "differencing out": while some communities in the sample offer relief to their members, others may not, but on the whole, across the 1,250 places sampled and the period under study—the bulk of the previous decade, prior to the economic recession—increasing immigration is not associated with increasing (or decreasing) criminality. These results contribute to the growing literature suggesting that the old disorganization view, grounded in the experiences of largely European immigrants settling into a less-pluralistic social landscape and finding employment within a still-industrial American economy, may not apply to the new waves of immigrants, who differ in important ways and who settle in a country dramatically different than the one encountered by those who came a century ago. The findings offered here build on work acknowledging such differences, though as will be discussed, they are not without their limitations.

Immigration and Biased Crime

A significant aim of this research was also to extend our understanding of the immigration-crime nexus by incorporating a focus on immigrant victimization. Few studies to date have investigated whether and to what degree the process of immigration results in increased crime against the foreign-born. In large part, the research that exists has drawn from qualitative interviews and the experiences of immigrant victims. While those studies have offered important contributions, the current research provides one of the first large-scale longitudinal analyses of immigrant victimization. As discussed in Chapter 1, the issue of immigrant victimization is of growing importance, as immigrants spread to newer areas of the country and at a time when much of the prevailing rhetoric posits their arrival as a threat.

Our understanding of the mechanisms by which immigration may contribute to immigrant victimization is still in its infancy, and as yet there is no well-developed theory to guide research. However, as the discussion in Chapter 2 sought to show, scholarly work in the area of group threat theory—traditionally applied to the residential movement of Blacks, and subsequently Latinos, in relation to whites—offers a sound base from which to draw expectations for foreign-born populations.

According to the extant research on group threat theory, as members of racial and ethnic minority groups move into areas populated primarily by members of dominant groups, the newcomers are likely to be met with conflict. Opposition, the findings suggest, is a product of the size of the incoming population—perceived and actual—and the existing economic conditions. Regarding the latter, scholars have noted that opposition increases during times of economic distress, at the individual level and particularly in the aggregate. Newcomers essentially provide a ready and easily identifiable scapegoat, whose arrival, at least for the preexisting populace, explains larger troublesome circumstances.

The analyses presented in Chapter 5 were designed to help clarify the extension of group threat theory to the minority group "immigrant" by addressing the question of whether increases in immigrant population size translate to increases in immigrant victimization. The dominant group was conceptualized as the population of native-born whites. Due in part to data constraints but also to differing key theoretical mechanisms, the independent variable was operationalized as the percent of the population that is foreign-born (and recent foreign-born), rather than an index of immigrant concentration, as was the case for the analyses of traditional crime. While there may be good reasons that an additional benefit of concentration is to insulate members from attack by outsiders, the concern here has been at a more fundamental level: whether the arrival of foreign-born persons triggers retaliation by the native-born population. Controlling instead for concentration would have incorporated potentially confounding forces, in effect testing whether the community resource perspective buffers against victimization, rather than whether presence engenders victimization.

As with traditional crime, analyses were conducted for the total and recent foreign-born populations within a broad sample of places across the U.S. To avoid methodological concerns and compensate for questionable data, these analyses were repeated within a smaller sample for which full hate crime data were available. For the period under study, 2000-2007, results conservatively indicate that changes in immigration exert no effect on the occurrence of immigrant hate crime victimization, and suggest that increasing immigration may in fact contribute to increased victimization.

The results of the primary analyses, using broader inclusion criterion of either two *or* three years of hate crime data summed for each time point, suggest divergent patterns for the effect of change in immigration on change in anti-immigrant hate crime, depending on when the immigrants arrived. Change in the percent of total foreign-born persons is negatively and significantly associated with change in the occurrence of anti-immigrant hate crime, a finding consistent across all four models of the analysis, controlling for a range of conceptually key predictors. In contrast, when the analyses were run using instead the percent of the population that is recently arrived foreign-born, the change in that population, while still negatively correlated, dropped from significance once controlling for measures of non-Hispanic white affluence and seasonal work. With this lone exception, the patterns of significant correlations were otherwise identical. Predictors of change in the occurrence of anti-immigrant hate crime were change in the adult-child ratio and change in the percent of the population that is non-Hispanic white (both positive and significant), as well as change in the percent of white families with income greater than $100,000 and change in the percent of seasonal workers (both negative and significant).

In sum, the findings suggest that established immigrants in an area, those who have resided in this country for more than five years, may provide a buffering effect against victimization. This finding, while at odds with the stated hypothesis, is in line with a variant of group threat theory: the defended neighborhoods thesis. According to this version, anti-immigrant acts of intimidation will diminish once a critical mass establishes residence in a community. The findings of a buffering effect, then may be an indication of a critical mass, and thus support the notion of defended neighborhoods.

Additionally, the findings for change in the percent non-Hispanic white and white affluence offer some important clarifications. While the occurrence of anti-immigrant hate crimes appears to parallel to a degree the presence of whites, it does so unevenly according wealth, and thus in part to social class. As the percent of wealthy white families increases, the occurrence of anti-immigrant hate crime decreases. The interpretation may be two-fold. On the one hand, the finding may suggest that owing to forces of residential segregation, wealthy whites and immigrants are unlikely to come into contact in their day-to-day lives. On the other hand, the finding may suggest that when and where these populations are in contact, immigrants are not seen as posing a threat by well-off white residents. This interpretation is in-line with research suggesting the opposition to out-groups is strongest when economic insecurity is highest; wealthy whites may be financially insulated from such insecurity and thus unlikely to define newcomers as threatening. Together, these findings suggest the need to refine the application of group threat theory to account for processes of acculturation and variations within dominant groups.

As was discussed in Chapter 5, these analyses may rightly be subject to criticism in the use of imbalanced yearly counts of hate crime. To address such concerns, two additional sets of analyses were conducted. First, the models for both total and recent foreign-born were re-estimated using change in the *average* annual hate crime incidence for each time point. The findings here were virtually identical to those obtained using total counts. Second, the models were re-estimated using a subset of places for which full data compliance was achieved; that is, only those places in which law enforcement agencies accurately reported annual crime data to the FBI for all of the years 1999-2001 and 2005-2007. This restriction effectively reduced the sample sizes by half but with the benefit of providing necessary data stability.

Compared to the results of the broader sample analysis, the findings for the reduced sample offer some interesting insights. Whereas the primary analysis found a buffering effect within the total foreign-population, no such effect was found for those places providing full annual data. Change in the percent of the population that is foreign-born in this subset exerted no significant effect once controlling for key predictor variables. Furthermore, rather than finding a nonsignificant effect of change within the recent foreign-born population, this secondary analysis indicated a moderately significant positive correlation, such that—as group threat theory predicts—increasing foreign-born residence in an area results in increasing conflict with the native-born population, here taking the form of anti-immigrant hate crime. Between the broad and restricted samples, the pattern of significance for the control variables remained fairly similar. For the second sample, change in non-Hispanic white affluence remained negative and significantly correlated with change in hate crime, while change in the non-Hispanic white population and the adult-child ratio remained positive and significant, with the latter being only somewhat so. Consistent with the lack of a buffering effect, the effect of seasonal work dropped from significance

Taken together, the results obtained using both samples paint a curious picture. On the one hand, results from the broader sample suggest that increasing immigration, and particularly the establishment of immigrants over time, may act as a buffer against victimization, perhaps by priming the native-born population to the acceptance of subsequent arrivals. On the other hand, the results from the restricted sample suggest that there may be no such buffering effect and that at least for the recent foreign-born, increasing numbers means increasing victimization.

While the two sets of places share a number of demographic similarities (Tables 5.1 and 5.8), they differ in two key ways. First, the places in the restricted sample tended to be larger in size; it may be that urbanization allows greater opportunity for different racial and ethnic groups to come into contact, and thus present greater opportunities for conflict. Alternatively, it may be that in our largest cities, perpetrators may find it easier to view the foreign-born as worthy of attack, or perhaps view their crimes as less likely to be noticed by local residents or law enforcement. Second, and somewhat more difficult to address, the two sets of places appear to differ in their reporting practices, introducing the important question of selection bias. Those places where hate crimes are more likely to be recorded were also the places where increasing immigration was more likely to lead to increasing anti-immigrant hate crimes. This concern will be addressed in more detail later in this chapter.

New Destinations: The Importance of Place and History
The final contribution of this research has been to begin to draw together the criminological research on immigration and the emerging scholarly interest in new immigrant destinations. Research on this latter topic is rooted in the notion that the process of immigrant incorporation may not be uniform across geographical space. More specifically, the process of immigrant incorporation is largely predicated on the availability of opportunities for and resources to the foreign-born population, and such availabilities are more common within traditional receiving areas than in places where the foreign-born are only recently-arrived. The rationale behind research on new destinations is conceptually akin to the assumptions of the community resource perspective, which again suggests that some immigrant communities are better able to provide resources to their members in order to assist the incorporation process and insulate from traditional criminogenic forces. Presumably, there is a temporal component to such well-organized locales: over time, such places develop and refine their networks of assistance. In this way, new destinations may be conceived of as special types of immigrant communities, wherein their networks of assistance and the range of resources they can offer are not yet fully developed. Consequently, in these areas we might expect less of a buffering effect of immigrant concentration on crime and its correlates.

Yet the results of the analyses of immigration and traditional crime differ little from the results obtained for the full sample of places. In none of the models for the new destination subset is there a significant effect of change in the independent variable on change in any of the three aggregate crime rates. As with the full sample analyses, there is virtually no difference in the pattern of results, whether the independent variable is change in the concentration of the total foreign-born or the recent foreign-born population. However, while the effect of immigration on crime appears similar across the full sample and the new destination subset, the patterns of association for the control variables are distinct. Within new destinations, there is no significant effect of change in the adult-child ratio on change in either overall or property crime rates and the change in socioeconomic disadvantage is only moderately significant. It would appear that while the explanation for crime differs within new destinations, on the whole immigrant concentration does not factor significantly in the account. In terms of the community resource perspective, it may be that as others have argued (Shihadeh and Barranco 2010b; Parrado and Kandel 2008), immigrants are drawn to these places by preexisting networks, such that even while in emergent stages, these communities buffer against criminality. The limits of such buffering, however, can be seen in the results of the negative binomial regressions of change in immigration on change in anti-immigrant hate crime incidence.

With regard to immigrant victimization and group threat theory, the logic is similar to that for the community resource perspective: new destinations may be less able to insulate their members from victimization on the basis of their immigrant status. Further, the salience of perceived threat may be heightened for native-born residents in places wherein immigration is a recent phenomenon, particularly in light of the climate of reception discussed in Chapter 1. Precisely because immigration to new destinations is so new, the native-born population would likely have only limited experience in such interactions, and may fill that void by drawing from the larger discourse, which is largely opposed to newcomers. Most simply, in the absence of experience to the contrary, anti-immigrant discourse may prime native-born residents to expect the worst, and may catalyze action to prevent such expectations.

The findings for immigration and anti-immigrant hate crime within new destinations differ in important ways from those obtained from the full sample analyses. As with those analyses, the effects were modeled for two sets of new destinations: a broader sample, for which data were available in at least two of the three years around each time point, and a restricted or sub-sample, for which full annual data compliance was achieved. Unlike the full sample analyses, among new destinations, results indicate no significant buffering effect of change in immigration on change in anti-immigrant hate crime once relevant controls are included, whether the measure of immigration is total or recent foreign-born. However, among the places for which full data was available, results indicate a *significant positive* effect of change in immigration—total *and* recent—on change in hate crime.

Taken with the findings for the total sample discussed earlier, these results suggest that the process of incorporation may be somewhat more precarious for immigrants in new destinations than for those who settle in more traditional receiving areas. While those in traditional areas may be protected by a buffering effect of established communities, and potentially viewed as less threatening by their native-born neighbors, such protection is not as likely a feature of immigrant communities in new destinations. These findings are in-line with expectations drawn from group threat theory; the recent movement of foreign-born populations into previously native-born-dominant communities appears to be a contentious issue, as increasing foreign-born populations are associated with increasing anti-immigrant hate crimes.

In sum, this research has sought to both refine our understanding of the immigration-crime relationship and to extend the discussion to include both immigrant victimization and the potentially distinct patterns occurring in traditional and new settlement destinations. The analyses discussed are not, however, without their limitations.

Limitations of the Current Research and Prospects for Future Study

Throughout the process of this research, a number of limitations have come to light that require discussion. Because the data used herein are drawn from secondary sources, the salient concerns center on issues of availability and treatment. This discussion should not be taken to undermine the results of the study, nor the conclusions drawn from them. In the case of the former, the analytical techniques employed and the study design itself were applied with accuracy as their primary aims. In the case of the conclusions, they have been drawn cautiously, with limitations of the data firmly in mind. Thus this discussion of the problems encountered is designed to put both into better perspective and to outline possible directions for future research.

An important limitation of this research is its treatment of the foreign-born as a homogenous category. Scholars have long called for research to disaggregate this population, most notably by country of origin, in order to better address the myriad forms of human and social capital, access to resources, and pre-migration experiences that may affect the process of incorporation and thus potentially rates of crime. In the planning stages of this research, disaggregation by country of origin was of primary concern. However, the spottiness of the data on this measure drawn from the ACS precluded its inclusion, relegating the analyses to testing only for the broad categories of overall and recent foreign-born. Future research may seek to extend aspects of this research by better accounting for variations within the foreign-born population.

In addition to limitations of the demographic data, there were significant obstacles with regard to the crime data that fundamentally altered the scope and direction of this project, as initially envisioned. Official measures of crime are notorious for what they leave out, namely crime that goes unnoticed by police or unreported by civilians (Watkins 2005). These "dark figures" have historically been problematic; as much products of police procedure as of actual rates of offending (Thrane, et al. 2008; Chambliss 1973). Problems of production include regional variations in offense definitions and underreporting due to computer problems, changes in record management systems, and personnel shortages, but also the potential for intentional manipulation of data in the interest of public image (Butterfield 1998). The situation may be particularly bad for hate crimes. In a given year, the number of hate incidents reported by the UCR may range from 6,000-10,000. According to a Department of Justice report, the actual incidence, as measured by the NCVS, may be 20 times higher (Harlow 2005). Part of the explanation is a large degree of underreporting, which may result in conservative estimates. Immigrants may be unlikely to report their victimization if they lack awareness either of their rights or of how actually to avail themselves of the justice system, and particularly if they lack fluency in English. Furthermore, some may distrust law enforcement, especially if they come from countries with histories of corruption and brutality (Davis and Henderson 2003), or they may fear retribution from the offending party if they contact law enforcement (Al-Mateen, Lewis, and Singh 2001).

Part of the explanation rests as well with law enforcement and members of the judicial system, in their decision-making powers to invoke the hate-crime designation. In some instances, reporting officers may be unaware or unsure of the requisite elements of a hate crime and thus unlikely to apply the designation. Additionally, others may forego the designation because of a lack of resources in terms of time, training, or cross-cultural awareness. Still others may leave it out due to past experience, whereby perhaps a previous victim subsequently recanted, or the court system declined to prosecute. Within the legal system, there are concerns as well, owing largely to the difficulty in proving the subjective bias in intent beyond a reasonable doubt. Prosecutors may decline to pursue the charge in certain instances, believing the evidence too weak to convince a jury. Additionally, defendants may plead out of the hate crime charge, or, if charged with multiple offenses, may plead guilty to some, but not to others.

With regard to hate crime victimization, the findings of this research have suggested the potential for a buffering effect of immigration, at least in some areas. But this research has not sufficiently addressed whether the effect is a product of concentration, or simply presence. To address the former, future research might seek to connect the literatures on community resource and group threat, providing a further test of the defended neighborhoods thesis. Similarly, this research has not adequately addressed the mechanisms by which that buffering takes places, leaving open the question of whether and to what degree it is a product of protection on the part of ethnic communities or a product of acceptance by native-born residents. Future research, particularly qualitative inquiries, might address this issue. Participant observation or in-depth interviews with residents of a multi-ethnic community comprised of a mix of both native- and foreign-born residents could help us better understand the patterns of interaction between the two and potential catalyst and solutions for conflict.

This research has provided insight into the application of group threat theory to the process of immigration, and has suggested the need to refine the perspective around variations within dominant groups, particularly social class. In the future, scholars might focus more squarely on this issue, to determine whether the significant positive effect of non-Hispanic white affluence is a product of segregation from immigrants or a lack of perceived threat. This would be an area in which qualitative research would again be quite helpful.

Another limitation of the hate crime analyses presented here is that the porosity of the data effectively precluded the ability to determine whether the crimes against the immigrant proxy groups were in fact committed by native-born persons. It is at least possible that the counts employed included instances wherein both the victim and offender were foreign-born. However unlikely such cases may be is unclear and unanswerable from the FBI's hate crime data. Yet in the interest of validity, this question is one that requires attention.

One of the most significant limitations, perhaps, has to do with the issue of selection bias, especially for the hate crime analyses. Recall that the results of the significant positive effect are based upon a limited sample for which full data was available. Essentially, those places wherein an anti-immigrant hate crime is most likely to be reported are the same places wherein such crimes are linked to increasing immigration. Potentially, the foreign-born in these areas might be more likely to report victimization, or law enforcement there more likely to record it. The same concerns are present with respect to traditional crime, albeit to a lesser degree. Future research might address the issue of selection bias by drawing data instead from the National Crime Victimization Survey, though this would not be a viable option for those interested in exploring hate crime research, nor those interested in aggregations smaller than the national-level. The FBI's National Incident Based Reporting System (NIBRS) is a promising source of data, though it has yet to be broadly adopted by law enforcement agencies.

Aside from locating alternative national data sources, future research might consider a qualitative analysis of a police department in a large city, which has failed to provide hate crime data. Such a study could offer insight into whether the lack of data is due to an objective lack of crimes, or the subjective coding out of the hate component. Future quantitative researchers might seek to replicate these analyses using more or different reporting years. It remains unclear both why individual departments refrained from providing data and also whether the omissions represent anomalies or trends. It may be that another combination of years might yield a greater number of usable cases. In collecting the data, it was evident that compliance with hate crime reporting, while still quite limited around the second time point, had grown considerably since the first. There is hope, at least, that this increase will continue, allowing future research to offer more refined results.

As has been discussed, the period under study in this research precluded the potentially confounding effects of the current economic recession. It would, however, be interesting to know the effects of the crisis on immigrant victimization and the buffering effects of ethnic communities. A change-over-time analysis using two time points, such as the ACS 2055-2007 and decennial census, or three time points, such as the 2000 and 2010 censuses and 2005-2007 ACS, might give a sense of how the confluence of factors such as job loss, stagnant wages, and stalled immigration have affected immigrant communities, and in turn crime and victimization.

Finally, some readers may raise questions on the geographical unit of analysis. Crime is a social activity that is not ecologically diffuse. It tends to occur overwhelmingly in certain areas while remaining quite rare in others. Cities and towns may consist of many neighborhoods that experience high rates of offending, as well as many that experience very low rates, though this should not be taken to mean that things "average out". Operating at an aggregate level could have the effect of glossing over variation in crime rates and may potentially give a distorted impression of the nature of crime in some cities and towns, leading to the creation or perpetuation of certain stereotypes. This has historically been the case with rankings of the nation's "Most Dangerous City" (Rosenfeld and Lauritsen 2008). While these are valid concerns, this research sacrifices a degree of specificity in favor of taking a broader look, but does so always with this limitation in mind.

On the other hand, a macro-level approach is necessary because immigrants enter an already established socioeconomic structure that is much broader than can be captured using tract-level data. As discussed, employment structure is an important factor when considering criminal offending. Since job networks extend across neighborhood boundaries (and of course even across city borders), micro analyses may miss the broader ecological impacts. Perhaps most importantly, this discussion should not be an either/or issue; our understandings of social phenomena are best augmented when macro- and micro-level analyses complement each other. Individual-level approaches generally show that immigrants engage in less crime than natives, but macro studies can help flesh out variations in this finding as well as possible explanations for it. Further, macro studies can uncover heretofore unexpected anomalies that inform and help guide future micro-level research.

Implications of the Current Research

Part of the impetus for this study was the growth in scholarly research over the last few years on immigration and traditional crime. One of the primary goals was to contribute to that research by providing an analysis of a broad national sample of places. The results of the analysis of traditional crime continue the parade of findings that immigration does not result in increasing rates of crime. This study confirms those results within 1,250 cities and towns of population greater than 20,000. The findings allow us to broadly state that across a wide range of places and over most of the previous decade, immigration did not contribute to rates of traditional crime. It is hoped that the equating of immigration with crime may be put to rest. Linking the two flaunts the results of the scientific process and is too often based on nonexistent or faulty evidence.

A second goal of this study was to provide a test of the tenets of social disorganization theory, which suggests that immigration contributes to higher rates of crime by disrupting normative informal controls. This disruption, according to the theory, indirectly leads to crime through factors such as population instability and poverty. The result of the analyses offered here suggest that immigration within the places sampled and over the period studied, did not result in increased crime either directly or indirectly. The absence of such an effect lends indirect support to the small but growing body of research on what has here and elsewhere been termed the community resource perspective. This view suggests that in some cases increasing immigrant concentration increases social cohesion and provides a number of physical and social resources to aid incorporation. In such a way, immigrant concentration is in fact an organizing, or re-organizing force (Shihadeh and Barranco 2013; Samson, 2002). At the aggregate level, the results of the traditional crime analyses presented here help build on the existing literature and encourage future research to continue refining our understanding of the mechanisms at work.

Another major aim of this research was to expand the discussion of immigration and crime to include immigrant victimization. To date, a relative few studies exist on the nature of the forms and ways in which immigrants are victimized once arriving in the U.S. (though for exceptions, see McDonald and Erez 2007; Miller 2007; Valenzuela 2006). Yet recurring news accounts of attacks on immigrants (cf. Akam 2009; Fahim 2009; Sacchetti 2009) coupled with recent reports at the local level (LCCR 2009; SPLC 2009) suggest the need to better understand this complex issue. This study sought to provide one of the first large-scale, systematic analyses of the correlates of immigrant victimization, in the form of anti-immigrant hate crime. The results of the analyses of immigration and biased crime offer in some ways conflicting results. While there is evidence to suggest that longer-term immigration may buffer against victimization—though the how and the why remain unclear—there is also evidence to suggest that increasing immigration, particularly among the recently arrived, leads to greater incidence of anti-immigrant hate crime. The conflict in the results presented here is clouded fundamentally by issues of data availability and begs the call for more, and more reliable, data on immigrant victimization. In the conflicting findings there is also opportunity. That hate crime incidence increases along with rates of immigration is consistent with group threat theory, while the finding of a buffering effect of established immigration is consistent with the defended neighborhoods thesis, a variant of group threat. In the future, researchers might help to clarify these dual findings.

The troubling state of affairs surrounding hate crime data warrants special discussion. Beyond the previously discussed issues of reliability are basic issues of availability. Less than one quarter of the nearly 2,100 places drawn from the ACS reported hate crime data for even two of the three years around both time points. Only roughly one in ten reported data for all six years. Additionally, there is the absence of a single dataset—official or otherwise—recording the occurrence of anti-immigrant hate crime. While concern with this topic is recent and scarce data to be expected, the virtual absence of data is a major limitation. Scholars interested in macrosocial trends are left with the unappealing choice between manipulating proxy measures and avoiding the research entirely. Understandably the absence of official records of anti-immigrant crime is tied to the fact that immigrant status is not a protected category of hate victimization under existing statute. Certainly the case might be made that it should be, but in the current political climate, such a call may well fall on deaf ears. Rather, it seems a more worthwhile endeavor to push for the establishment of an independent database recording attacks against immigrants.

Finally, this research sought to integrate criminological research on immigration with interest in new settlement destinations—places to which immigrants are only recently arrived. The findings, with regard to traditional crime, suggest again that the nature of immigrant communities—even those relatively new—may provide sources of aid, support, and organization to their members. Yet the findings from the analyses of hate crime data suggest also that new destinations may differ in important ways from traditional receiving areas. The finding of a positive significant effect within the restricted sample of new destinations offers important direction for future analysis and at least suggests it may be the consequence of a largely and often virulent anti-immigrant discourse. It is hoped that the results presented here offer fruitful directions for those interested in the role of place.

For policy-makers and the public, these results may hopefully be enlightening. The seeds of this research grew out of the gulf between academic studies finding no effect of immigration on crime, or in some cases a suppressive one, and public opinion and policies that remained firmly entrenched in the outdated and imprecise interpretation that immigrants lead to crime. In a way, these results suggest they might be right, though not nearly in the manner many would expect. While the results continue to confirm that immigration does not contribute to higher rates of traditional crime, they are among the first to show that the continued "myth of immigrant criminality," as Rumbaut and Ewing (2007) term it, may be responsible for anti-immigrant hate crimes. When increasing immigration is coupled with a largely anti-immigrant discourse, newcomers may be placed squarely in harm's way.

Supplementary Data Creation Information

Table A1a. Number of Cases by Reason Excluded, UCR Analyses

Reason for Exclusion	2000	2005-2007
Missing Census Data	12	12
	(1.48)	(1.48)
Missing UCR Data[1]	335	335
	(41.21)	(41.21)
Insufficient UCR Data[2]	190	154
	(23.37)	(18.94)
Missing Key Variable	1	273
	(0.12)	(33.58)
No Matching Pair	273	37
	(33.58)	(4.55)
Outlier	2	2
	(0.25)	(0.25)
	$n = 813$	$n = 813$

* Numbers in parentheses represent percentages

[1] No valid data reported for any of the three years in each time period.

[2] Less than two years of valid data reported within single time period.

Table A1b. Specification of Missing Variables by Time, UCR Analyses

Variable	2000	2005-2007
Percent Recent Foreign-Born	1	270
Percent Latino	-	86
Percent Less than High School	-	20
Pct Unemployed	-	71
Pct Management/Professional Occupations	-	102
Percent Seasonal Occupations	-	102
Total Missing	*1*	*273**

* Due to overlapping, counts of individual variables will not sum to the total number of missing cases.

Table A2a. Number of Cases by Reason Excluded, Hate Crime Analyses

	2000	2005-2007
Missing Census Data	12	12
	(0.73)	(0.73)
Missing HC Data[1]	987	954
	(60.11)	(58.10)
Insufficient HC Data[2]	423	401
	(25.76)	(24.42)
Missing Key Variable	1	81
	(0.06)	(4.93)
No Matching Pair	219	193
	(13.34)	(11.75)
Outlier	0	1
	(0.00)	(0.06)

Note: Numbers in parentheses represent percentages

[1] No valid data reported for any of the three years in each time period.
[2] Less than two years of valid data reported within single time period.

Table A2b. Specification of Missing Variables by Time, Hate Crime Analyses

Variable	2000	2005-2007
Percent Recent Foreign-Born	-	270
Percent NH White	-	274
White wealth	-	37
Season	-	102
Total Missing	*0*	*273**

* Due to overlapping, counts of individual variables will not sum to the total

Table A3a. Correlation Matrix for Variables Employed in Analysis of UCR Data

	Foreign-Born Index	Total Population (ln)	Male 15-29 (ln)	Adult-Child Ratio	Socioeconomic Disadvantage	Residential Stability	Management, Professional	Seasonal Occupations
Foreign-Born Index	1	0.16299	0.06761	-0.25675	0.46195	-0.11868	-0.2776	0.30787
Total Population (ln)	0.16299	1	0.13922	-0.04262	0.24419	-0.20464	-0.05593	-0.06314
Male 15-29 (ln)	0.06761	0.13922	1	0.24265	0.31601	-0.71668	-0.26276	0.14684
Adult-Child Ratio	-0.25675	-0.04262	0.24265	1	-0.30496	-0.27443	0.30671	-0.18975
Socioeconomic Disadvantage	0.46195	0.24419	0.31601	-0.30496	1	-0.39699	-0.63103	0.33411
Residential Stability	-0.11868	-0.20464	-0.71668	-0.27443	-0.39699	1	0.24093	-0.08596
Management, Professional	-0.2776	-0.05593	-0.26276	0.30671	-0.63103	0.24093	1	-0.24318
Seasonal Occupations	0.30787	-0.06314	0.14684	-0.18975	0.33411	-0.08596	-0.24318	1

Table A3h Correlation Matrix for Variables Employed in Analysis of Hate Crime Data

	Percent Foreign-Born	Total Population (ln)	Adult-Child Ratio	Percent Non-Hispanic White	White Wealth	Residential Stability	Seasonal Occupations
Percent Foreign-Born	1	0.16299	-0.25675	0.46195	-0.11868	-0.2776	0.30787
Total Population (ln)	0.16299	1	-0.04262	0.24419	-0.20464	-0.05593	-0.06314
Adult-Child Ratio	0.06761	0.13922	0.24265	0.31601	-0.71668	-0.26276	0.14684
Percent Non-Hispanic White	-0.25675	-0.04262	1	-0.30496	-0.27443	0.30671	-0.18975
White Wealth	0.46195	0.24419	-0.30496	1	-0.39699	-0.63103	0.33411
Residential Stability	-0.11868	-0.20464	-0.27443	-0.39699	1	0.24093	-0.08596
Seasonal Occupations	-0.2776	-0.05593	0.30671	-0.63103	0.24093	1	-0.24318

Table A4a. Place Level Population Coverages For Secondary Hate Crime Analysis - Places with Fully Compliant Data

	2000		2005-2007	
	Universe	Sample	Universe	Sample
Total Place-Level Population Wherein a Hate Crime Occurred	82,511,078 (100)	37,866,045 (45.89)[1]	91,077,851 (100.00)	39,938,255 (45.89)[1]
Foreign-Born Population	16,346,761 (52.55)[2]	7,606,786 (24.45)[3]	18,502,284 (49.69)[2]	8,457,937 (22.72)[3]
Recent Foreign-Born Population	4,005,975 (52.84)[2]	1,789,472 (23.60)[3]	4,630,114 (48.96)[2]	2,061,215 (21.79)[3]
Percent of Nation's Population Covered	29.32	13.46	30.49	13.37
	n = 642	*n = 205*	*n = 700*	*n = 205*

*numbers in parentheses represent percentages

[1] Indicates the percentage of the total U.S. population living in places wherein a hate crime occurred that is included in the data set

[2] Indicates the percentage of the U.S. population living in places wherein a hate crime occurred

[3] Indicates the percentage of the U.S. population included in the universe data set

Table A4 b. Statistical Profile of Places Excluded From and Included in (i.e. Fully Compliant Data) Secondary Hate Crime Analyses

	Excluded				Included / Full Data			
	2000		2005-2007		2000		2005-2007	
	Mean	Std Dev	Mean	Std Dev	Mean	Std Dev	Mean	Std Dev
Total Population	57,621	207,119	61,453	212,226	184,712	364,415	194,821	366,637
Percent Foreign-Born	12.14	11.67	14.05	12.09	16.73	11.39	18.45	11.45
Percent Recent Foreign-Born	2.99	3.02	4.04	3.39	4.01	2.74	4.61	2.81
Percent White	68.64	24.13	64.40	23.16	62.47	20.86	58.60	21.23
Percent Male Aged 15-29	10.80	3.83	11.15	3.91	11.72	3.56	12.04	3.57
Adult-Child Ratio	3.52	15.71	3.24	2.22	3.24	1.38	3.40	1.22
Residential Stability					0.00	1.74	0.00	1.76
Pct of HH Owner-Occupied	64.68	14.88	65.60	14.32	58.72	13.17	59.77	12.55
Pct of HH Occupied 2 years or more	78.02	7.05	77.97	7.07	76.34	6.51	76.45	6.43
Percent of White Households with Income Greater than $100k	15.24	11.42	23.36	14.22	17.01	9.37	25.76	11.55
Percent Seasonal Occupations	0.56	2.02	0.42	1.59	0.36	0.61	0.34	0.69
Total Count of Anti-Immigrant Offenses	1.87	7.40	1.44	3.72	9.90	35.28	6.10	14.63
	n = 1,860		*n = 1,860*		*n = 423*		*n = 423*	

Supplementary Analyses

Table B1. Fixed Effects (Within-City) Regression Models Predicting Violent Crime Rate (log-transformed), 2000-2007

Predictors	Model 1	Model 2	Model 3	Model 4
Recent Immigration Index	.008	.014	.007	.006
	(.018)	(.018)	(.018)	(.018)
City/Town Population (logged)		-.417***	-.390***	-.387***
		(.059)	(.059)	(.060)
Males Aged 15-29 (logged)		.107	.073	.068
		(.077)	(.079)	(.079)
Adult-Child Ratio (logged)		-.104	-.019	-.019
		(.103)	(.105)	(.105)
Disadvantage Index			.031***	.031***
			(.008)	(.008)
Residential Stability			-.019	-.019
			(.016)	(.016)
Managerial/Professional				-.002
				(.003)
Seasonal				-.005
				(.016)
Intercept	.006	.044	.039	.039
	(.009)	(.012)	(.012)	(.012)
Model Summary Information				
Between-Unit Variation	.951	.951	.951	.951
R^2 (Adj R^2)	.0002 (.000)	.040 (.036)	.052 (.047)	.052 (.046)
Total Number of Observations ($N \times T$)	2,504	2,504	2,504	2,504
Total Number of Cities/Towns (N)	1,252	1,252	1,252	1,252

$^\dagger p<.10$, $*p<.05$, $**p<.01$, $***p<.001$

Table B2. Fixed Effects (Within-City) Regression Models Predicting Property Crime Rate (log-transformed), 2000-2007

Predictors	Model 1	Model 2	Model 3	Model 4
Recent Immigration Index	-.015	-.012	-.015	-.013
	(.013)	(.013)	(.013)	(.013)
City/Town Population (logged)		-.209***	-.195***	-.200***
		(.043)	(.043)	(.044)
Males Aged 15-29 (logged)		.076	.068	.066
		(.056)	(.058)	(.058)
Adult-Child Ratio (logged)		.156*	.208**	.211**
		(.075)	(.077)	(.077)
Disadvantage Index			.020**	.020**
			(.006)	(.006)
Residential Stability			.001	.000
			(.012)	(.012)
Managerial/Professional				.000
				(.003)
Seasonal				-.014
				(.012)
Intercept	-.064	-.055	-.058	-.058
	(.007)	(.009)	(.009)	(.009)
Model Summary Information				
Between-Unit Variation	.943	.943	.943	.943
R^2 (Adj R^2)	.0001 (.0004)	.030 (.027)	.038 (.033)	.039 (.033)
Total Number of Observations (N x T)	2,504	2,504	2,504	2,504
Total Number of Cities/Towns (N)	1,252	1,252	1,252	1,252

† *p<.10,* *p<.05,* **p<.01,* ***p<.001*

Table B3. Fixed Effects (Within-City) Regression Models Predicting Violent Crime Rate (log-transformed) within New Destinations, 2000-2007, Recent Foreign-Born

Predictors	Model 1	Model 2	Model 3	Model 4
Recent Immigration Index	.005	.006	.004	.004
	(.025)	(.025)	(.025)	(.026)
City/Town Population (logged)		-.540***	-.505***	-.505***
		(.093)	(.097)	(.099)
Males Aged 15-29 (logged)		.114	.085	.080
		(.137)	(.142)	(.144)
Adult-Child Ratio (logged)		-.054	-.017	-.011
		(.184)	(.186)	(.187)
Disadvantage Index			.014	.014
			(.013)	(.013)
Residential Stability			-.020	-.021
			(.025)	(.026)
Managerial/Professional				-.001
				(.005)
Seasonal				-.010
				(.023)
Intercept	.026	.075	.069	.069
	(.015)	(.018)	(.018)	(.019)
Model Summary Information				
Between-Unit Variation	.943	.943	.943	.943
R^2 (Adj R^2)	.0001 (.000)	.060 (.053)	.063 (.053)	.064 (.050)
Total Number of Observations ($N \times T$)	1,146	1,146	1,146	1,146
Total Number of Cities/Towns (N)	573	573	573	573

$^{†}p<.10$, $*p<.05$, $**p<.01$, $***p<.001$

Table B4. Fixed Effects (Within-City) Regression Models Predicting Property Crime Rate (log-transformed) within New Destinations, 2000-2007, Recent Foreign-Born

	Model 1	Model 2	Model 3	Model 4
Predictors				
Recent Immigration Index	-.003	.001	-.001	.000
	(.018)	(.018)	(.018)	(.019)
City/Town Population (logged)		-.358***	-.334***	-.337***
		(.069)	(.072)	(.073)
Males Aged 15-29 (logged)		.020	.012	.009
		(.101)	(.104)	(.105)
Adult-Child Ratio (logged)		.137	.173	.181
		(.135)	(.136)	(.137)
Disadvantage Index			.018[†]	.018[†]
			(.009)	(.009)
Residential Stability			-.005	-.007
			(.019)	(.019)
Managerial/Professional				.000
				(.004)
Seasonal				-.014
				(.017)
Intercept	-.088	-.060	-.065	-.065
	(.011)	(.013)	(.014)	(.014)
Model Summary Information				
Between-Unit Variation	.926	.926	.926	.926
R^2 (Adj R^2)	.000 (.000)	.055 (.049)	.061 (.052)	.063 (.049)
Total Number of Observations ($N \times T$)	1,146	1,146	1,146	1,146
Total Number of Cities/Towns (N)	573	573	573	573

† $p<.10$, *$p<.05$, **$p<.01$, ***$p<.001$

Table B5a. Fixed Effects (Within-City) Negative Binomial Regression Models Predicting the Average Incidence of Anti-Immigrant Hate Crime, 2000-2007

Predictors	Model 1	Model 2	Model 3	Model 4
Percent Foreign-born	-.048***	-.016**	-.008	-.007
	(.004)	(.005)	(.005)	(.005)
City/Town Population (logged)		-.039	-.025	-.036
		(.039)	(.040)	(.040)
Males Aged 15-29		-.009	-.018	-.015
		(.014)	(.017)	(.017)
Adult-Child Ratio		.156***	.200***	.184***
		(.042)	(.045)	(.045)
Percent NH White		.027***	.028***	.028***
		(.003)	(.003)	(.003)
Residential Stability			.033	.031
			(.036)	(.036)
White Wealth			-.020***	-.021***
			(.004)	(.004)
Seasonal Work				-.078*
				(.040)
Intercept	-8.8052***	-10.9948***	-10.9758***	-10.7945***
	(.084)	(.592)	(.633)	(.636)
Model Summary Information				
Goodness of Fit (Value/DF)				
Deviance	1.008	.987	.987	.988
Scaled Deviance	1.000	1.000	1.000	1.000
Pearson Chi-Square	1.342	1.284	1.271	1.253
Scaled Pearson X2	1.332	1.301	1.287	1.268
Total Number of Observations (N xT)	846	846	846	846
Total Number of Cities/Towns (N)	423	423	423	423

NOTE: Population neither non-Hispanic white nor non-Hispanic Black (log transformed) used as offset.

† $p \leq .10$, * $p \leq .05$, ** $p \leq .01$, *** $p \leq .001$

Table B5h Fixed Effects (Within-City) Negative Binomial Regression Models Predicting the Average Incidence of Anti-Immigrant Hate Crime, 2000-2007, Recent Foreign-Born

	Model 1	Model 2	Model 3	Model 4
Predictors				
Percent Recent Foreign-born	-.138***	-.025	.005	.007
	(.017)	(.017)	(.018)	(.018)
City/Town Population (logged)		-.026	-.018	-.030
		(.039)	(.040)	(.040)
Males Aged 15-29		.004	-.013	-.010
		(.013)	(.017)	(.017)
Adult-Child Ratio		.127**	.178***	.164***
		(.042)	(.044)	(.044)
Percent NH White		.032***	.032***	.031***
		(.003)	(.003)	(.003)
Residential Stability			.038	.037
			(.037)	(.037)
White Wealth			-.022***	-.023***
			(.004)	(.004)
Seasonal Work				-.083*
				(.040)
Intercept	-9.0365***	-11.6598***	-11.395***	-11.1794***
	(.092)	(.551)	(.608)	(.612)
Model Summary Information				
Goodness of Fit (Value/DF)				
Deviance	1.037	1.003	.999	.999
Scaled Deviance	1.000	1.000	1.000	1.000
Pearson Chi-Square	1.422	1.382	1.349	1.323
Scaled Pearson X2	1.372	1.378	1.349	1.324
Total Number of Observations ($N \times T$)	846	846	846	846
Total Number of Cities/Towns (N)	423	423	423	423

NOTE: Population neither non-Hispanic white nor non-Hispanic Black (log transformed) used as offset.
† $p<.10$, *$p<.05$, **$p<.01$, ***$p<.001$

Table B5c. Fixed Effects (Within-City) Negative Binomial Regression Models Predicting the Average Incidence of Anti-Immigrant Hate Crime within New Destinations 2000-2007

Predictors	Model 1	Model 2	Model 3	Model 4
Percent Foreign-born	-.037***	-.012	.004	.004
	(.007)	(.008)	(.009)	(.009)
City/Town Population (logged)		-.141*	-.089	-.106†
		(.062)	(.061)	(.062)
Males Aged 15-29		-.059**	-.048†	-.046†
		(.020)	(.025)	(.025)
Adult-Child Ratio		.339***	.448***	.429***
		(.082)	(.084)	(.084)
Percent NH White		.023***	.021***	.021***
		(.005)	(.005)	(.005)
Residential Stability			.124†	.120†
			(.064)	(.064)
White Wealth			-.033***	-.034***
			(.008)	(.008)
Seasonal Work				-.113
				(.079)
Intercept	-8.777***	-9.4271***	-10.0165***	-9.7226***
	(.131)	(.957)	(.964)	(.980)
Model Summary Information				
Goodness of Fit (Value/DF)				
Deviance	1.029	.997	1.004	1.004
Scaled Deviance	1.000	1.000	1.000	1.000
Pearson Chi-Square	1.259	1.221	1.213	1.199
Scaled Pearson X2	1.223	1.224	1.208	1.194
Total Number of Observations (N x T)	346	346	346	346
Total Number of Cities/Towns (N)	173	173	173	173

NOTE: Population neither non-Hispanic white nor non-Hispanic Black (log transformed) used as offset.

† *p<.10*, **p<.05, **p<.01, ***p<.001*

Table B5d. Fixed Effects (Within-City) Negative Binomial Regression Models Predicting the Average Incidence of Anti-Immigrant Hate Crime within New Destinations 2000-2007, Recent Foreign-Born

	Model 1	Model 2	Model 3	Model 4
Predictors				
Percent Recent Foreign-born	-.111***	-.047†	.001	.002
	(.023)	(.024)	(.026)	(.026)
City/Town Population (logged)		-.142*	-.093	-.111†
		(.061)	(.061)	(.062)
Males Aged 15-29		-.055**	-.049*	-.047†
		(.020)	(.025)	(.025)
Adult-Child Ratio		.352***	.452***	.434***
		(.082)	(.084)	(.084)
Percent NH White		.022***	.020***	.020***
		(.004)	(.005)	(.005)
Residential Stability			.122†	.118†
			(.064)	(.064)
White Wealth			-.032***	-.033***
			(.008)	(.008)
Seasonal Work				-.112
				(.079)
Intercept	-8.7613***	-9.396***	-9.8636***	-9.56***
	(.137)	(.927)	(.932)	(.950)
Model Summary Information				
Goodness of Fit (Value/DF)				
Deviance	1.033	.996	1.000	1.000
Scaled Deviance	1.000	1.000	1.000	1.000
Pearson Chi-Square	1.221	1.197	1.200	1.186
Scaled Pearson X2	1.182	1.201	1.200	1.186
Total Number of Observations ($N \times T$)	346	346	346	346
Total Number of Cities/Towns (N)	173	173	173	173

NOTE: Population neither non-Hispanic white nor non-Hispanic Black (log transformed) used as offset.

† *p<.10 , *p<.05, **p<.01, ***p<.001*

References

Agnew, Robert. 1992. "Foundation for a General Strain Theory of Crime and Delinquency." *Criminology* 30: 47-87.

—. 2001. *Juvenile Delinquency: Causes and Control.* Los Angeles: Roxbury Publishing Company.

Agnew, Robert, Timothy Brenzina, John Paul Wright, and Francis T. Cullen. 2002. "Strain, Personality Traits, and Delinquency: Extending General Strain Theory." *Criminology* 40.

Akam, Simon. 2009. "Police Offer Reward in Beating of Mexican Immigrant in Brooklyn." *New York Times*, October 18.

Al-Mateen, Cheryl S., D.K. Lewis, and Nirbhay N. Singh. 2001. "Victims of Hate Crimes." Pp. 359-374 in *Comprehensive Clinical Psychology*, edited by A.S. Bellack and M. Hersen. New York: Pergamon.

Alaniz, Maria Luisa, Randi S. Cartmill and Robert Nash Parker. 1998. "Immigrants and Violence: The Importance of Neighborhood Context." *Hispanic Journal of Behavioral Sciences* 20: 155-175.

Alba, Richard, Ruben G. Rumbaut, and Karen Marotz. 2005. "A Distorted Nation: Perceptions of Racial/Ethnic Group Sizes and Attitudes Toward Immigrants and Other Minorities." *Social Forces* 84: 901-19.

Alba, Richard and Victor Nee. 1997. "Rethinking Assimilation Theory for a New Era of Immigration." *International Migration Review* 31: 826-74.

Alba, Richard D., John R. Logan, and Brian J. Stults. 2000. "How Segregated are Middle-Class African Americans?" *Social Problems* 47: 543-58.

Aliverti, Ana. 2012. "Making People Criminal: The Role of the Criminal Law in Immigration Enforcement." *Theoretical Criminology* 16: 417-434.

Allison, Paul D. 2005. *Fixed Effects Regression Methods for Longitudinal Data Using SAS.* Cary, NC: SAS Institute Inc.

Alsalam, Nabeel, and Ralph E. Smith. 2005. *The Role of Immigrants in the U.S. Labor Market.* Washington, D.C.: Congressional Budget Office (http://www.cbo.gov/ftpdocs/68xx/doc6853/11-10-Immigration.pdf).

Alvarez-Rivera, Lorna L., Matt R. Nobles, and Kim M. Lersch. 2013. "Latino Immigrant Acculturation and Crime." *American Journal of Criminal Justice.* Forthcoming.

Anderson, Elijah. 1999. *Code of the Street: Decency, Violence, and the Moral Life of the Inner City.* New York: Norton.

Associated Press. 1992. "Buchanan Supporters Claim Victory on Illegal Immigration Plank." Houston: The Associated Press.

—. 2007. "NW Ark police agencies sign agreement for immigration enforcement." *The Associated Press State & Local Wire.*

Beck, Roy. 1996. *The Case Against Immigration.* New York: Norton.

Berry, Brewton and Henry L. Tischler. 1978. *Race and Ethnic Relations.* Boston: Houghton Mifflin.

Biafora, Frank and George Warheit. 2007. "Self-Reported Violent Victimization Among Young Adults in Miami, Florida: Immigration, Race/Ethnic and Gender Contrasts." *International Review of Victimology* 14: 29-55.

Blalock, Hubert M. 1957. *Toward a Theory of Minority Group Relations.* New York: Wiley.

Bluestone, Barry. 1970. "The Tripartite Economy: Labor Markets and the Working Poor." *Poverty and Human Resources* 5: 15-35.

Blumer, Herbert. 1958. "Race Prejudice as a Sense of Group Position." *Pacific Sociological Review* 1: 3-7.

Blumstein, Alfred. 1995. "Youth Violence, Guns, and the Illicit Drug Industry." *Journal of Criminal Law and Criminology* 86: 10-36.

Bobo, Lawrence. 1988. "Group Conflict, Prejudice, and the Paradox of Contemporary Racial Attitudes." Pp. 85-114 in *Eliminating Racism,* edited by P.A. Katz and D.A. Taylor. New York: Plenum Press.

Borjas, George J. 1994. "The Economics of Immigration." *Journal of Economic Literature* 32: 1667-1717.

Brader, Ted, Nicholas A. Valentino, and Elizabeth Suhay. 2008. "What Triggers Public Opposition to Immigration? Anxiety, Group Cues, and Immigration Threat." *American Journal of Political Science* 52: 959-978.

Brauer, David A. 2006. *Projections of Net Migration to the United States.* Washington DC: Congressional Budget Office (http://www.cbo.gov/ftpdocs/72xx/doc7249/06-06-Immigration.pdf).

Burchfield, Keri B. and Eric Silver. 2013. "Collective Efficacy and Crime in Los Angeles Neighborhoods: Implications for the Latino Paradox." *Sociological Inquiry* 83(1): 165-176.

Burns, Peter and James G. Gimpel. 2000. "Economic Insecurity, Prejudicial Stereotypes, and Public Opinion on Immigration Policy." *Political Science Quarterly* 115: 201-225.

Bursik, Robert J., Jr., and Harold G. Grasmick. 1993. *Neighborhoods and Crime.* New York: Lexington.

Bursik, Robert J. 2006. "Rethinking the Chicago School of Criminology: A New Era of Immigration." Pp. 20-35 in *Immigration and Crime: Race, Ethnicity, and Violence*, edited by R. Martinez, Jr. and A. Valenzuela. New York: New York University Press.

Butcher, Kristin F. and Anne Morrison Piehl. 1997. "Recent Immigrants: Unexpected Implications for Crime and Incarceration." *NBER Working Paper No. W6067.* Available at SSRN: http://ssrn.com/abstract=226477.

—. 1998. "Cross-City Evidence on the Relationship between Immigration and Crime." *Journal of Policy Analysis and Management* 17: 457-493.

Butterfield, Fox. 1998. "Possible Manipulation of Crime Data Worries Top Police." *New York Times*, August 3, 1.

Byrne, James M. and Robert J. Sampson. 1986. *The Social Ecology of Crime.* New York: Springer-Verlag.

Card, David. 1990. "The Impact of the Mariel Boatlift on the Miami Labor Market." *Industrial and Labor Relations Review* 43: 245-257.

—. 2005. "Is the New Immigration Really So Bad?" *The Economic Journal* 115: 300-323.

Carter, Prudence. 2005. *Keepin' It Real: School Success Beyond Black and White.* New York: Oxford University Press.

Chambliss, William. 1973. "The Saints and the Roughnecks." *Society* 11: 24-31.

Chandler, Charles R., and Yung-Mei Tsai. 2001. "Social Factors Influencing Immigration Attitudes: An Analysis of Data from the General Social Survey." *The Social Science Journal* 38: 177-88.

Chiricos, Ted, Sarah Escholz, and Marc Gertz. 1997. "Crime, News and Fear of Crime: Toward an Identification of Audience Effects." *Social Problems* 44: 342-357.

Citrin, Jack, Donald P. Green, Christopher Muste, and Cara Wong. 1997. "Public Opinion Toward Immigration Reform: The Role of Economic Motivations." *The Journal of Politics* 59: 858-881.

Clark, William A.V. 1998. "Mass Migration and Local Outcomes: Is International Migration to the United States Creating a New Urban Underclass?" *Urban Studies* 35: 371-83.

Cohen, Jon and Pamela Constable. 2007. "U.S. Inaction Faulted, Immigration Polls Find; Md., Va. Residents Have Differing Views About How New Arrivals Affect Daily Life." *The Washington Post*, November 16, B01.

Cohen, Lawrence E., and Marcus Felson. 1979. "Social Change and Crime Rate Trends: A Routine Activities Approach." *American Sociological Review* 44: 588-608.

Cohrs, J. Christopher, and Monika Stelzl. 2010. "How Ideological Attitudes Predict Host Society Members' Attitudes Toward Immigrants: Exploring Cross-National Differences." *Journal of Social Issues* 66: 673-694.

Cramer, Maria, Maria Sacchetti, and Connie Paige. 2007. "Lawn work at Romney's home still done by illegal immigrants." *The Boston Globe*, December 4.

Crutchfield, Robert D. 1989. "Labor Stratification and Violent Crime." *Social Forces* 68: 489-512.

Crutchfield, Robert D., Ross L. Matsueda, and Kevin Drakulich. 2006. "Race, Labor Markets, and Neighborhood Violence." Pp. 199-220 in *The Many Colors of Crime: Inequalities of Race, Ethnicity and Crime in America*, edited by R.D. Peterson, L.J. Krivo, and J. Hagan. New York: New York University Press.

Cuevas, Carlos A., Chiara Sabina, and Riva Milloshi. 2012. "Interpersonal Victimization Among a National Sample of Latino Women." *Violence Against Women* 18: 377-403.

Davis, Robert C., and Nicole J. Henderson. 2003. "Willingness to Report Crimes: The Role of Ethnic Group Membership and Community Efficacy." *Crime and Delinquency* 49: 564-580.

DeJong, Gordon F., and Anna B. Madamba. 2001. "A Double Disadvantage? Minority Group, Immigrant Status, and Underemployment in the United States." *Social Science Quarterly* 82: 117-30.

Desmond, Scott A., and Charis E. Kubrin. 2009. "The Power of Place: Immigrant Communities and Adolescent Violence." *The Sociological Quarterly* 50: 581-607.

Dietrich, David R. 2012. "The Specter of Racism in the 2005–6 Immigration Debate: Preserving Racial Group Position." *Critical Sociology* 38: 723-745.

Doherty, Carroll. 2006. "Attitudes Toward Immigration: In Black and White." *Pew Research Center For the People and the Press.* Retrieved June 23, 2010 (http://pewresearch.org/ pubs/21/attitudes-toward-immigration-in-black-and-white).

Donato, Katherine M., Charles Tolbert, Alfred Nucci, and Yukio Kawano. 2008. "Changing Faces, Changing Places: The Emergence of New Nonmetropolitan Immigrant Gateways." Pp. 75-98 in *New Faces in New Places: The Changing Geography of American Immigration,* edited by D.S. Massey. New York: Russell Sage.

Donohue, Laura. 2012. "The Potential for a Rise in Wrongful Removals and Detention Under the United States Immigration and Customs Enforcement's Secure Communities Strategy." *New England Journal on Criminal & Civil Confinement* 38: 125-152.

Eggen, Dan and John Solomon. 2007. "Justice Dept.'s Focus has Shifted: Terror, Immigration are Current Priorities." *Washington Post,* October 17, A01.

Ernst, Robert. 1948. "Economic Nativism in New York City During the 1840s." *New York History* 46: 170-186.

Esbensen, Finn-Aage and Dena C. Carson. 2012. "Who Are the Gangsters?: An Examination of the Age, Race/Ethnicity, Sex, and Immigration Status of Self-Reported Gang Members in a Seven-City Study of American Youth." *Journal of Contemporary Criminal Justice* 28: 465-481.

Escobar, J.L. 1998. "Immigration and Mental Health: Why are Immigrants Better Off?" *Archives of General Psychiatry* 55: 781-2.

Espenshade, Thomas J. and Katherine Hempstead. 1996. "Contemporary American Attitudes Toward U.S. Immigration." *International Migration Review* 30: 535-570.

Fahim, Kareem. 2009. "2 Indicted in Fatal Beating of Ecuadorian Immigrant." *New York Times,* March 4. (http://www.nytimes.com/2009/03/04/nyregion/04ecuadorean.html).

Feldmeyer, Ben. 2009. "Immigration and violence: The offsetting effects of immigrant concentration on Latino violence." *Social Science Research* 38 (3): 717-731.

Felson, Marcus. 1996. "Routine Activity Approach." Pp. 20-22 in *Readings in Contemporary Criminological Theory,* edited by P. Cordella and L. Siegel. Boston: Northeastern University Press.

Fennelly, Katherine. 2008. "Prejudice Toward Immigrants In The Midwest." Pp. 151-178 in *New Faces in New Places: The Changing Geography of*

American Immigration, edited by D.S. Massey. New York: Russell Sage.

Fennelly, Katherine and Christopher Federico. 2008. "Rural Residence as a Determinant of Attitudes Toward U.S. Immigration Policy." *International Migration* 46: 151-190.

Fong, Eric, and Kumiko Shibuya. 2000. "Suburbanization and Home Ownership: The Spatial Assimilation Process in U.S. Metropolitan Areas." *Sociological Perspectives* 43: 137-157.

Fordham, Signithia. 1996. *Blacked out: Dilemmas of Race, Identity, and Success at Capital High.* Chicago: University of Chicago Press.

Freedburg, Louis. 1996. "Clinton and Dole's Dueling Immigration Ads." *San Francisco Chronicle*, July 7 (http://www.sfgate.com/opinion/article/ Clinton-and-Dole-s-Dueling-Immigration-Ads-2975932.php).

Frey, William H. 2009. "The Great American Migration Slowdown: Regional and Metropolitan Dimensions." in *Metropolitan Policy Program.* Washington, DC: Brookings Institute (http://www.brookings.edu/~/media/ files/rc/reports/2009/1209_migration_frey/1209_migration_frey.pdf).

Fussell, Elizabeth. 2011. "The Deportation Threat Dynamic and Victimization of Latino Migrants: Wage Theft and Robbery." *Sociological Quarterly* 52: 593-615.

Gamboa, Suzanne. 2009. "New face of offender in federal courts is Hispanic." *Associated Press*, Washington Dateline, February 18.

Gans, Herbert J. 1962. *The Urban Villagers.* New York: Free Press.

—. 1992. "Second-Generation Decline: Scenarios for the Economic and Ethnic Futures of the Post-1965 American Immigrants." *Ethnic and Racial Studies* 15: 173-92.

Gaouette, Nicole. 2007. "Campaign '08: GOP Debate Fallout; In GOP race, 'sanctuary city' is a dangerous place; The issue of shielding illegal immigrant from federal authorities has emerged as a point of attack for immigrants." *Los Angeles Times*, November 30.

Gordon, Milton M. 1964. *Assimilation in American Life: The Role of Race, Religion, and National Origins.* New York: Oxford University Press.

Gorman, Anna and Andrew Blankstein. 2007. "Massive sweep deports hundreds; More than 1,300 are arrested as U.S. officials target criminals in Southland." *Los Angeles Times*, October 3, A1.

Green, Donald P., Dara Z. Strolovich, and Janelle S. Wong. 1998. "Defended Neighborhoods, Integration, and Racially Motivated Crime." *American Journal of Sociology* 104: 372-403.

Griffith, David. 2008. "New Midwesterners, New Southerners: Immigration Experiences in Four Rural American Settings." Pp. 179-210 in *New Faces in New Places: The Changing Geography of American Immigration,* edited by D.S. Massey. New York: Russell Sage.

Hagan, John, Ron Levi, and Ronit Dinovitzer. 2008. "The Symbolic Violence of the Crime-Immigration Nexus: Migrant Mythologies in the Americas." *Criminology and Public Policy* 7 (1): 95-112.

Hagan, John and Alberto Palloni. 1998. "Immigration and Crime in the United States." in *The Immigration Debate: Studies on the Economic, Demographic, and Fiscal Effects of Immigration*, edited by J.P. Smith and B. Edmonston. Washington, DC: National Academy Press.

—. 1999. "Sociological Criminology and the Mythology of Hispanic Immigration and Crime." *Social Problems* 46: 617-632.

Hagan, Jacqueline and Scott Phillips. 2008. "Border Blunders: The Unanticipated Human and Economic Costs of the U.S. Approach to Immigration Control, 1986--2007." *Criminology and Public Policy* 7: 83 94.

Hamill, Sean D. 2006. "Altoona, With No Immigrant Problem, Decides to Solve It." *The New York Times*, December 7, A34.

Hargreaves, David H. 1967. *Social Relations in a Secondary School.* Routledge.

Harlow, Caroline Wolf. 2005. *Hate Crime Reported by Victims and Police.* Washington D.C.: U.S. Dept of Justice (http://bjs.ojp.usdoj.gov/content/pub/pdf/hcrvp.pdf).

Hegeman, Roxana. 2007. "Kansas lawmakers drafting bills to target illegal immigration." *The Associated Press State & Local Wire.* November 19.

Hendricks, Nicole, Christopher W. Ortiz, Naomi Sugie, and Joel Miller. 2007. "Beyond the Numbers: Hate Crimes and Cultural Trauma Within Arab American Immigrant Communities." *International Review of Victimology* 14: 95-113.

Hickman, Laura J. and Marika J. Suttorp. 2008. "Are Deportable Aliens A Unique Threat to Public Safety? Comparing the Recidivism of Deportable and Nondeportable Aliens." *Criminology and Public Policy* 7: 59-82.

Higgins, George E., Shaun L. Gabbidon, and Favian Martin. 2010. "The Role of Race/Ethnicity and Race Relations on Public Opinion Related to the Immigration and Crime Link." *Journal of Criminal Justice* 38: 51-56.

Hirschi, Travis and Michael Gottfredson. 1983. "Age and the Explanation of Crime." *American Journal of Sociology* 89: 552-584.

Hopkins, Daniel J. 2010. "Politicized Places: Explaining Where and When Immigrants Provoke Local Opposition." *American Political Science Review* 104: 40-60.

Human Rights Watch. 2009. *Forced Apart (By the Numbers): Non-Citizens Deported Mostly for Nonviolent Offenses.* New York: Human Rights Watch (http://www.hrw.org/en/reports/2009/04/15/forced-apart-numbers).

Huntington, Samuel P. 2004. *Who Are We? The Challenges to America's National Identity.* New York: Simon and Schuster.

Hurt, Charles. 2006. "Border fence cited as deterrent to crime." *The Washington Times,* July 21, A03.

Iguarta, Juan-Jose, and Lifen Cheng. 2009. "Moderating Effect of Group Cue While Processing News on Immigration: Is the Framing Effect a Heuristic Process?" *Journal of Communication* 59: 726-49.

Illinois Coalition for Immigrant and Refugee Rights. 2011. *Immigration Enforcement--The Dangerous Reality Behind "Secure Communities".* Chicago: Illinois Coalition for Immigrant and Refugee Rights (http://icirr.org/sites/default/files/ImmigrationEnforcementTheDangerou RealityBehindSecure%20Communities.pdf)

Immigration Policy Center. 2005. *Economic Growth and Immigration: Bridging the Demographic Divide.* Washington, D.C.: American Immigration Law Foundation.

Inciardi, James A. 1992. *The War on Drugs II.* Mountain View, CA: Mayfield Publishing.

King, Ryan D., Michael Massoglia, and Christopher Uggen. 2012. "Employment and Exile: U.S. Criminal Deportations, 1908-2005." *American Journal of Sociology* 117: 1786-1825.

King, Ryan D. and Darren Wheelock. 2007. "Group Threat and Social Control: Race, Perceptions of Minorities and the Desire to Punish." *Social Forces* 85: 1255-1280.

Kirk, David S. 2006. "Examining the Divergence Across Self-Report and Official Data Sources on Inferences About the Adolescent Life-Course of Crime." *Journal of Quantitative Criminology* 22: 107-29.

Kivisto, Peter. 2005. *Incorporating Diversity: Rethinking Assimilation in a Multicultural Age.* Boulder, CO: Paradigm Publishers

Kivisto, Peter and Georganne Rundblad (eds). 2000. *Multiculturalism in the United States: Current Issues, Contemporary Voices.* Thousand Oaks, CA: Pine Forge Press.

Koppel, Nathan. 1998. "Immigration lawyers irate over operation last call: A new INS roundup of immigrants convicted of multiple DWIs brings complaints." *Texas Lawyer,* October 5.

Kotkin, Joel. 2000. "Movers and Shakers." in *Urban Society,* 11th ed, edited by F. Siegel and J. Rosenberg. Guilford: McGraw Hill/Dushkin.

Kovandzic, Tomislav, Lynne M. Vieraitis, and Mark R. Yeisley 1998. "The Structural Covariates of Urban Homicide: Reassessing the Import of Income Inequality and Poverty in the Post-Reagan Era." *Criminology* 36: 569-599.

Kposowa, Augustine Joseph, Michelle A. Adams, and Glenn T. Tsunokai.2010. "Citizenship Status and Arrest Patterns in the United States: Evidence from the Arrestee Drug Abuse Monitoring Program." *Crime, Law, and Social Change* 53: 159-181.

Lapinski, John S., Pia Peltola, Greg Shaw and Alan Yang. 1997. "The Polls Trends: Immigrants and Immigration." *Public Opinion Quarterly* 2: 356 383.

Lauritsen, Janet L. 2001. "The Social Ecology of Violent Victimization: Individual and Contextual Effects in the NCVS." *Journal of Quantitative Criminology* 17: 3-32.

Leadership Conference on Civil Rights. 2009. *Confronting the New Faces of Hate: Hate Crimes in America.* Washington, DC: Leadership Conference on Civil Rights Education Fund. (http://www.protectcivilrights.org/pdf/reports/hatecrimes/lccref_hate_ crimes_report.pdf)

LeClere, Felicia B., Richard G. Rogers, and Kimberly D. Peters. 1997. "Ethnicity and Mortality in the United States: Individual and Community Correlates." *Social Forces* 76: 169-98.

Lee, Matthew R. and Tim Slack. 2008. "Labor Market Conditions and Violent Crime Across the Metro-Nonmetro Divide." *Social Science Research* 37: 753-768.

Lee, Matthew T., Ramiro Martinez, Jr., and Richard Rosenfeld. 2001. "Does Immigration Increase Homicide? Negative Evidence from Three Border Cities." *The Sociological Quarterly* 42: 559-580.

Levin, Jack, Gordana Rabrenovic, Vincent Ferraro, Tara Doran and Daniela Methe. 2007. "When a Crime Committed by a Teenager Becomes a Hate Crime: Results from Two Studies." *American Behavioral Scientist* 51: 258-70.

Levin, Jack and Gordana Rabrenovic. 2004. *Why We Hate.* Amherst, NY: Prometheus Books.

Levin, Jack and Jack McDevitt. 1993. *Hate Crimes: The Rising Tide of Bigotry and Bloodshed.* New York: Plenum Press.

—. 2002. *Hate Crimes Revisited: America's War on Those Who are Different.* Boulder, CO: Westview Press.

Levine, Robert A., and Donald T. Campbell. 1972. *Ethnocentrism.* New York: Wiley.

Lewis, Oscar. 1959. *Five Families: Mexican Case Studies in the Culture of Poverty.* New York: Basic Books.

Lichter, Daniel T., Domenico Parisi, Michael C. Taquino, and Steven Michael Grice. 2010. "Residential Segregation in New Hispanic Destinations: Cities, Suburbs, and Rural Communities Compared." *Social Science Research* 39: 215-230.

Lockwood, Dorothy, Anne E. Pottieger, and James A. Inciardi. 1995. "Crack Use, Crime by Crack Users, and Ethnicity." Pp. 212-34 in *Ethnicity, Race, and Crime: Perspectives Across Time and Place,* edited by D. F. Hawkins. Albany: SUNY Albany Press.

Logan, John R., Richard D. Alba, and Wenquan Zhang. 2002. "Immigrant Enclaves and Ethnic Communities in New York and Los Angeles." *American Sociological Review* 67: 299-322.

Luo, Michael. 2007. "G.O.P. Rivals Trade Charges on Illegal Immigration." *The New York Times,* November 21 (http://www.nytimes.com/2007/11/21/us/politics/21campaign.html).

Lutton, Wayne. 1996. "Immigration and Crime." Pp. 95-108 in *Immigration and the Social Contract: The Implosion of Western Societies,* edited by J. Tanton, D. McCormack, and J.W. Smith. Aldershot, England: Avebury.

MacDonald, Heather. 2004a. "The Illegal Alien Crime Wave." *City Journal* 14 (1) (http://www.city-journal.org/html/14_1_the_illegal_alien.html).

—. 2004b. "The Immigrant Gang Plague." *City Journal* 14 (3): 30-43 (http://www.city-journal.org/html/14_3_immigrant_gang.html).

MacLeod, Jay. 1987. *Ain't No Makin' It: Aspirations and Attainment in a Low Income Neighborhood.* Boulder, CO: Westview Press.

Marion, Nancy and Willard Oliver. 2012. "Crime Control in the 2008 Presidential Election: Symbolic Politics or Tangible Policies?" *American Journal of Criminal Justice* 37: 111-125.

Martinez, Ramiro Jr. 2000. "Immigration and Urban Violence: The Link Between Immigrant Latinos and Types of Homicide." *Social Science Quarterly* 81: 363-374.

—. 2002. *Latino Homicide: Immigration, Violence, and Community.* New York: Routledge.

—. 2006. "Coming to America: The Impact of the New Immigration on Crime." Pp. 1-19 in *Immigration and Crime: Race, Ethnicity, and Violence,* edited by R. Martinez Jr. and A. Valenzuela. New York: New York University Press.

Martinez, Ramiro Jr. and Matthew T. Lee. 2000. "On Immigration and Crime." in *Criminal Justice 2000: The Changing Nature of Crime, Volume 1*, edited by G. LaFree and R. Bursik. Washington, D.C.: National Institute of Justice.

Martinez, Ramiro Jr., Matthew T. Lee, and Amie L. Nielsen. 2004. "Segmented Assimilation, Local Context and Determinants of Drug Violence in Miami and San Diego: Does Ethnicity and Immigration Matter?" *International Migration Review* 38: 131-157.

Martinez, Ramiro Jr., and Amie L. Nielsen. 2006. "Extending Ethnicity and Violence Research in a Multiethnic City: Haitian, African American, and Latino Nonlethal Violence." Pp. 108-121 in *The Many Colors of Crime: Inequalities of Race, Ethnicity and Crime in America*, edited by R.D. Peterson, L.J. Krivo, and J. Hagan. New York: New York University Press.

Martinez, Ramiro Jr., Richard Rosenfeld, and Dennis Mares. 2008. "Social Disorganization, Drug Market Activity, and Neighborhood Violent Crime." *Urban Affairs Review* 43: 846-847.

Martinez, Ramiro Jr., Jacob I. Stowell, and Jeffrey M. Cancino. 2008. "A Tale of Two Border Cities: Community Context, Ethnicity, and Homicide." *Social Science Quarterly* 89: 1-16.

Martinez, Ramiro Jr., Jacob I. Stowell, and Matthew T. Lee. 2010. "Immigration and Crime in an Era of Transformation: A Longitudinal Analysis of Homicides in San Diego Neighborhoods, 1980-2000." *Criminology* 48: 797-829.

Massey, Douglas S. 1985. "Ethnic Residential Segregation: A Theoretical Synthesis and Empirical Review." *Sociology and Social Research* 69: 315 50.

Massey, Douglas S. and Nancy A. Denton. 1985. "Spatial Assimilation as a Socioeconomic Outcome." *American Sociological Review* 50: 94-106.

Massey, Douglas S. and Chiara Capoferro. 2008. "The Geographic Diversification of American Immigration." Pp. 25-50 in *New Faces in New Places: The Changing Geography of American Immigration*, edited by D.S. Massey. New York: Russell Sage.

McDonald, William F. 1997. "Crime and Illegal Immigration: Emerging Local, State, and Federal Partnerships." *National Institute of Justice Journal* 232: 2-10.

McDonald, William F. and Edna Erez. 2007. "Immigrants as Victims: A Framework." *International Review of Victimology* 14: 1-10.

Menjívar, Cecilia and Leisy J. Abrego. 2012. "Legal Violence: Immigration Law and the Lives of Central American Immigrants." *American Journal of Sociology* 117: 1380-1421.

Merrell, Melissa. 2007. *The Impact of Unauthorized Immigrants on the Budgets of State and Local Governments*. Washington, DC: Congressional Budget Office (http://www.cbo.gov/ftpdocs/87xx/doc8711/12-6-Immigration.pdf).

Merton, Robert K. 1938. "Social Structure and Anomie." *American Sociological Review* 3: 672-682.

Messner, Steven F. and Richard Rosenfeld. 2001. *Crime and the American Dream*, 3rd edition. Belmont, CA: Wadsworth.

Miller, Linda. 2007. "The Exploitation of Acculturating Immigrant Populations." *International Review of Victimology* 14: 11-28.

Modood, Tariq. 2007. *Multiculturalism*. Malden, MA: Polity Press.

Moore, Solomon. 2009. "Push on Immigration is Said to Shortchange Other Cases." *New York Times*, January 12, 1.

Morawetz, Nancy. 2000. "Understanding the Impact of the 1996 Deportation Laws and the Limited Scope of Proposed Reforms." *Harvard Law Review* 113: 1936-62.

Morenoff, Jeffrey D., Robert J. Sampson, and Stephen W. Raudenbush. 2001. "Neighborhood Inequality, Collective Efficacy, and the Spatial Dynamics of Urban Violence." *Criminology* 39: 517-559.

Morenoff, Jeffrey D. and Avraham Astor. 2006. "Immigrant Assimilation and Crime: Generational Differences in Youth Violence in Chicago." Pp. 36 63 in *Immigration and Crime: Race, Ethnicity, and Violence*, edited by R. Martinez, Jr. and A. Valenzuela. New York: New York University Press.

Mullen, Kevin J. 2005. *Dangerous Strangers: Minority Newcomers and Criminal Violence in the Urban West, 1850-2000*. New York: Palgrave MacMillan.

Muste, Christopher P. 2013. "The Dynamics of Immigration Opinion in the United States, 1992–2012." *Public Opinion Quarterly* 77(1): 398-416.

Newsom, Michael. 2011. "Law Maker Wants Wire Transfer Fee to Fund Border Fence." *Biloxi Sun Herald*, January 22. Retrieved February 9, 2011. (http://www.sunherald.com/2011/01/21/2797195/lawmaker-wants wire-transfer-fee.html).

Nielsen, Amie L. and Ramiro Martinez, Jr. 2006. "Multiple Disadvantages and Crime among Black Immigrants: Exploring Haitian Violence in Miami's Communities." Pp. 212-233 in *Immigration and Crime: Race, Ethnicity, and Violence*, edited by R. Martinez Jr. and A. Valenzuela. New York: New York University Press.

Oberle, Alex and Wei Li. 2008. "Diverging Trajectories: Asian and Latino Immigration in Metropolitan Phoenix." Pp. 87-104 in *Twenty-First Century Gateways: Immigrant Incorporation in Suburban America*, edited by A. Singer, S.W. Hardwick, and C.B. Brettell. Washington, D.C.: Brookings Institution Press.

Odem, Mary E. 2008. "Unsettled in the Suburbs: Latino Immigration and Ethnic Diversity in Metro Atlanta." Pp. 105-136 in *Twenty-First Century Gateways: Immigrant Incorporation in Suburban America*, edited by A. Singer, S.W. Hardwick, and C.B. Brettell. Washington, D.C.: Brookings Institution Press.

Olzak, Susan. 1992. *The Dynamics of Ethnic Competition and Conflict.* Stanford, CA: Stanford University Press.

O'Neil, Kevin and Marta Tienda. 2010. "A Tale of Two Counties: Natives' Opinions Toward Immigration in North Carolina." *International Migration Review* 44: 728-761.

Oppenheimer, Martin. 2008. "Does Immigration Hurt U.S.-Born Workers." *New Politics* 11: 90-99.

Osgood, D. Wayne. 2000. "Poisson-Based Regression Analysis of Aggregate Crime Rates." *Journal of Quantitative Criminology* 16: 21-43.

Osgood, D. Wayne, Janet K. Wilson, Patrick M. O'Malley, Jerald G. Bachman, and Lloyd D. Johnston. 1996. "Routine Activities and Individual Deviant Behavior." *American Sociological Review* 61: 635-655.

Ousey, Graham and Matthew R. Lee. 2007. "Homicide Trends and Illicit Drug Markets: Exploring Differences Across Time." *Justice Quarterly* 24: 48-79.

Ousey, Graham C. and Charis E. Kubrin. 2009. "Exploring the Connection between Immigration and Violent Crime Rates in U.S. Cities, 1980-2000." *Social Problems* 56: 447-473.

Pager, Devah. 2003. "The Mark of a Criminal Record." *American Journal of Sociology* 108: 937-75.

Park, Robert E. 1928. "Human Migration and the Marginal Man." *American Journal of Sociology* 33: 881-893.

Park, Robert E., and Ernest W. Burgess. 1924. *Introduction to the Science of Sociology.* Chicago: University of Chicago Press.

Park, Robert E., and Herbert A. Miller. 1921. *Old World Traits Transplanted.* New York: Harper and Brothers.

Parrado, Emilio A. and William Kandel. 2008. "New Hispanic Migrant Destinations: A Tale of Two Industries." Pp. 99-123 in *New Faces in New Places: The Changing Geography of American Immigration*, edited by D.S. Massey. New York: Russell Sage.

Passel, Jeffrey S. 2005. *Unauthorized Migrants: Numbers and Characteristics*. Washington, DC: Pew Hispanic Center (http://pewhispanic.org/files/reports/46.pdf).

——. 2006. *The Size and Characteristics of the Unauthorized Migrant Population in the US*. Washington, DC: Pew Hispanic Center.

Peguero, Anthony A. 2011. "Immigration, Schools, and Violence: Assimilation and Student Misbehavior." *Sociological Spectrum* 31: 695-717.

Pennell, Susan, Christine Curtis, and Jeff Tayman. 1989. *The Impact of Illegal Immigration on the Criminal Justice System*. San Diego, CA: San Diego Association of Governments.

Petersilia, Joan, Susan Turner, and Terry Fain. 2000. *Profiling Inmates in the Los Angeles County Jail: Risks, Recidivism and Release Options*. Santa Monica, CA: RAND (https://www.ncjrs.gov/pdffiles1/nij/grants/189733.pdf).

Peterson, Ruth D. and Lauren J. Krivo. 2000. "Macrostructural Analyses of Race, Ethnicity and Violent Crime: Recent Lessons and New Directions for Research." *Annual Review of Sociology* 31: 331-56.

Pew Hispanic Center. 2006. *Modes of Entry for the Unauthorized Migrant Population*. Washington, DC: Pew Hispanic Center (http://pewhispanic.org/files/factsheets/19.pdf).

Phillips, Julie A. 2002. "White, Black, and Latino Homicide Rates: Why the Difference?" *Social Problems* 49: 349-74.

Piore, Michael. 1970. "The Dual Labor Market: Theory and Implications." Pp. 55-59 in *The State and the Poor*, edited by S.H. Beer and R.E. Barringer. Cambridge, MA: Winthrop.

Planer, Jacinth. 2009. "Small town killing puts focus on crimes against Latinos." *Latino in America*. CNN. Retrieved October 24, 2009, (http://www.cnn.com/2009/CRIME/10/22/lia.shenandoah.killing/index.html).

Portes, Alejandro. 2007. "The Fence to Nowhere: More than ever, we need to craft an accord on migrant workers." Brooklyn, NY: Social Science Research Council. Retrieved January 26, 2009 (http://borderbattles.ssrc.org/Fence%20to%20Nowhere.pdf).

——. 2009. "CILS and Research on Children of Immigrants." Paper presented at the 79th Annual Meeting of the Eastern Sociological Society. Baltimore, MD.

Portes, Alejandro and Leif Jensen. 1992. "Disproving the Enclave Hypothesis." *American Sociological Review* 57: 418-420.

Portes, Alejandro and Min Zhou. 1993. "The New Second Generation: Segmented Assimilation and Its Variants." *Annals of the American Academy of Political and Social Science* 530: 74-96.

Portes, Alejandro and Ruben Rumbaut. 2006. *Immigrant America: A Portrait.* Los Angeles: University of California Press.

Portes, Alejandro and Alex Stepick. 1993. *City on the Edge: The Transformation of Miami.* Berkeley, CA: University of California Press.

Pratt, Travis C. and Francis T. Cullen. 2005. "Assessing Macro-Level Predictors and Theories of Crime: A Meta-Analysis." Pp. 373-450 in *Crime and Justice: A Review of Research*, edited by M. Tonry. Chicago: University of Chicago Press.

Press, Eyal. 2006. "Do Immigrants Make Us Safer?" *The New York Times*, December 3 (http://www.nytimes.com/2006/12/03/magazine/03wwln_idealab.html?pagewanted=all&_r=0).

Price, Marie and Audrey Singer. 2008. "Edge Gateways: Immigrants, Suburbs, and the Politics of Reception in Metropolitan Washington." Pp. 137-70 in *Twenty-First Century Gateways: Immigrant Incorporation in Suburban America*, edited by A. Singer, S.W. Hardwick, and C.B. Brettell. Washington, D.C.: Brookings Institution Press.

Pritchard, Justin. 2004. "Mexican-Born Workers More Likely to Die on Job: Risky Work, Compliant Attitude and Language Barrier Contribute to the Trend, AP Study Shows." *Associated Press*, March 14.

Quillian, Lincoln. 1995. "Prejudice as a Response to Perceived Group Threat: Population Composition and Anti-Immigrant and Racial Prejudice in Europe." *American Sociological Review* 60: 586-611.

Rabrenovic, Gordana. 2007. "When Hate Comes to Town: Community Response to Violence Against Immigrants." *American Behavioral Scientist* 51: 349-360.

Reid, Lesley Williams, Harald Weiss, Robert M. Adelman, and Charles Jaret. 2005. "The Immigration-Crime Relationship: Evidence Across US Metropolitan Areas." *Social Science Research* 34: 757-780.

Robbins, Ted. 2010. "Virtual U.S.-Mexico Border Fence At A Virtual End." *National Public Radio,* Retrieved February 11, 2011. (http://www.npr.org/templates/story/story.php?storyId=124758593).

Romer, Daniel, Kathleen Hill Jamieson, and Sean Aday. 2003. "Television News and the Cultivation of Fear of Crime." *Journal of Communication*

53: 88-104.

Rosenfeld, Richard, and Janet Lauritsen. 2008. "The Most Dangerous Crime Rankings." *Contexts* 7: 66-67.

Rumbaut, Ruben G. and Walter A. Ewing. 2007. "The Myth of Immigrant Criminality." Brooklyn, NY: Social Science Research Council. Retrieved January 22, 2009, (http://borderbattles.ssrc.org/Rumbault_Ewing/).

Sacchetti, Maria. 2009. "'Look How They Left Him': Brutal beating of immigrant, charges against six boys bring alarms in Lynn." *Boston Globe*, September 11.

Saltzman, Jonathan. 2006. "Illegal Immigrants toiled for governor: Guatemalans say firm hired them." *The Boston Globe*, December 1.

Sampson, Robert J. 2008. "Rethinking Crime and Immigration." *Contexts* 7: 28-33. Retrieved March 13, 2010. (http://contexts.org/articles/winter-2008/sampson/).

—. 2002. "Organized for What? Recasting Theories of Social (Dis)organization." Pp. 95-110 in *Crime and Social Organization*, edited by E. J. Waring, and D. Weisburd. New Brunswick, NJ: Transaction Publishers.

Sampson, Robert J., Stephen W. Raudenbush, and Felton Earls. 1997. "Neighborhoods and Violent Crime: A Multilevel Study of Collective Efficacy." *Science* 277: 918-924.

Sampson, Robert J., Jeffrey D. Morenoff, and Fenton Earls. 1999. "Beyond Social Capital: Spatial Dynamics of Collective Efficacy for Children." *American Sociological Review* 64: 633-660.

Sampson, Robert J., Jeffrey Morenoff, and Steven Raudenbush. 2005. "Social Anatomy of Racial and Ethnic Disparities in Violence." *Public Health Matters* 95: 224-232.

Sampson, Robert J. and John H. Laub. 2003. *Shared Beginnings, Divergent Lives: Delinquent Boys to Age 70.* Cambridge, MA: Harvard University Press.

—. 1993. *Crime in the Making: Pathways and Turning Points Through Life.* Cambridge, MA: Harvard University Press.

Sampson, Robert J. and Lydia Bean. 2006. "Cultural Mechanisms and Killing Fields: A Revised Theory of Community-Level Inequality." Pp. 8-36 in *The Many Colors of Crime: Inequalities of Race, Ethnicity and Crime in America*, edited by R.D. Peterson, L.J. Krivo, and J. Hagan. New York: New York University Press.

Sampson, Robert J. and William J. Wilson. 1995. "Toward a Theory of Race, Crime, and Urban Inequality." Pp. 177-89 in *Race, Crime, and Justice: A Reader*, edited by S.L. Gabbidon and H.T. Greene. New York: Routledge.

Sayad, Abdelmalek. 2004. *The Suffering of the Immigrant.* Malden, MA: Polity Press.

Scheve, Kenneth F. and Matthew J. Slaughter. 2001. *Globalization and the Perceptions of American Workers.* Washington, DC: Institute for International Economics.

Schulenberg, Jennifer L. 2003. "The Social Context of Police Discretion with Young Offenders: An Ecological Analysis." *Canadian Journal of Criminology and Criminal Justice* 45: 127-157.

Semyonov, Moshe, Rebeca Raijman, and Anastasia Gorodzeisky. 2006. "The Rise of Anti-foreigner Sentiment in European Societies, 1988-2000." *American Sociological Review* 71: 426-499.

Seper, Jerry. 2007. "States urged to act on illegal aliens; Irate at federal failure to address the issue, an Ohio sheriff calls for a crackdown." *The Washington Times,* June 10, A01.

—. 2008. "ICE effort snares 1,808 in six states; Most being quickly deported." *The Washington Times,* June 3, A03.

Shaw, Clifford R. and Henry D. McKay. 1942. *Juvenile Delinquency in Urban Areas.* Chicago: University of Chicago Press.

Shihadeh, Edward S. and Raymond E. Barranco. 2010a. "Leveraging the Power of the Ethnic Enclave: Residential Instability and Violence in Latino Communities." *Sociological Spectrum* 30: 249-269.

—. 2010b. "Latino Employment and Non-Latino Homicide in Rural Areas: The Implications of U.S. Immigration Policy." *Deviant Behavior* 31: 411-439.

—. 2013. "The Imperative of Place: Homicide and the New Latino Migration." *Sociological Quarterly* 54: 81-104.

Shihadeh, Edward S., and Lisa Winters. 2010. "Church, Place, and Crime: Latinos and Homicides in New Destinations." *Sociological Inquiry* 80: 628-649.

Shihadeh, Edward S., and Graham Ousey. 1996. "Metropolitan Expansion and Black Social Dislocation: the Link Between Suburbanization and Center City Crime." *Social Forces* 75: 649-66.

Sidanius, Jim and Felicia Pratto. 1999. *Social Dominance: An Intergroup Theory of Social Hierarchy and Oppression.* New York: Cambridge University Press.

Sides, John and Jack Citrin. 2007. "How Large the Huddled Masses? The Causes and Consequences of Public Misperceptions about Immigrant Populations." Paper presented at the 65th Annual Meeting of the Midwest Political Science Association. Chicago, Illinois.

Sidoti, Liz. 2007. "Thompson Criticizes Immigration Measures." *The Washington Post*, May 25. Retrieved January 11, 2011. (http://www.washingtonpost.com/wp-dyn/content/article/2007/ 05/25/ AR2007052501415_pf.html).

Simcox, David. 1997. "Major Predictors of Immigration Restrictionism: Operationalizing 'Nativism'." *Population and Environment* 19: 129-143.

Simon, Rita J. and Susan Alexander. 1993. *The Ambivalent Welcome: Print Media, Public Opinion, and Immigration.* Westport, CT: Praeger.

Simon, Rita J. and James P. Lynch. 1999. "A Comparative Assessment of Public Opinion toward Immigrants and Immigration Policies." *International Migration Review* 33: 455-467.

Simon, Rita J. and Keri W. Sikich. 2007. "Public Attitudes toward Immigrants and Immigration Policies across Seven Nations." *International Migration Review* 41: 956-962.

Singer, Audrey. 2008. "Twenty-First-Century Gateways: An Introduction." In *Twenty-First-Century Gateways: Immigrant Incorporation in Suburban America*, edited by A. Singer, S.W. Hardwick, and C.B. Brettell. Washington, D.C.: Brookings Institution Press.

Smith, Heather A. and Owen J. Furseth. 2008. "The 'Nuevo South': Latino Place Making and Community Building in the Middle-Ring Suburbs of Charlotte." Pp. 281-307 in *Twenty-First Century Gateways: Immigrant Incorporation in Suburban America*, edited by A. Singer, S.W. Hardwick, and C.B. Brettell. Washington, D.C.: Brookings Institution Press.

Smith, James P. and Barry Edmonston, ed. 1997. *The New Americans: Economic, Demographic, and Fiscal Effects of Immigration.* Washington, DC: National Academy Press.

Sniderman, Paul M., Louk Hagendorn, and Markus Prior. 2004. "Predisposing Factors and Situational Triggers: Exclusionary Reactions to Immigrant Minorities." *American Political Science Review* 98: 35-49.

South, Scott J. and Steven F. Messner. 1986. "Structural Determinants of Intergroup Association: Interracial Marriage and Crime." *American Journal of Sociology* 91: 1409-30.

South, Scott J., Kyle Crowder, and Erick Chavez. 2005. "Migration and Spatial Assimilation among U.S. Latinos: Classical versus Segmented Trajectories." *Demography* 42: 497-521.

Southern Poverty Law Center. 2009. *Climate of Fear: Latino Immigrants in Suffolk County, NY.* Montgomery, AL: Southern Poverty Law Center. (http://www.splcenter.org/images/dynamic/main/splc_suffolk_report_lores .pdf).

Stowell, Jacob I., Steven F. Messner, Kelly F. McGeever, and Lawrence E. Raffalovich. 2009. "Immigration and the Recent Violent Crime Drop in the United States: A Pooled, Cross-Sectional Time-Series Analysis of Metropolitan Areas." *Criminology* 47: 889-928.

Sullivan, Eileen. 2009. "Immigrant roundups snare nonviolent offenders." *Associated Press*, Washington Dateline. February 5.

Sutherland, Edwin H. 1947. *Principles of Criminology, 4th ed.* Philadelphia: J.B. Lippincott Company.

Taylor, Paul S. [1932] 1970. *Mexican Labor in the United States.* New York: Arno Press and New York Times.

Thomas, William I. and Florian Znaniecki. 1918. *The Polish Peasant in Europe and America.* Urbana: University of Illinois Press.

Thrane, Lisa, Xiaojin Chen, Kurt Johnson, and Les B. Whitbeck. 2008. "Predictors of Police Contact Among Midwestern Homeless and Runaway Youth." *Youth Violence and Juvenile Justice* 6: 227-39.

Tolnay, Stewart E., E. M. Beck, and James L. Massey. 1989. "The Power Threat Hypothesis and Black Lynching: 'Wither' the Evidence?" *Social Forces* 67 (3): 634-641.

Tonry, Michael, ed. 1997. *Ethnicity, Crime, and Immigration: Comparative and Cross-National Perspectives.* Chicago: University of Chicago Press.

Tonry, Michael. 1997. "Ethnicity, Crime, and Immigration." Pp. 1-29 in *Ethnicity, Crime and Immigration: Comparative and Cross-National Perspectives*, edited by M. Tonry. Chicago: University of Chicago Press.

Tversky, Amos and Daniel Kahneman. 1973. "Availability: A Heuristic for Judging Frequency and Probability." *Cognitive Psychology* 5: 207-232.

U.S. Census Bureau. 2009. *American Community Survey.* (http://www.census.gov/acs/www/).

U.S. Dept. of Homeland Security. 2012. *Activated Jurisdictions.* Washington, DC: U.S. Dept. of Homeland Security (http://www.ice.gov/doclib/secure-communities/pdf/sc-activated2.pdf).

—. 2006. *Immigration Enforcement Actions: 2005. Annual Report.* Washington, DC: U.S. Dept. of Homeland Security (http://www.dhs.gov/xlibrary/assets/statistics/yearbook/2005/Enforcement_AR_05.pdf).

U.S. Dept. of Justice, Federal Bureau of Investigation. 2001. *Uniform Crime Reporting Program Data [United States]: Offenses Known and Clearances By Arrest, 1999 [Computer file].* Compiled by the U.S. Dept. of Justice, Federal Bureau of Investigation. 2nd ICPSR ed. Ann Arbor, MI: Inter-University Consortium for Political and Social Research [producer and distributor]. doi: 10.3886/ICPSR03158.

—. 2002. *Uniform Crime Reporting Program Data [United States]: Offenses Known and Clearances By Arrest, 2000 [Computer file]*. Compiled by the U.S. Dept. of Justice, Federal Bureau of Investigation. ICPSR ed. Ann Arbor, MI: Inter-University Consortium for Political and Social Research [producer and distributor]. doi: 10.3886/ICPSR03447.

—. 2003. *Uniform Crime Reporting Program Data [United States]: Offenses Known and Clearances By Arrest, 2001 [Computer file]*. Compiled by the U.S. Dept. of Justice, Federal Bureau of Investigation. ICPSR ed. Ann Arbor, MI: Inter-University Consortium for Political and Social Research [producer and distributor]. doi: 10.3886/ICPSR03723.

—. 2007. *Uniform Crime Reporting Program Data [United States]: Offenses Known and Clearances By Arrest, 2005 [Computer file]*. Compiled by the U.S. Dept. of Justice, Federal Bureau of Investigation. ICPSR04721-v1. Ann Arbor, MI: Inter-University Consortium for Political and Social Research [producer and distributor]. doi: 10.3886/ICPSR03721.

—. 2008. *Uniform Crime Reporting Program Data [United States]: Hate Crime Data, 2001 [Record-Type Files] [Computer file]*. ICPSR23781-v1. Ann Arbor, MI: Inter-University Consortium for Political and Social Research [distributor]. doi: 10.3886/ICPSR23781.

—. 2008. *Uniform Crime Reporting Program Data [United States]: Hate Crime Data, 2005 [Record-Type Files] [Computer file]*. ICPSR23441-v1. Ann Arbor, MI: Inter-University Consortium for Political and Social Research [distributor]. doi: 10.3886/ICPSR23441.

—. 2008. *Uniform Crime Reporting Program Data [United States]: Hate Crime Data, 2006 [Record-Type Files] [Computer file]*. ICPSR22406-v1. Ann Arbor, MI: Inter-University Consortium for Political and Social Research [distributor]. doi: 10.3886/ICPSR22406.

—. 2008. *Uniform Crime Reporting Program Data [United States]: Offenses Known and Clearances By Arrest, 2006 [Computer file]*. Compiled by the U.S. Dept. of Justice, Federal Bureau of Investigation. ICPSR22400-v1. Ann Arbor, MI: Inter-University Consortium for Political and Social Research [producer and distributor]. doi: 10.3886/ICPSR22400.

—. 2009. "Hate Crime in the United States." Washington, D.C.: U.S. Department of Justice. Retrieved March 31, 2009 (http://www.fbi.gov/ucr/ucr.htm#hate).

—. 2009. *Uniform Crime Reporting Program Data [United States]: Hate Crime Data, 1999 [Record-Type Files] [Computer file]*. ICPSR23800-v1. Ann Arbor, MI: Inter-University Consortium for Political and Social Research [distributor]. doi: 10.3886/ICPSR23800.

—. 2009. *Uniform Crime Reporting Program Data [United States]: Hate Crime Data, 2000 [Record-Type Files] [Computer file].* ICPSR23783-v1. Ann Arbor, MI: Inter-University Consortium for Political and Social Research [distributor]. doi: 10.3886/ICPSR23783.

—. 2009. *Uniform Crime Reporting Program Data [United States]: Hate Crime Data, 2007 [Record-Type Files] [Computer file].* ICPSR25107-v1. Ann Arbor, MI: Inter-University Consortium for Political and Social Research [distributor]. doi: 10.3886/ICPSR25107.

—. 2009. *Uniform Crime Reporting Program Data [United States]: Offenses Known and Clearances By Arrest, 2007 [Computer file].* ICPSR25101-v2. Ann Arbor, MI: Inter-University Consortium for Political and Social Research [distributor]. doi: 10.3886/ICPSR25101.

U.S. Immigration Commission. 1911. *Immigration and Crime.* Vol. 36. Washington, DC: U.S. Government Printing Office

U.S. Industrial Commission. 1901. *Special Report on General Statistics of Immigration and the Foreign Born Population.* Washington, DC: U.S. Government Printing Office.

Valenzuela, Abel Jr. 2006. "New Immigrants and Day Labor: The Potential for Violence." Pp. 189-211 in *Immigration and Crime: Race, Ethnicity, and Violence,* edited by R. Martinez, Jr. and A. Valenzuela. New York: NYU Press.

Vallas, Steven P., Emily Zimmerman, Shannon N. Davis. 2009. "Enemies of the State? Testing Three Models of Anti-Immigrant Settlement." *Research in Social Stratification and Mobility* 27: 201-217.

Vartabedian, Ralph and Nicholas Riccardi. 2008. "Campaign '08: The Republicans; McCain has home fences to mend." *Los Angeles Times,* February 4.

Velez, Maria B. 2006. "Toward an Understanding of the Lower Rates of Homicide in Latino versus Black Neighborhoods: A Look at Chicago." Pp. 91-107 in *The Many Colors of Crime: Inequalities of Race, Ethnicity and Crime in America,* edited by R.D. Peterson, L.J. Krivo, and J. Hagan. New York: New York University Press.

Vigil, James Diego. 2002. *A Rainbow of Gangs: Street Cultures in the Mega City.* Austin, TX: University of Texas Press.

Wadsworth, Tim. 2010. "Is Immigration Responsible for the Crime Drop? An Assessment of the Influence of Immigration on Changes in Violent Crime Between 1990 and 2000." *Social Science Quarterly* 91: 531-553.

Wagner, Peter. 2003. *The Prison Index: Taking the Pulse of the Crime Control Industry.* Northampton, MA: Prison Policy Initiative.

Waldinger, Roger. 1996. *Still the Promised City? African-Americans and New Immigrants in Post-Industrial New York.* Cambridge, MA: Harvard University Press.

—. 1997. "Black/Immigrant Competition Re-Assessed: New Evidence from Los Angeles." *Sociological Perspectives* 40: 365-86.

Wang, Xia. 2012. "Undocumented Immigrants as Perceived Criminal Threat: A Test of the Minority Threat Perspective." *Criminology* 50: 743-776.

Warner, W. Lloyd, and Leo Srole. 1945. *The Social Systems of American Ethnic Groups.* New Haven, CT: Yale University Press.

Waters, Mary. 2009. "The New York Second Generation Study." Paper presented at the 79th Annual Meeting of the Eastern Sociological Society. Baltimore, MD.

Watkins, Adam M. 2005. "Examining the Disparity Between Juvenile and Adult Victims in Notifying the Police: A Study of Mediating Variables." *Journal of Research in Crime and Delinquency* 42: 333-353.

Welch, Kelly, Allison Ann Payne, Ted Chiricos, and Marc Gertz. 2011. "The Typification of Hispanics as Criminals and Support for Punitive Crime Control Policies." *Social Science Research* 40: 822-840.

Whyte, William Foote. 1943. *Street Corner Society: The Social Structure of an Italian Slum.* Chicago: University of Chicago Press.

Williams, Paul and Julie Dickinson. 1993. "Fear of Crime: Read All About it? The Relationship Between Newspaper Crime Reporting and Fear of Crime." *British Journal of Criminology* 33: 33-56.

Wilson, William Julius. 1987. *The Truly Disadvantaged: The Inner City, The Underclass, and Public Policy.* Chicago: University of Chicago Press.

Winders, Jamie. 2008. "Nashville's New "Sonido": Latino Migration and the Changing Politics of Race." Pp. 249-273 in *New Faces in New Places: The Changing Geography of American Immigration*, edited by D.S. Massey. New York: Russell Sage.

Wirth, Louis. 1945. "The Problem of Minority Groups." in *The Science of Man in the World Crisis*, edited by R. Linton. New York: Columbia University Press.

Wolfe, Scott E., David C. Pyrooz, and Cassia C. Spohn. 2011. "Unraveling the Effect of Offender Citizenship Status on Federal Sentencing Outcomes." *Social Science Research* 40: 349-362.

Zarrugh, Laura. 2008. "The Latinization of the Central Shenandoah Valley." *International Migration Review* 46: 19-58.

Zhou, Min. 1997. "Segmented Assimilation: Issues, Controversies, and Recent Research on the New Second Generation." *International Migration Review* 31: 975-1008.

Index

CPSIA information can be obtained at www.ICGtesting.com
Printed in the USA
LVOW07*2229171114

414215LV00005B/12/P